FOREMOTHERS OF
THE WOMEN'S
SPIRITUALITY MOVEMENT

Foremothers of the Women's Spirituality Movement

Elders and Visionaries

EDITED BY

Miriam Robbins Dexter and Vicki Noble

AMHERST, NEW YORK

*We dedicate this book to the
foremothers who are no longer with us:
Margot Adler (1946-2014) , Mary Daly (1928-2010),
Kay Gardner (1941-2002), Marija Gimbutas (1921-1994),
Susan Gray (Susan Gitlin-Emmer) (1949-2008),
Patricia Monaghan (1946-2012),
Shekinah Mountainwater (1939-2007),
Layne Redmond (1952-2013),
Adrienne Rich (1929-2012), Gabrielle Roth (1941-2012),
Monica Sjöö (1938-2005), Merlin Stone (1931-2011),
Donna Wilshire (1933-2012), Diane Wolkstein (1942-2013),
and Morning Glory Zell-Ravenheart (1948-2014)*

TABLE OF CONTENTS

LIST OF FIGURES

ACKNOWLEDGEMENTS

Vicki and Miriam would like to thank Toni Tan and Michelle Wright for all of their hard work in helping us to birth this book and bringing it to completion.

We would also like to thank all of the authors for their inspiring and moving contributions, and for their patience and alacrity in responding to comments and edits.

Miriam is so grateful to her husband, Greg Dexter, for his ability to be a sounding-board—to both the technicalities and the content of this book, for being another pair of eyes in proofreading, and for always being there; and her children, Leah Robbins and Jake Robbins, for their years of showing interest in and supporting her work.

Foremothers of the Women's Spirituality Movement

PREFACE

GRASSROOTS UPRISING TO GRADUATE DEGREES IN WOMEN'S SPIRITUALITY

Vicki Noble

We became inspired to edit this anthology in order to remember and honor the foremothers of the 1970s Women's Spirituality movement. Women's Spirituality (also known at times as feminist or Goddess spirituality) organically grew from the revolutionary Second Wave women's movement in the United States; thus it was mainly composed (at first) of middle class white women, many of whom had abandoned the Judeo-Christian religions of their upbringing after awakening to the extent of institutionalized sexism, racism, and homophobia contained therein. This mass exodus of contemporary middle class women from organized religion in America was a radical event that has never been given the attention it deserves.

We can understand now, in hindsight, the power of white privilege and the many ways that the movement did not (could not) speak to most women of color at the time. (See Luisah Teish's piece.) While much insightful analysis and valuable critique has come forth to deconstruct the issue over the years, the importance of such a spontaneous and radical uprising of women should not be thrown out altogether. White women, for all their ingrained blindness to racial and class issues at the time, can still be given credit for the courageous act of leaving organized patriarchal religion and inventing a new spirituality with Goddess at the center (See Carol Christ's piece). Surely such privilege was well used as a springboard for transformative and revolutionary events?

When Karen Vogel and I moved to Berkeley in 1976, we had a potent intuition of the work that lay ahead for us. Our impassioned research (should I say, obsession?) into the ancient civilizations of the Goddess took several years and involved not only the utilization of Bay Area libraries and used bookstores, but included psychic training, yoga, natural medicine, shamanism, and art. We delved into the Western Magical Tradition, creating the *Motherpeace* tarot drawings the following year.[1] We felt that we were remembering something crucial that had been suppressed and forgotten by our culture. And although we were fairly isolated as we began the project, by the time it was finished, we were actively part of the burgeoning social and spiritual movement that sprang from the fertile soil of 1970s Berkeley. Our west coast feminist agent, representing radical feminists of the time (See Mary Mackey, this volume), made an earnest effort to sell our unusual project in New York, and when that effort initially failed, we printed the cards ourselves; shortly after that, Harper & Row (later HarperSanFrancisco) wrote me a letter offering to publish the book I was writing.[2] It was a time of such creative awakening that we knew we would permanently change the world. Karen and I wrote a novel together (unpublished), called *When It's Good, It's Good, When It's Bad, It's Over*, at the end of which, all the women in the world woke up laughing.

What I remember most from that time is the thrill of being part of a grassroots uprising, momentous and larger than ourselves. The women featured in this book were reconceptualizing religion to include priestesses and rituals honoring a female divinity, while other feminist women were creating independent venues to channel the exuberant creativity that had exploded with the general rise of the women's movement. A whole field of women's (wimmin's, womyn's) music brought female vocalists and musicians into the foreground, supported by independent feminist labels (such as Olivia and Redwood Records) producing albums, women's coffee houses and other performance venues; it was during this time that women's music festivals were born, the Michigan Women's Music Festival (produced by Lisa Vogel) being the most famous and enduring (1976 to the present), where the *Motherpeace* cards made their debut in the summer of 1981.

Feminist music played continuously in the background of our lives: Holly Near, Chris Williamson, Meg Christian, Margie Adam; LPs with names like "Lavender Jane Loves Women" and rock groups like Fanny. We went to concerts and once saw the young, androgynous punk rocker, Patti Smith, in UC Berkeley's Zellerbach Hall; later, Karen modeled her version of the *Motherpeace* Magician after Smith. One night I remember us listening to Kay Gardner's flute album, *Mooncircles*, all night long! (To be fair, I think I should also tell you that we had just eaten psilocybin mushrooms.) We went to Take Back the Night marches in San Francisco, organized by Hallie Austen Iglehart (in this volume). We heard live poets like Judy Grahn (in this volume) and Susan Griffin, giving electrifying readings at local Bay Area women's coffee houses; we met Mary Daly, whose book, *GynEcology* was inspirational for my drawing of the Hierophant card. Karen and I often read whole books aloud to each other, such as Marge Piercy's visionary novel, *Woman on the Edge of Time* and Jean Auel's *Clan of the Cave Bear*. For five years, we shared an active visionary life of "big dreams" and psychic events leading to our healing work in the world.

When I later married Jonathan Tenney and gave birth to our son, Aaron, who has Down Syndrome, I wrote *Down is Up for Aaron Eagle*.[3] In my forties, I founded and directed a school for women healers in the Berkeley-Oakland area; and while the Motherpeace school was active, we published a full-color quarterly journal called *SnakePower*[4] and I edited an anthology of essays on Female Shamanism, *Uncoiling the Snake*.[5] I traveled and taught around the country and eventually around the world, co-leading tours of women on pilgrimage trips to ancient Goddess sites.

One of the most powerful things to come out of the experience of running the Motherpeace school was the development of what I call the Transformational Healing Ritual. Because I had second- and third-year students in a weekly class for nine months of the year, our time together became a laboratory for experimenting with hands-on healing. We invited women and men from around the Bay Area who were struggling with life-threatening or debilitating illnesses to come to the school and let us work on them; Marija Gimbutas was our first. Over the years, we invented a vibrant collective process utilizing drumming, chanting, and hands-on healing to simulate ancient and tribal healing rituals performed by indigenous people around the world. In the early 1990s, I took this ritual on the road with Canadian singer-songwriter, Jennifer Berezan, whose musical collaboration helped create a beautiful and safe container for the ritual; we offered it wherever we were invited to teach. Now almost twenty years later, I rank it as one of my most potent contributions to the women's community; when twenty or more women gather in a room to raise the "snake power" and bring down the "big energy," the heat rises and people get well—healers as well as those who come for the healing.

Since 1980, I have practiced Tibetan Buddhism, and it has always been my goal to somehow integrate Buddhism with Feminism. And though feminists often see Buddhism as just another male religion, if all the men in the world would become Buddhists (who are pacifists), we would instantly have world peace. This is different from Christianity, Judaism, Islam, and Hinduism, which have become more fundamentalist over time, seeking to dominate and control women, and fighting with each other almost nonstop. I love the vibrant colors and sounds contained in the rich chanting and visualization practices, especially the potent female iconography and mandala practices dedicated to Dakinis (flying female deities representing freedom and enlightenment). I have spent the last fifteen years adapting Tibetan invocations to the Dakinis for my Western (non-Buddhist) women students, because I believe women need a strong method of grounding and centering in the Sacred Female. My loosely-woven *sangha* (group of like-minded practitioners) in Italy has been going strong for nearly a decade, involving hundreds of Italian women dedicated to the practices I have developed for them; this is an ongoing source of great satisfaction to me. I recently teamed up with another renegade Tibetan Buddhist, Prema Dasara, whose dances of the twenty-one Taras are world-renowned.

I was fortunate to teach in two unique graduate programs in Women's Spirituality, first in San Francisco (at CIIS and New College) and finally in Palo Alto (ITP: the Institute for Transpersonal Psychology, now known as Sofia University). Graduate school allowed the original scholarship of several decades of Goddess studies to anchor, provided faculty slots for movement leaders, and delivered scores of Masters and PhD degrees to women specializing in the subject (see Mara Keller and Elinor Gadon in this volume). This allowed me to put the content I had developed into serious graduate courses, which required students to go deep and integrate the work into a thesis project at the end of their studies. Now, in 2015, these programs—as they have been conceived and sustained— are in jeopardy. New College, where I taught in the Women's Spirituality program directed by Dianne Jenett, Judy Grahn, and D'vorah Grenn, went bankrupt and closed in 2008. Magician-like, the co-directors worked tirelessly to get the program successfully transferred to ITP/Sophia, but in a period of years, a corporate structure was put in place for the school to become a "for profit" institute, with programs (including ours) going online, faculty and staff being let go, and precious electives dropped. Due to these changes, I have recently resigned my position there, and now, sadly, the program has ceased to exist. At CIIS, the name has been changed from Women's Spirituality to "Gender, Spirituality, and Social Justice," which conveniently takes the *woman* out of it. Nonetheless, two decades of graduate degrees in Women's Spirituality was a good run!

Looking back over the years, I can only feel gratitude for being part of the special history of Women's Spirituality, one that has become somewhat muted over time and is in danger of being erased or forgotten by mainstream American culture. I am honored to give back to the movement by bringing together these authors and leaders of that time to tell their stories and share their visions. My hope for this book is that it might demonstrate the cohesion that existed then—and exists still —beneath the apparent randomness of our various contributions and artistic offerings. May it bear fruit in the next generation!

Blessed be.

NOTES

1. Vicki Noble and Karen Vogel, *The Motherpeace Tarot Deck* (Stamford, CT: US Games Systems, 1983). The deck was first self-published in 1981, and in 1983 US Games Systems took over the publishing of the cards.
2. Vicki Noble, *Motherpeace: A Way to the Goddess Through Myth, Art, and Tarot* (San Francisco: HarperSanFrancisco, 1983).
3. Vicki Noble, *Down is Up for Aaron Eagle* (San Francisco: HarperSanFrancisco, 1994).
4. Vicki Noble, *SnakePower: A Journal of Ancient and Contemporary Female Shamanism* (San Francisco: HarperCollins, 1993).
5. Vicki Noble, *Uncoiling the Snake: Ancient Patterns in Contemporary Women's Lives (A Snakepower Reader)* San Francisco: HarperCollins, 1993).

INTRODUCTION

ON MY PATH

Miriam Robbins Dexter

This anthology reflects the voices of foremothers of the Women's Spirituality movement, which began for most in the 1970s but for some even earlier! These women are artists, activists, scholars, ritualists—and some are all of these and more. Vicki and I asked each woman to write about how and when she came to be involved in the Women's Spirituality movement, what she thinks has been accomplished in this movement, and what she is passionately focused upon at this time: labors of love which we believe reflect the present and even the future directions of the Women's Spirituality movement. One of the most important goals of our anthology is to inspire the next generations of women.

FOLLOWING THE PATH

It was not necessarily a conscious choice which led me to Feminist Spirituality, and, decades later, to co-edit this book. Instead, it was following the path laid out before me, one step at a time. I had always thought that I would go to the University of California, Berkeley, but because of some personal choices I made, I found myself as an undergraduate at the University of California, Los Angeles (UCLA). I enjoyed my undergraduate work in Classics, studying Latin, Greek, and then having a chance to take a year of Sanskrit. While in Graduate school I discovered the program in Indo-European Studies, and within a few months I had found my true scholarly home. Indo-European Studies includes the study of ancient Indo-European languages, linguistics, myth, and archaeology. For a myth class, I wrote a paper, "Indo-European Female Figures and the Principles of Energy." I do not know why I picked female figures —Goddesses[1] and heroines. This was in the early 1970s, before I began meditating, so I was probably pretty dense about my life path. That paper became the core of my doctoral dissertation and led to a rich and fruitful association with the Lithuanian-born archaeologist, Marija Gimbutas, whose work on ancient civilizations of the Goddess in Old Europe has been so foundational for scholars in Women's Spirituality.

I had finished my course work and was ready for my comprehensive exams in 1975. Along with other course work, I had been taking archaeology classes with Marija since 1969, and when she heard that my dissertation was to be on Indo-European Female Figures—by that time she was already writing about female figures—she had herself placed on my doctoral committee. I recall that, during my oral exam, which was attended by my whole committee, each time Marija would ask an archaeological question which would cause me to hesitate, she would quickly gloss over it and ask me another. She was clearly determined that I would pass my orals and get on with the business of writing the dissertation.

Because of the composition of my doctoral Committee—including Jaan Puhvel, who taught many of the language courses and all of the myth courses for the Indo-European Studies program at UCLA at that time—I had to research both myth and archaeology, using primary sources which I translated from many Indo-European languages; thus, for my doctoral dissertation,[2] I was already doing Archaeomythology, even before the term came into use. For the first time in my life I loved the process of writing as well as the research—so much so that I have spent over three and a half decades continuing the work.

What is interesting now in hindsight is that at UC Berkeley there was no program offering the study of multiple Indo-European languages together with mythological texts and no Marija Gimbutas to cause me to tie it all together with archaeology. The Goddess had placed me upon my path whether I wanted to be there or not!

MARIJA GIMBUTAS

As I was finishing my dissertation, Marija invited me to her first international Indo-European conference, in Dubrovnik, Yugoslavia. She was definite that I was to write a paper based upon the second chapter of my dissertation, the "Assimilation of Proto-Indo-European Female Figures into the Indo-European pantheons." I had found, while writing the dissertation and doing linguistic analyses, that the patriarchal Indo-Europeans worshipped very few female figures before their migrations: the dawn Goddess, the sun maiden (and in some areas the sun Goddess), the earth Goddess, and the river Goddess, Danu: all representing naturalistic phenomena. Every other Goddess—significantly, all of the "Great"-Goddesses, such as the Greek Athena, Germanic Freyja, Hindu Devī and others—belonged to the pre-Indo-European cultures, the indigenous peoples of Europe and Western Asia, some belonging to Marija's "Old Europe." Thus, Marija was responsible for my first international conference, as well as my very first publication,[3] consisting of the work I produced for the conference.

As a way to repay a fraction of what Marija did for me in her life, shortly after she passed away, in 1994, I accepted rather a large task: I was asked by three different people to edit works by and for her,[4] including the final manuscript she was working on at the time of her death, *The Living Goddesses.*[5]

For more than a decade, I enjoyed writing about the Indo-European Goddesses who represented naturalistic phenomena. During this time, I published *Whence the Goddess: A Source Book,*[6] which continued the studies of my doctoral dissertation. Then other, more powerful and more potent Goddesses began calling me. My friend Starr Goode, who had long been researching the Irish Sheela na gigs, and I wrote about the Sheelas,[7] Starr discussing their fascinating background and I translating some Old Irish texts which seemed to discuss similar figures. The Sheelas were *apotropaic*—protecting those in their care from their enemies, and from harm—and this sparked my interest in other such Goddesses. I decided to find out more about the Greco-Roman Medusa, another apotropaic female figure, by translating every text I could find about her, in chronological order.[8] At about the same time, the Sinologist Victor Mair contacted me and suggested that we write about apotropaic Eurasian female figures together, sparking a conference paper[9] and publication of our book, *Sacred Display: Divine and Magical Female Figures of Eurasia,*[10] which in 2010 won the first Association for the Study of Women and Mythology (ASWM) Sarasvatī award for best nonfiction book. More recently, we published an online, open-source monograph continuing the research.[11] These Goddesses and heroines do a "sacred display" of their genitalia, thereby bringing good fortune, protection against one's enemies, and fertility to the societies who honor them.

These female figures continue to fascinate me. In the earliest Upper Palaeolithic they were found in or near galleries occupied by depictions of felines, or by human-feline figurines, and that association has continued into the present (the Hindu Great-Goddess Durgā/Kālī, Devī, still worshipped in India today, is accompanied by either a lion or a tiger).

Thus the female genitalia have been regarded as sacred by some peoples for at least forty thousand years.

Over the years many women in various fields of Women's Spirituality have inspired me. I loved Anne Key's memoir of her time serving as priestess of the Sekhmet temple (established by Genevieve Vaughan) in Nevada; she is also a publisher of women's spirituality books, along with Candace Kant. Reverend Ava Park and Reverend Xia Judy Tatum have founded and established contemporary Temples of the Goddess in Orange County and Pasadena, wonderfully serving their communities; Anique Radiant Heart, originally a jazz singer who now uses her voice in honor of the Goddess, has opened a similar temple in Australia. Also serving their communities are Karen Tate, Anniitra Ravenmoon and Jayne DeMente, who host radio talk shows in Los Angeles, where they interview women who have produced books in Women's Spirituality. Particular writers in our field—in addition to the works of those who have written essays for this anthology—have brought me joy and inspiration over the years, including the poet/psychiatrist Janine Canan's anthologies of poetry, *Her Magnificent Body*[12] and *She Rises Like the Sun*,[13] the novelist Marion Zimmer Bradley's *Mists of Avalon* (1984),[14] which I spent a month reading in the wilderness in Canada in the 1990s; and Barbara Ardinger's highly entertaining and exceptionally funny *Finding New Goddesses: Reclaiming Playfulness in Our Spiritual Lives.*[15]

In what I see as amazing good fortune, the Goddess has allowed me to teach as well as write about her: I taught courses at UCLA, "Ancient Goddesses and Heroines," for sixteen years, following thirteen years of teaching Latin, Greek, and Sanskrit courses at the University of Southern California (USC). In the late '80s, I began to circle with women, following a wonderful class on the Craft with Susan Gray (Susan Gitlin-Emmer, who wrote an excellent book on the Germanic runes, *Lady of the Northern Light: A Feminist Guide to the* Runes.)[16]

As I look back upon my path I feel truly blessed, because my life's work and my spirituality have been united. I am humbled and grateful for the opportunity to co-edit this volume, and for the participation of all the amazing women who have contributed essays.

NOTES

1. In this volume, we have chosen to capitalize Goddess, Witch, Wicca, Shaman, Indigenous Mind, Mother Earth, and other religious terms.

2. Miriam Robbins (Dexter), *Indo-European Female Figures,* Doctoral Dissertation, University of California, Los Angeles. University Microfilms, 1978.

3. Miriam Robbins (Dexter), "The Assimilation of Pre-Indo-European Goddesses into Indo-European Society." *Journal of Indo-European Studies* 8, no.1-2: 19–29.

4. Marija Gimbutas, *The Kurgan Culture and the Indo-Europeanization of Europe: Selected articles from 1952 to 1993,* ed. Miriam Robbins Dexter and Karlene Jones-Bley (Washington, DC: Institute for the Study of Man—Journal of Indo-European Studies Monograph #18, 1997); *Varia on the Indo-European Past: Papers in Memory of Marija Gimbutas,* ed. Miriam Robbins Dexter and Edgar C. Polomé (Washington, DC: The Institute for the Study of Man—Journal of Indo-European Studies Monograph #19, 1997).

5. Marija Gimbutas, *The Living Goddesses,* ed. and supplemented by Miriam Robbins Dexter (Berkeley/Los Angeles: University of California Press, 1999).

6. Miriam Robbins Dexter, *Whence the Goddesses: A Source Book* (New York: Pergamon. Athene Series, 1990).

7. Starr Goode and Miriam Robbins Dexter, "Sexuality, the Sheela na gigs, and the Goddess in Ancient Ireland," *ReVision* 23, no. 1 (2000): 38–48. Miriam Robbins Dexter and Starr Goode, "The Sheela na gigs, Sexuality, and the Goddess in Ancient Ireland," *Irish Journal of Feminist Studies* 4, no. 2, ed. Mary Condren (2002): 50–75.

8. Miriam Robbins Dexter, "The Ferocious and the Erotic: 'Beautiful' Medusa and the Neolithic Bird and Snake," *Journal of Feminist Studies in Religion* 26, no.1 (2010): 25–41.

9. Miriam Robbins Dexter and Victor H. Mair, "Apotropaia and Fecundity in Eurasian Myth and Iconography: Erotic Female Display Figures," In *Proceedings of the Sixteenth Annual UCLA Indo-European Conference, 2004,* ed. Karlene Jones-Bley, Angela della Volpe, Martin Huld, and Miriam Robbins Dexter. (Washington, DC: Institute for the Study of Man—Journal of Indo-European Studies Monograph No. 50, 2005): 97-121.

10. Miriam Robbins Dexter and Victor H. Mair, *Sacred Display: Divine and Magical Female Figures of Eurasia* (Amherst, New York: Cambria Press, 2010).

11. Miriam Robbins Dexter and Victor H. Mair, *Sacred Display: New Findings. Sino-Platonic Papers*, September, 2013. http://www.sino-platonic.org.

12. Janine Canan, *Her Magnificent Body* (South San Francisco, California: ManrootPoems, 1986).

13. Janine Canan, ed., *She Rises Like the Sun* (Freedom, California: Crossing Press, 1989).

14. Marion Zimmer Bradley, *Mists of Avalon* (New York: Ballantine,1984).

15. Barbara Ardinger, *Finding New Goddesses: Reclaiming Playfulness in Our Spiritual Lives* Toronto: ECW Press, 2003).

16. Susan Gitlin-Emmer, *Lady of the Northern Light: A Feminist Guide to the Runes* (Freedom, California: Crossing Press, 1993).

Part I

Scholars

CHAPTER 1

OUR QUEST FOR
SPIRITUAL AUTHENTICITY

Charlene Spretnak

When the waves of newly discovered women's history rippled through
the emergent feminist movement in the early 1970s, some women felt
that the historical revelations bore only minimal relevance to urgent
issues of justice for women in all areas of modern life. For others of us,
learning of the historical documentation and prehistoric evidence—that
numerous cultures had honored the females as conduits to the sacred
cosmos in which they were embedded; that sacral presence and processes
had been perceived as concentrated in one or more female forms (that
is, Goddesses); and that religious rituals connecting the people with the
sacred whole were conducted by clan mothers or priestesses—felt like a
thrilling shock of cosmic electricity. An unknown inner dimension of us
sprang awake, intensely vital and utterly resilient. Why did those of us
who initiated the Women's Spirituality movement respond in this way

to the unexpected inheritance of female sacrality birthed in deep nature and deep time? It felt almost as if we were a long-dispersed sisterhood suddenly drawn together, suddenly so alive.

THE SIRENS' SONG

My initial encounter with history that was quite different from what I knew of (patriarchal) religion and culture came when I read the mass-market paperback edition of *The First Sex*[1] by Elizabeth Gould Davis in the spring of 1974. Riding home from a *vipassana* (mindfulness) meditation retreat in New Mexico in a Volkswagen, I spent the long trip, when not driving, reading that book in the backseat and yelling over the engine noise to the two women in the front seat, "Wow! Listen to this! This is incredible!" I later became aware that Davis had made leaps between some of the evidence and some of her conclusions, but it was she who drew back the heavy drapery that had hidden so much about women in cultural history.

In *The Odyssey*, Homer depicts the Sirens as *femmes fatales* who lure sailors to their death on a rocky shore—but in the *Metamorphoses* Ovid describes Sirens as companions of Persephone when she gathered the flowers of spring. Those are the ones I met in 1975 in Berkeley. Walking down Telegraph Avenue one day, I saw a posted flier about a workshop on women's spirituality and mythology, to be led by someone named Hallie Iglehart in her home. I went. We sat in a circle as she shared her intriguing findings about female mythology and her sense of one's personal mythology. One of the attendees I met at a subsequent workshop at Hallie's was Carol P. Christ. Through her I met Mara Lynn Keller. Something grand was being born.

I also met Merlin Stone in Berkeley shortly after her book *When God Was a Woman*[2] (1976) was published, and we became friends. I had begun researching the pre-Olympian myths of Greece, which became the book *Lost Goddesses of Early Greece*.[3] That year Carolyn Shaffer organized what was the first large conference on the women's spirituality movement, drawing speakers from New York, Texas, and Minneapolis, as well as the Bay Area: *The Great Goddess Re-Emerging*. The event was hosted by the University of California at Santa Cruz Extension. Presenters included Merlin Stone, Carol P. Christ, Kay Turner, Mary Beth Edelson, Z. Budapest, Hallie Iglehart, Nor Hall, Gloria Orenstein, and me. (Unfortunately, heads rolled: the staff person at UCSC Extension who had approved this marvelously energetic conference was fired soon afterward, apparently because of some spontaneous bare-breasted dancing on a terrace.) The year 1978 was also when the artist Mary Beth Edelson convinced the *Heresies* magazine collective in New York to let her organize a theme issue on Women's Spirituality; they reluctantly agreed, only to see it sell more copies than any other issue. Also that year I sought out Marija Gimbutas after reading her book *The Gods and Goddesses of Old Europe: 6500–3500 BC*;[4] she kindly answered my questions that afternoon, as our friendship began. In 1979, both *The Spiral Dance*[5] by Starhawk and *Drawing Down the Moon*[6] by Margot Adler were published. A few years later came *Jambalaya*,[7] by Luisah Teish and *The Sacred Hoop*,[8] by Paula Gunn Allen.

We were an entirely grassroots phenomenon, a characteristic that was reflected in the quarterly, nomadic magazine *WomanSpirit* (1974-1984). The most beautiful periodical of the movement, without fail, came out of Austin, Texas: *Lady-Unique-Inclination-of-the-Night*, edited by Kay Turner and her chums. Boston and the Bay Area were the two largest areas of concentration of the Women's Spirituality movement in the early years, but when the two editors of *Chrysalis* magazine set out from Los Angeles in the mid-1970s to make a cross-country survey of feminist communities, they were surprised to find in town after town that interest in Women's Spirituality seemed to be everywhere. In 1978, they invited me to write the introduction to a feature in *Chrysalis* (Issue 6), entitled "Women's Survival Catalogue: Spirituality," which presented twenty-two pages of annotated listings of books, articles, organizations, and events. In only a few years we had created a vast banquet.

CULTIVATING THE AUTHENTIC

After that heady beginning, the Women's Spirituality movement continued to work out the myriad implications of a female-honoring ontology, cosmology, and spiritual perspective. We felt that framing a critique of patriarchal religion, as Mary Daly had done early on in *The Church and the Second Sex*,[9] was merely a first step, a point of departure for a search—within women's religious heritage and within ourselves— for communion with the ineffable, a search that felt deeply authentic. We soon discovered that the critique of male-centered religion was a point of bifurcation: many women who agreed with the critique decided to remain in religious institutions in order to reform them, whereas many others of us, including Mary Daly, felt compelled to execute a collective swan dive into the uncharted waters of female-based spirituality and cosmology to see what we would find. It was unfortunate that there was some tension between these two groups (mostly from a few feminist theologians toward the renegades), but that largely dissipated over time.

What did our movement accomplish? Even with the extensive bibliography of insights that have been articulated by authors in Women's Spirituality over forty years, most of our effect flourished beyond that, in the unquantifiable realm of women's inner lives, in our newly grounded presence in a male-dominant culture, in our sense of being part of a profound sisterhood with deep historical roots, and in our activist dreams for a better world. Much of this range of intangibles is underlain by the revolutionary *naming* we achieved, which was extraordinarily liberating: we grasped that patriarchal religion—with its hierarchical institutions ruled over by a male god as Commander-in-Chief—was not simply "religion" but, rather, a *type* of religion that had evolved as a comfortable fit with the male psyche. This decentering of male-oriented religion freed women to evolve our own modes of deep communion with the sacred whole.

Because women demonstrate repeatedly on tests of perception, even when given cross-culturally, that we tend to perceive the gestalt of a situation or a pattern, it made perfect sense to us that a spirituality that was authentic to us would celebrate dynamic interrelatedness, that is, the relational nature of reality—and beauty, always beauty: the momentary awe at the softness of a baby's skin, the green colors of a spring garden, the palpable presence of old friends, even over the telephone. We created rituals and made small altars in our homes on which we set objects that spark gratitude, connection, and a calm joy. Some of us were drawn to Goddesses, or Wicca, or world mythology; some were not. By forming our circles, always exploring and expanding to learn from diverse perspectives, we found our way.

Why Is There No Book About...

Every once in a while, I wished a certain book existed—so I wrote it. The first time this need occurred to me was in 1976 when I was driving in my car with my pre-school daughter and she became very excited at the sight of a white sign featuring a red horse with wings, the logo of Mobil Oil. I explained that the flying horse was named Pegasus and that he was from a very old story called a myth. I told her that we could go to the library and take out a book of myths to read at home. At the library, however, I discovered that all their books on Greek mythology presented only the patriarchal versions, with most of the females depicted as duped, duplicitous, or contorted with jealousy at a male's infidelity—not at all suitable for an impressionable little girl. I knew from my reading that there were older, Goddess-centered myths, which—as the famed classicist Jane Ellen Harrison put it—constituted a stratum at once more primitive and more permanent than the Olympian myths conveyed by Homer. I did research for about a year in the Classics library on the campus of the University of California at Berkeley. Eventually, I had tracked down a substantial amount of archaeological and other documentation about the pre-Olympian Goddesses. With that data, I reconstructed the earlier myths based on the characteristics, objects, places, and practices associated with each Goddess. This book was titled *Lost Goddesses of Early Greece: A Collection of Pre-Hellenic Myths* (1978).[10]

The following year, it became apparent that the exuberant growth of the Women's Spirituality branch of the feminist movement was considered thoroughly deplorable by members of a different branch: socialist/Marxist feminists. In articles, some of them opined that Women's Spirituality was counter-revolutionary and a dead weight on the feminist movement because it lured women into a self-absorbed, apolitical state of mind, removing them from the struggle. This depiction, I knew, was not accurate. So I compiled and edited an anthology, a chorus of voices organized into three categories: Discovering a History of Power, Manifesting Personal Power, and Transforming the Political. Half of the fifty articles were reprinted from Women's Spirituality magazines, and half were commissioned for the book. *The Politics of Women's Spirituality*[11] came out in 1982 and went through several printings. In the early 1990s the publisher invited me to write a Preface about the movement, which I titled "The First Twenty Years;" it is included in the 1994 edition, with cover art by Mayumi Oda.

In the late 1980s, I wished there were a book that would take on the modern assumption that religions are merely marginal in the modern era and would never be the source of practical solutions to the problems of modernity. In particular, I wished there were a book that presented the special focus, or gift, of various spiritual traditions that are relevant to solving the crises of our time—and I wished that Goddess spirituality would be recognized for its gifts on equal footing with the other traditions. I also wished there were a book that would cut through the assumptions of extreme social constructionism (also called then deconstructive post-modernism), one that would include an ecofeminist refutation of the "decon" belief that any cultural connections made between women and nature, whether historical or contemporary, cancel the possibility that women can be cultural agents in any given society. All of these issues

I addressed in a book entitled *States of Grace: The Recovery of Meaning in the Postmodern Age.*[12]

After not paying much attention for about thirty years to the patriarchal religion in which I had been raised, Roman Catholicism, I stuck a toe back in during the early 2000s. Imagine my surprise to find that they had all but eliminated the Great Mother figure at the heart of the faith, a sacred-mother-and-son religion. In order to modernize the church, bishops and other Council Fathers from around the world had been called to Rome in 1962–1965 to the Second Vatican Council to bring the church into the present day, as Pope John XXIII had put it when he convened the historic gathering. In the areas of theology and liturgy, the Council Fathers voted to make it all more rational (that is, more text-based and far less involved in communion with the ineffable through sculpture, paintings, poetic prayers, heavenly music, and the scent of incense). It was obvious to me that the Virgin Mary, though not a Goddess, carried forth into the modern era many of the characteristics of Goddess religions in the eastern Mediterranean basin: producing a son via parthenogenesis who became a great leader and died but arose. Even more importantly, Mary's bountiful spiritual presence had symbolic, mystical, and cosmological dimensions—all of which the modernizers had thrown out the window, even as they made wise and overdue decisions in the other areas they voted on. Clearly, there needed to be a book about this loss. I weighed in with *Missing Mary.*[13]

In the mid-1990s, I learned that art historians and other art world professionals generally hold that there is no spiritual content in modern art because, beginning with the Impressionists' first exhibition in 1874, modern art had made a great leap across the chasm *away from* tradition, religion, and bourgeois values. In spite of that narrative, I knew that scores of famous modern artists had had spiritual interests that played out in their creation of radically new art forms. Over seventeen years I did research, which revealed that more than 150 prominent historical modern artists and more than one hundred prominent contemporary artists made their spiritual interests central in their art. This research became the book *The Spiritual Dynamic in Modern Art*.[14] Among the many artists I was especially charmed by were Remedios Varo and Leonora Carrington, who, after painting in the male-dominated Surrealist scene in Paris, created a small women's spirituality community in Mexico City with two other artists and painted mystical works with woman and female agency at the center. In Varo's extraordinary works especially, a variety of Goddess-like figures typically perform extraordinary feats of creation or scientific discovery with utter nonchalance.

I am grateful every day for the abundant blessings generated by the Women's Spirituality movement throughout these forty years.

NOTES

1. Elizabeth Gould Davis, *The First Sex* (New York: Penguin, 1972).
2. Merlin Stone, *When God Was a Woman* (New York: Barnes and Noble, 1976).
3. Charlene Spretnak, *Lost Goddesses of Early Greece: A Collection of Pre-Hellenic Myths* (New York: Beacon Press, 1978).
4. Marija Gimbutas, *The Gods and Goddesses of Old Europe, 6500-3500 BC: myths and cult images* (Los Angeles: University of California Press, 1974). (Republished in 1982 as *The Goddesses and Gods of Old Europe.*)
5. Starhawk, *The Spiral Dance* (New York: Harper and Row, 1979).
6. Margot Adler, Drawing Down the Moon (New York: Viking, 1979).
7. Luisah Teish, *Jambalaya* (San Francisco: HarperOne, 1985).
8. Paula Gunn Allen, *The Sacred Hoop* (New York: Beacon, 1986).
9. Mary Daly, *The Church and the Second Sex* (New York: Harper & Row, 1968).
10. Charlene Spretnak, *Lost Goddesses of Early Greece: A Collection of Pre-Hellenic Myths.*
11. Charlene Spretnak, ed., *The Politics of Women's Spirituality.* (New York: Anchor/Doubleday, 1982).
12. Charlene Spretnak, *States of Grace: The Recovery of Meaning in the Post-modern Age* (San Francisco: HarperSanFrancisco,1991).
13. Charlene Spretnak, *Missing Mary* (New York: Palgrave Macmillan, 2004).
14. Charlene Spretnak, *The Spiritual Dynamic in Modern Art* ((New York: Palgrave Macmillan, 2014).

Chapter 2

The Life and Work of a Feminist Goddess Theologian

Carol P. Christ

Along with the loving voices of my mother, grandmother, and aunt, the eerie cries of the peacocks on the roof must have been one of the first sounds I heard when I was brought from the hospital to my grandmother's home at the back of the Los Angeles County Arboretum. Mother love and the mystery and beauty of nature nourished me in my childhood years. When I was fourteen, my baby brother died. His death launched a too early and lifelong search for the meaning of life, which led me to the study of the Hebrew Bible in my undergraduate years. The juxtaposition of anger and compassion in the God of the Hebrews appealed to me at the time, perhaps because it mirrored my experience with my father. My undergraduate thesis on nature imagery in the prophets argued that their insistence that the trees of the field would clap their hands on the day of redemption was not a metaphor "for something other than" an affirmation of the deeply spiritual connection between divinity, humanity, and other forms of life. The term "pathetic fallacy," the error of attributing feeling to plants or animals, was introduced to me during my oral examination. Much later I coined the term "apathetic fallacy," the error of not attributing feeling to other than human forms of life.

I went to Yale to study the Hebrew Bible and was soon discouraged from that pursuit by the professor with whom I had chosen to study. I landed in theology, where I was still the only woman in the program. I was young and pretty and "looked like Twiggy" and not taken seriously as a student. In those days professors and students felt entitled to tell me at every turn that I "probably would not finish my degree" and that if I did, they "would hire a man with a family" over me. I took courses on Karl Barth and St. Thomas Aquinas during my first year, and though not assigned, read their disquisitions on women, hoping to gain insight into why I was being treated as if I did not have a mind in my body. What I found was that "the great" theologians of Roman Catholicism and Protestantism agreed that woman was created to be obedient to and subordinate to man. Aquinas followed Aristotle in proclaiming that females had a lesser rational capacity than males. No wonder my rational mind was not being taken seriously by my colleagues! Barth argued that God created "man" to have "initiative, precedence, and authority" in relation to "woman," just as God had in relation to man. When I attempted to discuss these ideas with my boyfriend, he laughed and said that no one took that part of Barth's work seriously. I knew from my own experience that such views were widely held, but I often felt that I must be crazy. As I write these words decades later, my body reminds me that the constant dismissal of my mind—my ideas, insights, and questions— at Yale was a profound trauma that is still not fully healed.

I suspected then that there was some relationship between the maleness of God and male domination, an idea that was dismissed even by the majority of those invited to the first Conference of Women Theologians at Alverno College in 1971. This conference was held at the same time

Mary Daly published "After the Death of God the Father,"[1] in which she stated that the God who "is dead" is the Father in whose realm women would always come in second. Hers were among the first published words that validated my questions. At the conference, I suggested that we form a women's caucus at the next annual meetings of the American Academy of Religion; thus an academic feminist community that sustained my early writing was born. Back at Yale, I told my advisor that I was thinking of writing about women's spiritual quest in the novels of Doris Lessing in my dissertation, but he turned that idea down. However, he accepted an analysis of the early works of Elie Wiesel—who at that time was a little known writer on the theological implications of the holocaust.

I was looking for God the Mother when I moved to New York City in 1972 to teach at Columbia University. I began my own search for sources that had not been part of my education. I was disappointed that the Greek Goddesses were under the thumb of the warrior God Zeus, and because I was vehemently opposed to the Vietnam War, I was not attracted to the Devī of the *Devī Māhātmyam* slaying hordes of demons with her sword. I was shocked to discover in Raphael Patai's *The Hebrew Goddess*[2] that when the prophets railed against those who worshipped "on every high hill and under every green tree" they were castigating worshippers of Asherah. My faith was challenged. Most of the others in the New York Feminist Scholars in Religion, which I founded in 1974 with Anne Barstow, dismissed the "need" for "God-She." But when I came back from a sabbatical in California in the fall of 1976, Anne Barstow and Naomi Goldenberg and I spoke to the group about the Goddess. Our presentations unleashed an enormous energy and argument about whether it was necessary to leave Judaism and Christianity.

In the interim, several important things had happened. In the spring of 1974, while writing about Elie Wiesel's anger at God for abandoning the Jews during the holocaust, I started feeling my own anger at God for the history of the male domination of women. One night, I lay down on my bed and cried out: Why did you let women be raped and beaten and abused? Why did you allow our voices to be silenced? Why did you not send us a prophet or a savior? Where were you when women were suffering? In the silence that followed, I heard what I have described as a "still small voice" in my mind. It said, "in God is a woman like yourself. She too has suffered and had her history stolen from Her." This experience redoubled my quest for a God like myself—in whose image I was created. My questions, ideas, and hopes were also being validated in my teaching as they never were at Yale, in powerful courses on women and religion that had the force of "revelation" for me and for my students.

Visiting Mama Bears Bookstore in Oakland, California during my sabbatical in 1975–1976, I picked up copies of *The Gods and Goddesses of Old Europe*[3] by Marija Gimbutas, the first issues of *WomanSpirit* magazine (1974), and an early version of Z Budapest's manifesto for the Goddess movement, *A Feminist Book of Lights and Shadows.*[4] During the year, I took classes on healing and women's wisdom with Hallie Iglehart (Austen), and one of the first workshops offered by Starhawk. Starhawk's naming of "the Goddess" and the rituals she created with us confirmed for me in a way nothing else had that I was right to be seeking "Her."

I read Merlin Stone's *When God Was a Woman*[5] as soon as it was published, transfixed by her re-imagining of Goddess history—a story I had never heard in all my years of studying religion! At the same time, I was invited by a friend to a performance of Ntozake Shange's *for colored girls who have considered suicide/when the rainbow is enuf.* I too had considered suicide in response to the multiple traumas I had suffered in my twenties at the hands of men; I felt my skin tingle when a tall (like me) black woman rose from her despair to sing, "i found god in myself/ and i loved her fiercely/i loved her fiercely."

Naomi Goldenberg encouraged me to join her in proposing a closed seminar (we were afraid of going public) at the American Academy of Religion in the winter of 1977, where we would invite Z Budapest and Starhawk to present papers on the Goddess along with us. Naomi and I wrote our papers in my living room just before the conference. I can still remember our excitement and fear as we asked each other continually, "Can I say this?" In the end we did read everything we had written. At the conference I met Marie Cantlon and John Loudin of HarperSanFrancisco and introduced them to Starhawk. I "went public" with my essay, "Why Women Need the Goddess," in the spring of 1978 when I read it to 500 cheering women and a few men as the keynote address at the "Great Goddess Re-Emerging" conference at the University of Santa Cruz—which was covered on page three of the *Los Angeles Times.* The two decades of Harper publishing books in Women's Spirituality began with the publication of *Womanspirit Rising*[6] (in which "Why Women Need the Goddess" was included), co-edited with my friend from graduate school Judith Plaskow, and Starhawk's *The Spiral Dance .*[7]

My book on women's spiritual quest, *Diving Deep and Surfacing,*[8] was published a year later. During those heady years when I was speaking at universities and to church groups several times a month, I was also being distanced by my feminist colleagues in the academy who were beginning to close ranks as Christian feminists; their subtle and not so subtle snubs reopened old wounds. When a senior feminist colleague told me to give up my dream of teaching graduate students in the field of religion because my work (which she said she respected greatly) was too radical, I decided to leave the university and move to Greece. My last year in the academy was spent at Harvard Divinity School where the serious threat by a senior faculty member that the hiring of Elisabeth Schussler-Fiorenza in New Testament would be "over his dead body" and the inability of the women faculty to respond to a paper I had presented publically because as one of them said "we could never do anything like that at Harvard" made it clear to me that I did not really even want a job at Harvard.

My story and theological reflections on my journey from God to Goddess were published as *Laughter of Aphrodite,*[9] just before I left Harvard. When I moved to Greece, I took with me a contract to write a systematic Goddess theology along with many questions about whether or not theology was the appropriate mode in which to write about the

Goddess. In my lecture at Harvard I had posed but not answered the theological question about whether the Goddess is a personal presence who cares about individuals and the fate of the world or simply the name we give to the forces of birth, death, and renewal that undergird all of life. When I wrote the first draft of my Goddess theology, my editors responded that "something" was missing. My inability to figure out what this was, combined with my disappointment with the Goddess Aphrodite that I have written about elsewhere, made it impossible for me to finish the book. I toyed with writing poetry or fiction but instead I put my energies into a second volume co-edited with Judith Plaskow, *Weaving the Visions*,[10] and fixing up the apartment I had purchased in Athens.

Then in 1991 my mother died. The experience I had as she died changed my life. *As my mother died, the room filled with love.* Until that moment I had often felt I was not loved enough. From that moment to this, I have known that love is everywhere and that the divine power is love. Like many others, I had equated love with "finding my true love" and had discounted other forms of love. Once I gave up that delusion, I realized that love is everywhere.

An invitation to write about my mother's death opened the wellsprings of my creativity and the memoir that was titled *Odyssey with the Goddess*[11] (my title was *A Serpentine Path*) came pouring out of me. Once I finished the memoir I realized that I had the answer to the question I posed during my Harvard speech. I understood that the Goddess is love, or as I stated: *"Goddess is the intelligent embodied love that is the ground of all being."*[12] I had found the "something" that was missing in the earlier draft of my Goddess theology. Duh...it was just a little bit difficult to write a Goddess theology without resolving the theological question of the nature of divinity! With new insight firmly planted in my mind, I dove enthusiastically into the task of writing a Goddess theology. I covered the important theological topics: "God," "man," the world, and ethics. It was not an easy task, because I had no body of earlier work on the subject to refer to, to question, to agree or disagree with. I recognized that the question of epistemology or "how do we know" had to be dealt with before I could begin. I developed a theory of "embodied thinking" and argued theology begins in experience and is challenged and confirmed in community.

In the process of writing *Rebirth of the Goddess*,[13] I realized that I am a theologian after all: I like to think about and discuss the meaning of life in philosophical terms. However, I reject the notion that rational thinking can ever appeal to transcendent principles. Like everything else in life, thinking is rooted in the body, in relationships, in communities, in history. Therefore, theology must always include narrative elements. And its conclusions must always be prefaced with something like: from my standpoint and taking into account a wide number of other standpoints, it seems to me that...

Because I was completing my Goddess theology in splendid isolation from other academics (and that may have been necessary), my theological companion Judith Plaskow and my editor Marie Cantlon were the only ones who had read it. I wondered: was the book I had written a theology? Would it be recognized as such by other scholars? I decided to send it to the two male theologians with whom I had had my most recent contact: Gordon Kaufmann and John Cobb, who had jointly led a theological seminar I had participated in while at Harvard. I boxed up the hard copy, added a letter, and waited with trepidation. Gordon, who had responded positively when I criticized his work in my Harvard lecture, said that my book was precisely the kind of theology that is needed in our time. John wrote back that I had written a process theology and invited me to visit him the next time I came to California.

Because John lives near where my family lives, I visited him the next year. When I told him that I had never seriously studied process theology and that I had only referred to the single book by Charles Hartshorne that I had ever read from memory, John responded that this made my achievement even more amazing: I had worked my way through to the major insights of process philosophy on my own. These include the relational nature of reality, the affirmation of change, the notion that divinity cannot be omnipotent because it is not the only actor in the universe, and the idea that feeling—and feeling the feelings of others— permeates the world. My study of process philosophy and the strong affinity I felt for the work of American philosopher Charles Hartshorne led me to write *She Who Changes* (2003),[14] in which I argued that process philosophy's relational worldview provides a framework for many of the assertions of feminist spirituality and theology. It made me very happy to realize that ways of thinking that some have called "women's way of knowing" can be shown to be rational ways of thinking that explain the metaphysical basis of all of reality. It would be an understatement to say that process philosophy has provided a firm foundation for my theological thinking.

I wrote *She Who Changes* during the internet age, and the exchange of chapters by email with Judith Plaskow began a dialogue about the nature of Goddess or God that culminated in a nearly-completed book tentatively titled *Divinity in the World: Conversations in Embodied Theology*.[15] While writing about the nature of Goddess in terms of Hartshorne's idea that the divinity is the most relational of all relational beings and the most sympathetic of all sympathetic individuals in the universe, I assumed that Judith would agree with me. At the same time, she must have thought that she could convince me of her view that divinity is an impersonal power of creativity that undergirds everything in the world—including all good and all evil. We decided to write a book exploring our differences and exposing our theological agreements and disagreements. Because neither of us could convince the other to change her opinions with rational or moral arguments, we concluded that the roots of theology in experience must be discussed. We model a new way of doing theology that takes seriously the dictum of *Womanspirit Rising* that "theology begins in experience."[16] In the process, we have discovered that our theological views are rooted in deeply held experiences, while at the same time that no single experience or group of experiences can be shown to be "the cause" of our different, yet equally complex and reasonable, views of Goddess or God and the world.

NOTES

1. Mary Daly, "After the Death of God the Father: Women's Liberation and the Transformation of Christian Consciousness," in *Womanspirit Rising: A Feminist Reader in Religion*, ed. Carol P. Christ and Judith Plaskow (San Francisco:Harper & Row, 1979), 53-62.
2. Raphael Patai, *The Hebrew Goddess* (New York: Avon, 1967).
3. Marija Gimbutas, *The Gods and Goddesses of Old Europe, 6500-3500 BC: myths and cult images* (Los Angeles: University of California Press, 1974).
4. Zsusanna Budapest, *The Feminist Book of Lights and Shadows*, ed. Helen Beardwoman. (Venice, California: Luna Publications, 1975).
5. Merlin Stone, *When God Was a Woman* (New York: Barnes and Noble, 1976).
6. Carol P. Christ, "Why Women Need the Goddess," in *Womanspirit Rising: A Feminist Reader in Religion*, ed. Carol P. Christ and Judith Plaskow (San Francisco:Harper & Row, 1979), 273–287.
7. Starhawk, *The Spiral Dance* (New York: Harper and Row, 1979).
8. Carol P. Christ, *Diving Deep and Surfacing: Women Writers on Spiritual Quest* (Boston: Beacon Press, 1980).
9. Carol P. Christ, *The Laughter of Aphrodite* (Berkeley: University of California Press, 1987).
10. Judith Plaskow and Carol P. Christ, eds., *Weaving the Visions: New Patterns in Feminist Spirituality* (San Francisco: Harper and Row, 1989).
11. Carol P. Christ, *Odyssey with the Goddess: A Spiritual Quest in Crete* (New York: Continuum, 1995).
12. Carol P. Christ, *Rebirth of the Goddess: Finding Meaning in Feminist Spirituality* (New York: Addison-Wesley, 1997), 107.
13. Carol P. Christ, *Rebirth of the Goddess: Finding Meaning in Feminist Spirituality* (New York: Addison-Wesley, 1997).
14. Carol P. Christ, *She Who Changes* (New York: Palgrave Macmillan, 2003).
15. Fortress Press, 2016.
16. *Womanspirit Rising: A Feminist Reader in Religion*, ed. Carol P. Christ and Judith Plaskow (San Francisco:Harper & Row, 1979), 5-9.

CHAPTER 3

RESURGENCE

Max Dashú

When I began on this path, no movement was visible yet, but we were there, breaking through the surface. As we emerged from our female spiritual exile under patriarchy, women were looking around to discern the lay of the land. We knew how much we did not know, how much had been stolen from us in our long bondage. But our understanding was good, and it was this: we saw that Goddess had been overthrown, crushed, trampled. In us, women, feminists, witches, she had been punished, hated and reviled, and beaten down into an unconsciously defensive crouch. Our state of alienation and emergency had been so profound that we could barely name it. Now we turned ourselves around and embraced the task of setting ourselves free. It was a momentous return.

In 1971, a group of female squatters spent a summer camping in the woods behind a Vermont commune, aiming to recover and discover our witchen ancestry. We chanted, sat around the fire, danced under the moon, and had long conversations about how we could free ourselves. This was going on in other places, too, although these early spiritual feminist dawnings were hardly ever recorded anywhere. They happened before named groups and formal organizations came into existence. We were wild, passionate, and rebelliously anarchic. We began finding each other and coalescing into an incipient movement. In 1976, a hundred of us gathered at the Siskiyou WomanSpirit festival in northern California, dancing in ecstatic joy to drums around a fire, lolling on rocks along a stream.

I participated in many circles, both in the coalescing women's land movement and in city full moon circles where we trance-danced. I also went on quests to the land, away from the man-made, into mountains and forests, to rivers and seashores. I drank them in, chanting and dancing. I came to release pain, to stretch open, to expand my strength: to learn freedom. I roamed the wilderness and sat out on great rocks in silence.

It was a challenge for an epileptic non-driver to get out of the city, hitchhiking and learning to backpack as a woman alone. I had to overcome fears that were both realistic and culturally induced. I bushwhacked off-trail and concealed my fireless camp, wary of a certain breed of two-legged. I learned to listen closely, casting a safety radar, observing birdcalls and sounds of approach. And in the untamed mountains, the nectar poured into me like a long rain, among the gnarled junipers with their amber-stained wood (see figure 1).

Painting and drawing were a big part of my spiritual life in the '70s. My primary theme was sacred dance, the movement of power through women's bodies and how this streaming profoundly transforms our consciousness. I gave away many of my pictures in those days, without keeping copies. They hung on walls and altars all over the West Coast. Some were published in *Womanspirit* magazine, the pagan mag *Nemeton*, and various feminist journals; others in Judy Grahn's *She Who*, my own *Witch Dream* comix, *We'moon* Calendar, and *Daughters of the Moon* Tarot.

My search for free women had begun in 1970, when I left college to research women's history. I scanned the cultural record then available, loaded with kings, gods, and warriors. Paging through countless books and journals, I searched for images and knowledge about real women, while culling out the dominionist misrepresentations. I tried to discover where in the world egalitarian societies could be found, which necessitated studying the history of war and empire. Learning about Indigenous history and cultures—especially the mother-right societies, so rich in orature commemorating female founders and leaders—was a central element of this research.

How had women in the past, and in various cultures, connected with earth, water, wind and fire, with animals and plants and with each other? What did their ceremonial practices look like? I found multitudes of female figurines, in innumerable forms, over most of the planet. These ancestral Mothers appeared as the defining icons of the oldest cultures—and yet so little attention was paid to them. That was the unselfconscious sexual politics of the gatekeepers. I thought that the spiritual and political belonged together, were in fact deeply intertwined. This went against the prevailing tide which saw them as oppositional, though many feminists I knew felt the same way.

As the Fates would have it, I became a historical consultant for Donna Deitch's first film, in 1973–1974. She wanted a section on women's history in her feminist documentary, *Woman to Woman*. We went to UCLA and other university libraries searching for archaeological images and shooting slides to use in the film. I learned copy photography and wound up with about 300 slides, the seedlings of the Suppressed Histories Archives.

In 1974, I began doing slideshows at feminist coffeehouses and book-stores. The first happened at A Woman's Place bookstore in Oakland, with Sandy Ajida on congas, Kay Sato on koto, and Cynthia Fitzpatrick on flute. Other shows followed up and down the West Coast (including one on witches for Starhawk's Reclaiming collective). Showing sacred images to women, I witnessed their visceral reaction of recognition, of loss and anger that the female Divine had been locked away from view. They were elated to find that these heritages existed, and they expressed delight in experiencing what untrammeled female power looks like (see figure 2).

That is how I started teaching with images. First there was one show, then four, then eight. As I added new images, they kept fissioning off into new shows, until there were over a hundred. I began by presenting slideshows on women's history, mother-right cultures, and Goddesses in feminist bookstores, coffeehouses, and women's centers. In 1981, I began to break into universities, mostly through the Women's Centers that feminists founded. Since then, I have done hundreds of visual presentations at colleges, community centers, schools, museums, galleries, churches, prisons, festivals, and conferences. Titles include *Female Icons, Ancestral Mothers; Deasophy: Goddess Wisdom; Woman Shaman; Mother-Right and Gender Justice; Female Rebels and Mavericks; Witches and Pagans; Treasures of African Women,* and *Rebel Shamans: Indigenous Women Confront Empire.*

Traveling up and down the West Coast, I was seeking to recover the shamanic dimensions of *wycce-cræft.* It was clear to me that women of European descent needed to recover and restore our own heritages. Only through a direct relationship with Nature—the ultimate wellspring from which all those traditions grew—would we be able to illuminate the deep wisdom that survived in folk tradition, in the historic residues of sculpture, embroidery, manuscripts; of songs, stories, proverbs and spells. We longed to reintegrate these strands, to reclaim demonized female power and the long-persecuted pagan folk religions. Many early feminists reclaimed the name Witch, seeing witches as embodiments of female power and rebellion. "You are a Witch by saying aloud, 'I am a Witch' three times, and *thinking about that.* You are a Witch by being female, untamed, angry, joyous, and immortal."[1] So we proudly called ourselves witches.

Many women were influenced by the neo-pagan Wiccan revival, with its restoration of the old solar holydays and cross-quarters. Doreen Valiente's magnificent "Charge of the Goddess" inspired many: "For She is the soul of nature, who gives life to the universe...from Her all things proceed, and unto Her all things must return; and before Her face, let thine innermost divine self be enfolded in the rapture of the infinite...For behold, She has been with thee from the beginning; and She is that which is attained at the end of desire."[2] The Wiccan label soon lost its attraction when I found out that it was a 20th century renaming from an Anglo-Saxon word meaning "male witch." Many feminist witches have moved beyond the Celtic/Saxon emphasis of Wicca to reaffirm their Italian, Slavic, Norse, Jewish, and other ethnic heritages. Wiccan chants or ballad-style circle songs did not appeal to me; I lean toward wild minor-key melodies and rhythms that animate sacramental dance and open up the ecstatic.

It's easy to miss how many currents of influence were flowing. Female spiritual seekers delved into yoga, ecstatic *bhajans*, and the Thousand Names of Lalitā and Kālī. We pursued Buddhist meditation and mantras, Taoist philosophy, and qigong. We tasted exaltation in Peruvian *sanjuanitos*, the voices of Miriam Makeba and Letta Mbulu, Irish airs and Slavic dances.

We went as deep as we could to recover the ancient names and mother tongues, searching for the sacraments of long past ancestors. We gazed at the ancient statues, rock paintings, ceramics and seals, to glean snatches of the ceremonies of far-passed time. They taught us. The old clay figurines showed us how women painted up for ritual. We saw the kind of offering vessels they used, in the shape of breasts or women or animals. Ceramic paintings showed us women's circle dances, processions with branches, spirals and cascades of energy, rain on fields. Now we are longing to hear again the songs, the medicine songs, *oriki*, and *varðlokkur*, to recreate the haunting refrains of journey music.

What are our remedies? We've learned, often through sheer need answered by synchronicity. One is the restorative power of immersion into "living waters," as the Hebrew women of old called the fresh streams and pools. We smudge to cleanse our bodies and spaces, with Artemisia (moxa, desert sage, mugwort), with copal and myrrh and palo santo. We lie down on the earth and heal with herbs and stones. We open our inner sight by gazing into embers and mirrors and bowls of water. We draw and lay out the cards; divide and gather the yarrow stalks; cast the cowries, the cocos, the "bones." We observe our sacred days of the week, the lunar month, the quarterly and yearly, marking the revolution of time. "Are we not olden, olden, olden?"[3]

A longing for the female Divine has been pouring forth from many cultural directions. Women have been rediscovering and recreating liberatory female spiritual culture from their ancestral heritages. In the African streams, women have embraced drumming and entered the path of Ifá, of Lucumí and Santería, and of the ancient Kemetic spiritual philosophies. A movement to restore the *Kohanot* (Hebrew priestesses) is growing among Jewish women, amidst a flowering of music, poetry, and other cultural expressions of feminist Judaic culture. The Mexicanas are plunging into *curanderismo* and restoring *cultura indígena*. We resonate to rhythms that call up the *devatā* and dakinis (*ḍākinīs*), the *faerie*, the *zar*, the *bori* and orisha.

We draw inspiration from the *bembes* and teachings of Luisah Teish, from the Pinay way-showers of the babaylan restoration, from drum priestesses like Edwina Lee Tyler and Ubaka Hill, from the mass incantations convened by Jennifer Berezan and the pagan Celtic anthems of Ruth Barrett. We rejoice in the majestic torch-bearers descending to the stage at Michfest, the annual Women's Sundance in New Mexico, the Two-Spirit powwows in Oakland, and the drum circles at Idle No More demonstrations for Indigenous sovereignty, in the middle of urban shopping centers.

Each woman needs to find her authentic place to stand, grounded in her own heritages. We don't have to recreate a historical period gone by, but sipping from the elixir of cellular memory and continuity has a power that moves us forward in the present. We remember, too, the historical and cultural reasons why not all sacred ways might be shared. The guiding principle is being invited in; the guardians of a tradition decide whether to include outsiders—or not. This awareness bypasses the shoals of cultural appropriation. Respect leads to the real shore of community. There we can each bring what we carry into the circle, to learn from each other and be mutually strengthened.

We are growing incantation and litanies, a body of ceremonial practice to draw on. We need room for variability, a way to move within the structure as who we really are. We are developing shared containers that offer this, without pressing anyone to do things in ceremony that they do not feel moved to say or do. Now we need to take the next step in manifesting Council, ways of coming together that go beyond paid conferences. That is a challenge, because women don't control public space; very few of us have land or temples. Everything costs money.

One of the hardest challenges to our co-creations comes from mass-market stereotypes, with their pervasive pornification of anything female and powerful. A web search for "Goddess," "priestess," or "female shaman" brings up torrents of pictures and videos of simpering Barbies whose unrealistic bodies are contorted into pin-up poses. (Searches in Russian, Japanese, Chinese, and Spanish all yield the same results.) This contamination affects impressionable girls and women who do not perceive the distorting lens of hyper-sexualization because it is all around them. Of course, sexuality is sacred! But the impossibly narrow stereotype of pouting models spreads lies about the Female. This insidious tyranny of market forces teaches girls and women to hate their bodies, and rather than inhabiting them, to perform as feminine consumables. It is more imperative than ever to decolonize the Female and to hold her sacred (see figure 3).

In 1978, I began writing the *Secret History of the Witches*, to uncover the original spiritual traditions of Europe. I traced the Matronae, knotwork, Sheela-na-gigs, Fatas and faery traditions of my ancestral lands. I found women's hearth sacraments, herb chants and healing ways, ceremonies of spinning and weaving; and incantations, sweathouses, birth rites, and funereal keening. It was equally crucial to document w*hat happened in Europe*: the attacks on female power, the loss of pagan culture, the witch persecutions and the resulting Terror. We need to understand how women were vanquished, and how Europe colonized the world. The long unfolding of the witch hunts is the prehistory of the racist imperial settler patriarchy we are living under now. I know this is hard stuff for people to look at, and some will say it is negativity. But what I know from history is that without shining a light on the poisons, they keep causing terrible harm. My book is still unpublished after all this time because the process of recovery is endless. I keep adding and revising, expanding and fleshing out detail as new knowledge comes to light. But that could go on forever, so I'm going to publish the first volumes soon. After a good shaking from the Fates, I'm ready to pour out what I have gathered in the past forty-five years, out on the web, in photo essays and video streams, into books and DVDs. I want to paint again, and to composite my art with digital images in video animations. This is my way of loving the world, all her peoples, their cultural treasures, sacraments, and insights.

Looking forward, I see our resurgence expanding. Women have broken down cultural barriers and opened liberatory pathways, drumming and dancing, co-creating ceremonies, and dreaming again into ancestral wisdom. It is time to grow into procession, in defense of earth and water and forest, of humans and animals. It is time to bring our banners, masks, staffs, drums, and sacred anthems to call people together to the reverence of Mother Earth. It is time to spend all-night vigils in the womb of intention, meditating in concentrating awareness and entering into the vastness of infinite renewal (see figure 4).

And oh, what happens when we sway, shake, whirl—when we roll our hips and throw up our arms? When we moan, collectively wail, breathe it out, pant the fire-breath and bathe ourselves in *prana*? When we massage and brush, brush off, brush away illness, when we activate our bodies with intention: what then happens to our consciousness? "There we enter into the Presence where knowing and healing come."[4] And there guidance showers upon us, because the Universe is a numinous, resonant, and responsive Being.

NOTES

1. NYC W.I.T.C.H, 1970, in Robin Morgan, ed., *Sisterhood Is Powerful: An Anthology of Writings from the Women's Liberation Movement* (New York: Random House, 1970), 540.
2. Original Doreen Valiente version of the Charge of the Goddess: http://www.controverscial.com/The Charge of the Goddess.htm, via John Belham-Payne, designated conservator for Doreen Valiente.
3. Judy Grahn, "Plainsong from an older woman to a younger woman," Personal manuscript copy, Oakland, 1972.
4. Max Dashú, "The Meanings of Goddess" 2007. Goddess Pages, Spring 2007. Glastonbury UK: 2007 http://www.goddess-pages.co.uk/index.php/2007-issues/2-spring-2007/item/59-the-meanings-of-goddess-part-1.

CHAPTER 4

MY SPIRITUALITY HOLDS THE MEANING OF LIFE FOR ME

Elinor W. Gadon

My memory of my earliest consciousness of a "women's spirituality" as a distinct phenomenon—gendered, unique, separate from the generalized "spirituality" that was a theme in the History of Religion I studied—was a part of my own growing awareness of my embodied, gendered being. As Adrienne Rich had informed us, our minds were located in our bodies, and mine was physiologically female. This was in the '80s. I was teaching World Religion at the Harvard University Divinity School. Carol Gilligan of the Education School addressed the faculty on her ongoing research and theory, in which she claimed that women had a different hierarchy of ethical values than men. This was in response to her mentor, Lawrence Kohlberg, whose highly regarded scale of ethics was based on his research of his male undergraduate students' responses to some critical issues he had presented to them. He established a scale of seven, which culminated in abstract justice. Women, when given the same test, seldom scored above four, which was concerned with the context in which ethical decisions were made. The highest ethical value was abstract justice.

The conclusions of Gilligan's research were based on her women students' responses to the same questions that her mentor had asked his male students, published as *In A Different Voice;*[1] the book turned out to be a best seller, its paperback edition selling a half a million copies, the largest number in the press's history. Women, it would seem, had a different moral calculus than their male peers. Gilligan's analysis suggested that this was so because women's decisions were contextualized while the men's were based on the hierarchical notion of abstract justice.

This was in the heyday of an emerging powerful Women's Consciousness Movement in which the right to claim our own tradition of moral reasoning was liberating. Furthermore, it was an embodied consciousness, as Rich had identified. Immanence, not transcendence, was the goal. This was in the face of monotheistic religions, whose allegiance is to a god separate from his creation.

Meanwhile, I was becoming aware that spirituality and religion were not the same, that the academic study of world religions was based on scripture/texts, probably all written by men, and the women's religious experience was at that time mostly a dark, unknown continent. Women's experience of the sacred had been left out of this study. My initial foray into this mystery was connected to the emerging Goddess Movement. Women all over the country were meeting in small groups outside of churches and synagogues, creating their own rituals celebrating such uniquely female life events as first menstruation and childbirth. While some were looking to established traditions like that of Wicca, others were breaking new ground, based on their own experiences of an embodied sacred, an earth-based spirituality, rather than the transcendent one eulogized by world religions.

I was also influenced by a year's residence in India in 1967–68, and my non-academic study, observation and participation in Hindu and

Buddhist rituals. As a formally educated art historian, my previous entry into religion had been through the visual arts. In India, the visual arts were paramount and there was an explosion of color, images of Gods and Goddesses everywhere. Religious experience was sensual and an integral part of life, not just added on, as was so often the case in contemporary Western culture. The deity was within, embodied, not out there in the heavens.

The Goddess was omnipresent in the subcontinent, an object of men's as well as women's devotion, a force for regeneration, embodied, and, like nature, both benign and destructive. Alas, there was little correlation between Her glory and the status of women. However, unlike Western attitudes towards female sexuality, which are burdened by Eve's role in the primordial parent's Fall from Paradise and disobedience to God the Father, female sexuality in Hinduism is auspicious. In order for most rituals in this religious tradition to be propitious, a man needs a wife by his side.

For me, spirituality grounds my worldview and holds the meaning of life. I understand myself as part of a larger whole that circles out in ever widening spheres to infinite space. I feel responsible to the minute territory that is mine, to tend to during my lifetime. Somehow I survived decades of emotional and psychological chaos, as I struggled to find my balance after the ravages of a failed marriage, twenty-five years of responsible mothering in a time of social and sexual revolution, and gender bias in graduate school that included sexual assaults from male faculty. My whole being has been enriched by claiming my spiritual space as my own, a potent source of empowerment.

I documented the Women's Spirituality Movement in my book, *The Once and Future Goddess: A Symbol for our Time,*[2] in which I traced the iconography of the female as sacred from the Palaeolithic into the present day. The process of writing my book took me from the East Coast to California, because I wanted to meet some of the women writing books about and developing rituals and practices in this new spirituality. My background as a historian of religion at Harvard had taught me that women's experiences had been left out of what we called "religion" at the time. I interviewed key players, such as Vicki Noble, Starhawk, Hallie Austen, and Carol Christ—all women who were actively recovering women's earth-based traditions from ancient times and making them appropriate for our time.

In California, I taught for a while at California College of Arts and Crafts in Oakland (CCAC), until the president of CIIS (California Institute of Integral Studies) in San Francisco offered me a job there. Lawrence Rockefeller had given five million dollars to the university to establish two new programs, one in ecology and one in women's studies. CIIS was a non-traditional graduate school and the foundational pedagogy of the program was to be experiential, rather than teaching simply from books. I spent a year interviewing students on the campus to see what was happening there and what kinds of issues they might wish to see included in the new women's graduate program. I decided to call it Women's Spirituality, meaning earth-based spirituality rather than "up there."

To launch the Master's program, we offered a 10-day intensive in the summer of 1993 with three guest teachers: Starhawk, Luisah Teish, and Vicki Noble. Thousands of inquiries came from all over the United States in response to this graduate program that did not exist anywhere else, where women could get a Master's degree (and later a PhD) in the subject. I thought the program should also embrace other social sciences, such as anthropology and history, all coming from the point of view of women's experiences, and integrating body, mind, and spirit. At one time the program received more inquiries than any other program at the University. But eventually, even in this collaborative and nontraditional program facilitated by women for women, there were ego struggles, which was a very disillusioning experience for me.

Recently, I have completed a manuscript on my research into the Village Goddesses of India; it is the culmination of my own research and thinking in terms of Women's Spirituality, with the foundation of my understanding going back to the indigenous worship of Nature. There is now extensive evidence, from scholars such as the late Danish physicist, Neils Bohr, showing that trees and rocks generate energies that are palpable. With our growing understanding of climate change and our place in the physical environment, it is all the more important for us to honor and respect this ancient spiritual approach.

As we are redefining gender, opening up other possibilities of what it means to be a man or woman, so too are we enlarging spirituality. This is good news in a time of increasing violence in culture. We are far more aware of sexual abuse, particularly of women and children. The good news is that the emerging generations are less concerned with materialism, and more aware of the climate crisis, the destruction of our environment and atmosphere—the very air we breathe to stay alive—as well as the integration of all of life: human, animal, plant. The growing understanding that our natural resources are finite, not necessarily renewable, prompts a responsible citizenship committed to sustainability.

NOTES

1. Carol Gilligan, *In a Different Voice* (Boston: Harvard University Press, 1998).
2. Elinor Gadon, *The Once and Future Goddess: A Sweeping Visual Chronicle of the Sacred Female and Her Reemergence in the Cultural Mythology of Our Time* (New York: HarperOne, 1989).

CHAPTER 5

WOMEN'S SPIRITUALITY AND HIGHER EDUCATION

Mara Lynn Keller

My life's work as an educator is to practice and teach feminist social justice, women's spirituality, philosophy and religion. When I was a girl, I wanted to be a doctor or minister, but I was born in 1944 during the Second World War, and the Second Wave of Feminism had not reached me by the time I went to college, so those paths were not open to me. I chose to be a college teacher.

My mother raised me to be a devout Christian and to value all religions. At Gettysburg College I earned a BA degree in Biblical Literature and History, with a minor in Philosophy. I developed a strong interest in World Religions, which prompted me to break with the Christian tenet that only Christians could enter the Kingdom of Heaven. I could not believe a just and loving God would condemn most people in the world to Hell because they had not elected the salvation offered by Christianity; or if He would, then He was not worthy of devotion. I completed an MA in Philosophy at Purdue University and a PhD in Philosophy at Yale University. In studying Philosophy and Religion, I was seeking the deepest and wisest meaning of life, for myself, to share with others.

As a young and idealistic white, middle-class woman responding to the social turmoil of the 1960s, I joined the Civil Rights Movement that sought justice for poor people and people of color in the United States, and I became active in the student movement, protesting against racism, sexism, and war. Exclusion of women from higher education was widespread at the time. At Yale, I became part of the wave of women who pushed open the realms of higher education to women. Along with other women graduate students and faculty, I initiated a sex-discrimination suit against Yale.

At the University of California at Riverside I taught Philosophy and organized with other women to create Women's Studies on campus and Women Centers both on campus and in the community. After moving to Berkeley, I taught Philosophy and Women's Studies at San Francisco State University (1977-1996), where I also co-founded and coordinated the Global Peace Studies program (1990-1994). At SFSU, I co-taught *Women, Myth and Ritual* with Carol Lee Sanchez and developed *Women and Nature* for the Women's Studies program and *Woman and Spirit* for the Philosophy Department.

There was a strong and diverse women's movement in the San Francisco Bay Area, and I belonged to several women's spiritual groups with Carol Christ, Starhawk, Vicki Noble, Charlene Tschirhart, Patrice Wynne, Bonnie MacGregor, and others. We co-created rituals based in Goddess mythology, connecting us to powers of nature and providing the opportunity to share spiritual leadership.

In 1981, when I was summer faculty with the Aegean Women's Studies program directed by Ellen Boneparth, I co-created a Demeter-Persephone ritual at Eleusis with Carol Christ, Patrice Wynne, and sixty other women.

When my mother Mary died on Winter Solstice, 1982, my women's circle created a ritual for my mother and me, honoring her life and our love for one another. It included a laying-on-of-hands that addressed my grief in an embodied way. It honored the loving bonds of mother and daughter in ways Christianity had not been able to do, with its focus on Father and Son. In1985, at the American Academy of Religion meetings, I presented a paper on the Eleusinian Mysteries of Demeter and Persephone.[1] In 1989, I traveled to Greece with my partner Bob Spurgeon, where we visited as many Demeter sites as possible on the Greek mainland and islands.

Working with Riane Eisler and Margaret Papandreou of Greece, I was a key organizer for the First International Minoan Celebration of Partnership on the island of Crete in 1992. It brought together some 600 scholars, artists, and political activists from around the world to create effective means for building relationships and institutions for a more-partnership and less-dominator future. I presented "A New Dating and Naming System for Pre-Mycenaean Crete."

In 1993, I joined the Philosophy and Religion faculty at the California Institute of Integral Studies (CIIS), an innovative graduate institute in San Francisco committed to the education of body, mind, and spirit in service to individuals, community, and the Earth. I taught the *History of Western Thought* from a feminist perspective. More significantly, I participated in creating the new Women's Spirituality program.

WOMEN'S SPIRITUALITY STUDIES AT THE CALIFORNIA INSTITUTE OF INTEGRAL STUDIES

The academic study of Women's Spirituality at CIIS was founded in 1993 by Elinor Gadon as one of the first places in the world where one can pursue an MA or PhD in Women's Spirituality. From the beginning, the program was multicultural and committed to community service, with students contributing thousands of service hours to local non-profit agencies. Goddess Studies have been an important part of the program.[2]

I created classes on the *Goddesses of Prehistory* (co-taught with Joan Marler), *Eleusinian Mysteries of Demeter and Persephone*, and *Goddess-and-God Civilization of Ancient Crete.*[3]

I became director of the Women's Spirituality MA and PhD program at CIIS (1998–2008) and worked with Lucia Birnbaum, Arisika Razak, Charlene Spretnak, and many others to build a womanist-feminist curriculum focused in Women's Mysteries, Sacred Arts and Healing; Women and World Religions;[4] and Feminist and Ecofeminist Philosophy and Activism. Many of the leading voices of the Women's Spirituality movement have taught with us, including Paula Gunn Allen, Jennifer Berezan, Carolyn Brandy, Ana Castillo, Carol P. Christ, Randy Conner, Riane Eisler, Rose Wognum Frances, Heide Goettner-Abendroth, Susan Griffin, Mary Mackey, Ani Mander, Joan Marler, Patricia Monaghan, Vicki Noble, Victoria Rue, Peggy Reeves Sanday, Starhawk, Luisah Teish, Elizabeth Ursic, Amina Wadud, and Afia Walking Tree. In 2010, some of our faculty and students joined other Goddess scholars in creating an ongoing Goddess Studies section for the American Academy of Religion western division.

In twenty-one years we educated one hundred and twenty-seven graduates, ninety-three MA students and thirty-four PhD students, of whom we are very proud! They are carrying Women's Spirituality into the larger world through diverse avenues: academic teaching and writing, healthcare, spiritual counseling, spiritual artwork, and work in non-profits. Their master's theses and doctoral dissertations are extraordinary and valuable in developing Women's Spirituality as an academic field. This next generation of scholars includes Susan Carter, Joan Cichon, Lisa Christie, Eahr Joan, Pairin Jotisakulratana, Anne Key, In Hui Lee, Marybeth Moser, Marguerite Rigoglioso, Lori Swick, Karen Villanueva, and Annette Williams.

Continuing the emphasis of directors Elinor Gadon and Rose Frances, we produced special events of women's sacred arts and scholarship, showcasing the work of Cristina Biaggi, Jalaja Bonheim, Miriam Robbins

Dexter, Brooke Medicine Eagle, Judy Grahn, Mayumi Oda, and Alice Walker. In 1998, Joan Marler and I produced the conference *From the Realm of the Ancestors: Language of the Goddess*, in honor of archaeomythologist Marija Gimbutas. In 2002, I co-produced with Jennifer Berezan her ritual concert *Returning to the Mother of Us All*. With filmmakers Donna Read and Starhawk, I produced the West Coast Premiere gala for *Signs out of Time: the Story of Archaeologist Marija Gimbutas* (2004). With artist and art curator Tricia Grame, I produced and sometimes co-curated nine art exhibits (2000 to 2009), from *Woman as Symbol,* with fifty artists, to *Ineffable / Woman: A Bi-coastal Conversation,* showing a dozen women artists from San Francisco and New York, in collaboration with Ceres Art Gallery. In addition, I created courses on *Women's Visionary Film*[5] and *Women's Visionary Poetry and Fiction,* co-taught with poet and novelist Mary Mackey.

Supporting the multicultural value of educational travel, I promoted *Women's Spirituality Journeys.* I was faculty for the International Women's Studies Institute between 1981 and 2007, with educational tours to Greece, Hawaii, Turkey, the Baltics, and Spain. In 2001, I coordinated and co-taught a CIIS course on "Sacred Cosmologies and Ancient Greek Mysteries" in Athens, Eleusis, and Madouri, the ancestral island home of renowned Greek poet and scholar Nanos Valaoritis and his artist wife Marie Wilson. Afterwards, Joan Cichon and her husband Nikos Karneros led a tour to Crete and they introduced Bob and me to the special seaside village of Mochlos, where we returned for two of my sabbaticals. Bob has been a strong supporter and champion of Women's Spirituality.

In this beautiful setting, I continued researching and writing about ancient Crete and also worked on my two book manuscripts: *The Greater Mysteries of Demeter and Persephone,* a poetic spiritual quest narrative about a young woman's initiation into the death and rebirth ceremonies of the ancient Eleusinian Mysteries; and *The Eleusinian Mysteries and Greek Goddess Traditions,* a companion volume that documents my reconstructions of the Thesmophoria (rites of fertility and renewal for women only), the Lesser Mysteries (rites of Spring, rites of atonement), and the Greater Mysteries, also known as the Eleusinian Mysteries. During my 2005 sabbatical, Bob and I were married by Unitarian lay-minister and friend Bonnie MacGregor in Demeter's temple in Eleusis.

THE RELIGION/SCIENCE DIVIDE AND EMBODIED WOMEN'S SPIRITUALITY STUDIES

Science and religion have often been at odds. One of the theoretical challenges in bringing together a spiritually and politically engaged graduate program in Women's Spirituality is creating an interface among the methodologies of religious studies, women's studies, social sciences, and physical sciences.[6] Studies of religion often focus on traditions that believe in transcendent truths and divine revelations, received in unique individual and communal, subjective spiritual experience. The sciences usually focus on objective empirical data, while attempting to exclude researcher bias.

In embodied Women's Spirituality Studies, we respect and combine the relatively subjective dimensions of spiritual experiences, along with the relatively objective empirical data of the social and physical sciences. For example, in our courses on Women's Mysteries, Sacred Arts, and Healing, we draw upon direct spiritual experiences with mystical intuition, art-making, interpretation of dreams, ritual, bodywork, dance, music, and women's visionary poetry, fiction, and film. And we join these with scientific and social scientific knowledge regarding women's life-cycles, blood mysteries, and healing arts.[7] Embodied spirituality and empirical science can work together.

Fortunately, in this postmodern era, many academic disciplines acknowledge the subjective agency of the researcher. We use Feminist Standpoint and Transdisciplinary approaches that include the embodied researcher as a self-reflexive agent who selects and shapes the research process, creatively interprets and presents the findings, and also holds the intention that the researcher, subjects researched, and audience may experience a personal, social, and/or spiritual transformation because of the study. When we emphasize the interpretive or hermeneutical dimensions of the work, we acknowledge the creative lens of the researcher as well as our commitment to the integrity of the subjects being researched.

ESSENTIALISM, ANTI-ESSENTIALISM, AND NATURE-EMBEDDED WOMEN'S SPIRITUALITY

There are several stumbling blocks for Women's Studies and Gender Studies programs in the United States that have hindered them from including Women's Spirituality in their curricula. First, most employ secular humanist plus social scientific and scientific frameworks that exclude religious beliefs and practices (except perhaps as social/historical artifacts). They do not attempt to integrate mind with body and spirit. Another stumbling block is the doctrine pervasive in Women and Gender Studies that any attempt to posit distinguishing characteristics of a group is "essentializing" and therefore incorrect.

Anti-essentialists think it is inaccurate to make assertions about all women, claiming there are no essential characteristics that define women as such, only socially-conditioned features that differentiate women from one another, according to gender, race, class, age, sexual orientation, and physical abilities. However, by the same logic, there would be no essential characteristics defining men as distinct from women, or humans as distinct from other species, or groups like women of color or lesbians in contrast to white women or heterosexual women, or womanists from feminists. In contrast, spiritual feminists often invoke notions of the sacredness of women, of Goddess archetypes and Goddesses, the Sacred Feminine, and the Feminine Divine, as if the terms *women* and *feminine* and *Goddess* have special, even essential meanings.

The social-constructionist, anti-essentialist critique of woman/feminine/Goddess essentialism correctly points out that it is a mistake to over-generalize about women and assume all women are the same—as happened in the early stages of Second Wave Feminism that argued that "all women are oppressed" or "all women are sisters." This did not take into account important personal, economic, racial, and political differences among women. We need to be as specific and nuanced as possible in our discussions of women, men, differently gendered persons, and other-than-human species. At the same time, it is important to use categories in practical and beneficial ways, and not eliminate categories and generalities altogether. I believe it is a mistake to do away with all general identifiers for women. These can be understood as approximate and corrigible truths, rather than absolute truths.

A nature-embedded and embodied Women's Spirituality can resolve at least some of the divisions between essentialism and anti-essentialism. It politically affirms diversity (pluralism) and also celebrates women's eco-bio-psycho-spiritual commonalities (unity). Essential women's spirituality is pro-body and pro-spirit and pro-ecosocial-justice. As embodied beings, each woman experiences differing characteristics of gender, race, class, age, sexual orientation, physical abilities, and spiritual sensibilities. And at the same time all of us are embedded in nature and the cosmos. Women all share a human nature and a woman-nature, rooted in the tremendous creativity of the cosmos. We can acknowledge the differences of body, place, and culture, and at the same time affirm the variable yet enduring and essential experiences of women, including our embodied physical, mental, and spiritual energies.

Diverse women around the world have spiritual feelings about experiences that women (but not men) have primarily or exclusively, like sexuality via a female body, menstruation, ovulation, pregnancy, birth-giving, breast-feeding, and other behaviors associated with sexuality and sexual procreation. Millions of women honor these profound experiences as sacred feminine experiences. Sometimes they connect these to the powers of a Goddess or Goddesses. This forms the chosen spirituality of many women and men around the world. Why are these gestures of faith by people believing in the sacredness of women, women's experiences, and Goddesses, denied? Is such dismissal not an act of religious prejudice?

Understanding the particularities of our own lives serves us in understanding others' lives. This in turn helps us form reliable alliances for social transformation toward a visionary future that is more inclusive, just, humane, healthy, compassionate, creative, ecologically balanced, and loving.

Women have contributed spiritual gifts and leadership in families and communities around the world since the beginning of human culture. It is important that the study of Women's Spirituality, including Goddess Studies, find an accepting home in academia, alongside the study of other major human accomplishments. At their best, religions in general and women's spirituality in particular keep the divine sparks of love, compassion, and social justice alive in individuals and societies. These qualities find expression in a myriad of ways, worthy of preserving and transmitting in informal and formal educational endeavors. I intend to continue my commitment to Women's Spirituality in Higher Education as long as I live, through teaching, writing, and sharing ritual and eco-social spiritual activism.

NOTES

1. Mara Lynn Keller, "The Eleusinian Mysteries of Demeter and Persephone: Fertility, Sexuality and Rebirth," *Journal of Feminist Studies in Religion* 4, no. 1 (Spring 1988): 27–54. Mara Lynn Keller, "The Ritual Path of Initiation into the Eleusinian Mysteries," *The Rosicrucian Digest*, 87 (Special issue on Eleusis), no. 2 (2009): 28–42. http://www.rosicrucian.org/publications/digest/digest2_2009/04_web/07_keller/07_keller.pdfAccessed 1/12/2015.

2. Mara Lynn Keller, "Goddesses around the World," *Common Ground* 113 (Fall 2002): 16, 18–19,137–138; Mara Lynn Keller, "Goddess Spirituality," in *Encyclopedia of Psychology and Religion*, Vol 1, ed. D.A. Leeming, 2nd ed. (New York/Heidelberg/Dordrecht/London: Springer, 2014), 729–735.

3. Mara Lynn Keller, "Crete of the Mother Goddess: Communal Rituals and Sacred Art," *ReVision: A Journal of Consciousness and Transformation* 20, no. 3 (Winter 1998): 12–16.

4. Mara Lynn Keller, "Violence against Women and Children in Scriptures and in the Home," in *The Rule of Mars: Readings on the Origins, History and Impact of Patriarchy*, ed. Cristina Biaggi, Manchester CT: Knowledge, Ideas & Trends, 2005: 225–240.

5. Mara Lynn Keller, "*Sorceress:* Mythic Archetype of the Wise Woman Healer during the European Middle Ages," *Association for the Study of Women and Mythology Conference Proceedings.* (Las Vegas, Nev.: Goddess Ink, Ltd., Forthcoming.)

6. Mara Lynn Keller, "The Interface of Archaeology and Mythology: A Philosophical Evaluation of the Gimbutas Paradigm," in *From the Realm of the Ancestors: Essays in Honor of Marija Gimbutas*, ed. Joan Marler, Manchester, CT: Knowledge, Ideas, Trends, Inc., 1997: 381–398.

7. Mara Lynn Keller, "Rosen Method Bodywork—Spiritual Dimensions: A Conversation with Marion Rosen and Gloria Hessellund," *Creation Spirituality Magazine* (November 1993), 28–31.

CHAPTER 6

WOMEN'S SPIRITUALITY: FROM DOMINATION TO PARTNERSHIP

Riane Eisler

I had no idea there was a women's spirituality until I began the research that led me to write *The Chalice and the Blade: Our History, Our Future.*[1] That research took over a decade, from the mid-1970s to the mid-1980s, and it showed that much that people today think new and radical, such as the women's spirituality movement, has very ancient roots.

Many people have written that they kept having "aha" experiences when reading *The Chalice and the Blade.* That is how it was for me as I did my research. Suddenly things that seemed random and disconnected began to make sense. I began to see patterns in our past and present that had been ignored: patterns in which the status of women plays a key role. I also saw that many of our problems today stem from a radical cultural shift in the direction of civilization during our prehistory.

This re-reading of history has been empowering to me as well as to others. It verified that a better future is possible. And it led to something I had not anticipated: I gradually began to reconnect with the realm of the spiritual, a realm I had abandoned when I was in my early teens.

SPIRITUALITY LOST

My loss of spirituality came when I was twelve. My parents and I had been living in Cuba, refugees from the Nazis after they took over my native Vienna. My father had been taken away by the Gestapo, but by a miracle my mother obtained his release, and shortly after that we fled from the city where I was born, taking with us only what we could carry. It was hard as a child to understand why Jews like me were hunted with license to kill. It was hard suddenly having to live in the Havana slums, where, as gradually became apparent, anti-Semitism was also in the air. But I knew that we were the lucky ones, the only ones in my family who had escaped from Europe. So every night I prayed to God to protect those left behind from whom there was no news. I was careful, as children will be when they pray, to mention every name of my aunts, uncles, cousins, and grandparents, afraid that if I forgot one name God would not hear me. Then, after World War II ended, I learned that most of them had been killed. And I saw the newsreels of the concentration camps, the skeletal bodies piled one on top of the other and the just as skeletal handful of hollow-eyed survivors who, unlike six million other Jews, had somehow survived the Holocaust.

I could not fathom how God (or for that matter the rest of the world) could let such horrors happen. At that point, God died for me.

I still went to synagogue with my parents, and I still felt Jewish, which I do to this day. But it was also at that point that everything I had been taught about religion and spirituality no longer made sense.

I still loved the beautiful chanting of the Hebrew prayers and the ritual of the Torah being taken around the synagogue. I especially loved it when my mother baked bread on Fridays, when that wonderful aroma of her *chalah* filled the house. I loved it when she lit the candles on the Shabbat, chanting the prayer of welcome to the *Kalah* (bride) as she circled her hands over the lit candles in that beautiful ritual—the only one, I began to realize, performed by a woman, not a man.

MY RETURN TO SPIRITUALITY

I did not realize until years later, while I was doing my research for *Sacred Pleasure: Sex, Myth, and the Politics of the Body,*[2] that the ritual I so loved was a remnant from a time when women were priestesses. When I read the *Hymns of Inanna* (the Sumerian Goddess of Love and Procreation), I understood that the *Kalah* or bride was the Goddess, and that like Inanna's earlier sacred marriage to Dumuzi (whom Inanna managed to bring back every year from the dead), what my mother performed was an ancient celebration of the sacred marriage, most probably of the Goddess Asherah or Ishtar and her divine husband—a rite still performed in biblical times.

Even before my study of ancient religions, I had hints about "mystery cults" where a Goddess such as the Egyptian Isis or the Greek Demeter not only gave life but also had the power to bring the dead back to life. But it was only as I delved deeply in pursuit of our ancient feminine spiritual heritage, first for *The Chalice and the Blade* and then for *Sacred Pleasure*, that I found strong evidence from both archaeology and mythology of a much earlier time when the world was imaged as a Great Mother who gave and renewed life, like the cycles of vegetation, once again to be reborn.

Judging from the profusion of female figurines and other images from the European Upper Palaeolithic, going back to around 40,000 years ago, all the way to the middle of the Neolithic (around 5000 years ago), when farming was already the norm, and even after that in the highly sophisticated, technologically advanced civilization of Minoan Crete, the mythical focus seems to have been on the creative powers inherent in woman's body. But there are also male images, and there is no hint that men were dominated by women in these societies.. As archaeologist Ian Hodder wrote about his excavations of the Neolithic site of Çatalhöyük in his article for the *Scientific American* in 2004,[3] based on dietary and bone analyses there are no signs that differences between women and men were translated into differences of status or power. As he remarked with some surprise, the evidence suggests a society in which sex is relatively unimportant in assigning social roles.

However, during a time of great upheavals and mass migrations in our prehistory, there was a fundamental shift in the mainstream of our cultural direction. We begin to see the disappearance of the once ubiquitous female figurines, as well as a new social structure of rigid rankings of domination—starting with the ranking of male over female —along with signs of chronic warfare. In short, we see evidence of a fundamental cultural shift from a *partnership model* to a *domination model* of society.

I introduced these new social categories as well as the concept of the *partnership/ domination continuum* (because orientation to either model is always a matter of degree), as there were no names for these two contrasting cultural configurations. In addition, because our language did not have a gender-specific term for a society where women and men are equal partners, I coined the terms *gylany* and *gylanic* (*gy* for *gyne* or woman and *an* for Greek *aner, andros* or man, with the letter l standing for linking rather than ranking). All we had were *patriarchy* and the old definition of *matriarchy*, which has popularly been interpreted to mean the opposite of patriarchy to describe cultures where women rather than men dominate, though feminist scholars dispute this interpretation.[4] By contrast, in the partnership or *gylanic* model, partnership between women and men is the template for all relationships.

The knowledge that there was a time when women were not subordinate, and, rather than a supreme (or only) male deity, female deities were widely venerated, gradually led me to reconnect to that amorphous realm we call spirituality—but in a way that is very different from how it is presented in the religions that developed after the shift toward the domination model.

In domination systems, spirituality is largely a means of escaping from what in the Christian Middle Ages was termed our earthly "vale of tears." That so-called age of faith oriented closely to the domination side of the continuum, with its Inquisition, Crusades, chronic wars between "nobles," the oppression of serfs, and the rigid subordination of women. So life was indeed a vale of tears. And since the Church proclaimed this the "divinely ordained" order and people were tortured and killed for trying to change it, the only way out was in an afterlife.

I want to emphasize that this use of religion to maintain hierarchies of domination is by no means unique to the West. Beliefs in reincarnation serve a similar function in Hinduism, which was used to maintain a caste system and the rigid subordination of women. Further, the Koran says men should beat wives for disobedience,[5] and Muslim men are promised forty virgins for killing in the name of Allah—as terrorists are to this day.[6]

By contrast, partnership spirituality is both immanent and transcendent. It acknowledges realms beyond human comprehension but focuses on creating a good life here on earth.

More partnership-oriented prehistoric societies do not seem to have made the artificial distinction between spirituality and nature that came later, with man and the spiritual placed above woman and nature in a hierarchy of domination. For these earlier people, everything was imbued with the divine, including nature.

So when I think of spirituality today, I think of the life-supporting and enhancing powers in the universe. And I think of a morality of caring rather than coercion.

Above all, for me spirituality is putting love into action. I think the highest spiritual calling is not just to develop ourselves spiritually, but to serve others. Indeed, what I call spiritual courage is standing up against injustice out of love (as my mother did to the Gestapo when they took my father away, risking her own life to get him back).

CULTURAL AND SPIRITUAL TRANSFORMATION

Over the years, my work has increasingly focused on ways to accelerate the shift to the partnership side of the partnership/domination continuum. I say "accelerate" because fortunately we do not have to start from square one.

Over the last centuries, there has been strong movement toward partnership. All the progressive social movements—from the "rights of man" movement challenging the "divinely ordained" right of kings to rule over their "subjects" to the feminist movement challenging the "divinely ordained" right of men to rule over the women and children in the "castles" of their homes to the civil rights and anti-colonial movements challenging the "divinely ordained" right of one race to rule over an "inferior" one, all the way to the environmental movement challenging the "divinely ordained" right of man to rule over the rest of nature—have challenged traditions of domination. They are all parts of the partnership movement. And so also is the women's spirituality movement which seeks to reconnect us with the feminine divine, reintegrate women into the priesthoods, and imbue spirituality—and life—with "feminine" values such as empathy and caring.

Of course, there are also partnership teachings in our sacred scriptures. Many Jewish and Christian teachings contain a core of caring and empathy. We can use these passages to counter the domination dogma of a spirituality and morality of control and punishment with a partnership spirituality of caring and empathy.

I saw these partnership teachings applied by my parents, when after the Holocaust they gave whatever they could to the handful of our relatives who were not killed so the latter could emigrate to Israel. My parents modeled for me that real love is empathic and that service is integral to spirituality.

The problem is that the in-group vs. out-group rankings integral to domination systems require insensitivity, cruelty, and violence, which is why these are often idealized in the scriptures we inherited from more rigid domination-oriented times.

A sign of movement toward partnership is the growing realization that the old idea of a male God and of men (made in his image) to dominate women, children, and nature could be the swan song for us as a species. Another important sign is the growing recognition that the devaluation of women and the stereotypically feminine is a major obstacle to a more just and truly spiritual world.

This takes me to a central finding from my research: that cultures where women have higher status, as they did in prehistoric societies with powerful female deities, are more generally egalitarian and peaceful. So a major theme in my work is that raising the status of women worldwide is not only essential for women and girls; it is essential for men and boys —and for building a world where both women's and men's capacities for empathy and caring, rather than for insensitivity and cruelty, are culturally supported rather than inhibited.

Because empathy and caring are in domination systems considered "soft" or "feminine"—and hence not appropriate for "real men"—we have inherited a skewed system of values. And this gendered system of values affects everything.

As I show in *Tomorrow's Children: A Blueprint for Partnership Education in the 21st Century*[7] (which provides resources for a gender-balanced education), it negatively affects education. As I detail in *The Power of Partnership: Seven Relations that will Change Your Life*[8] (which won the Nautilus best self-help book prize), it negatively affects all our relationships—from intimate to international. As I document in *The Real Wealth of Nations: Creating a Caring Economics*[9] (which has informed much of my recent teaching, speaking, advocacy, and organizational work), it led to economic systems that cannot effectively meet either our material or spiritual needs.

I have spoken about these critical issues from many platforms, ranging from the United Nations General Assembly and the United States State Department to diverse conferences worldwide. I have highlighted them in hundreds of articles, book chapters, and op-eds. While I love doing keynotes for women's conferences and working with women's organizations, I have also made a special effort to engage men and to bring these insights about the critical importance of "women's issues" into international organizations that have asked me to join, such as the World Future Council and the Club of Rome. And as president of the Center for Partnership Studies (CPS), I initiated a number of important programs designed to lay foundations for a more partnership-oriented world.

I co-founded CPS's "Spiritual Alliance to Stop Intimate Violence (SAIV)" with Nobel Peace Laureate Betty Williams as a forum for faith and other spiritual leaders to speak out against entrenched traditions of intimate violence. Because religious institutions have all too often condoned and even commanded violence against women and children, mobilizing enlightened religious leaders to condemn it is essential. As part of the movement toward partnership, an increasing number of faith leaders and communities already offer support for victims of this violence. Through SAIV, they can more effectively join together to prevent this violence, which not only blights and takes the lives of millions of women and children but also provides a "school" for using violence to impose one's will on others—be it in intimate or international relations.

Another important CPS initiative I am also passionately committed to is the "Caring Economy Campaign (CEC)." The CEC demonstrates the importance of investing in caring for people, starting in early childhood, through paid parental leave, caregiver tax credits, Social Security for caregivers, and subsidies for childcare. A centerpiece of the CEC is the development of new "Social Wealth Economic Indicators (SWEIs)," that show the enormous economic value of the work of care and early education, as well as focusing attention on marginalized populations, such as women, children, and people of color.

Policy support for caregiving work is essential to cut through cycles of poverty, because worldwide, women still do the bulk of this work for very low wages in the market and for free in homes—largely accounting for the disproportionate poverty of women. The CEC offers resources, training, and advocacy opportunities, including an online Leadership Training program that to date has certified leaders from seventeen nations, and the CEC Coalition now includes organizations representing sixteen million people.

These programs bring together women and men who want to put spirituality into action as agents of cultural transformation.[10]

Let us join together to build foundations for a time where all of life is imbued with that sense of caring connection to one another and to nature that is at the core of women's spirituality. Let us invoke the divine feminine in us all to inspire and guide us in moving toward a partnership world.

NOTES

1. Riane Eisler, *The Chalice and the Blade: Our History, Our Future* (San Francisco: Harper and Row, 1987).
2. Riane Eisler, *Sacred Pleasure: Sex, Myth, and the Politics of the Body* (San Francisco: Harper San Francisco, 1995).
3. Ian Hodder, "Women and Men at Çatalhöyük," *Scientific American* (January 2004), 77-83.
4. Editor's note: the currently accepted definition of the word "matriarchy" is "mother in origin, mother at the center" rather than "mother-rule." See Goettner-Abendroth in this volume. Compare, for example, the equalitarian, Indonesian Minangkabau peoples, who call themselves a matriarchate.
5. *Quran*, chapter 4 (An-Nisa), verse 34.
6. The specific Hadith (the second most authoritative type of document in Islam after the Quran) in which the number of virgins is specified is Hadith Al-Tirmidhi in the Book of Sunah (volume IV, chapters on The Features of Paradise as described by the Messenger of Allah, chapter 21, About the Smallest Reward for the People of Paradise.) The same hadith is also quoted by Ibn Kathir in his Quranic commentary (Tafsir) of Surah Al-Rahman: "The Prophet Muhammad was heard saying: 'The smallest reward for the people of paradise is an abode where there are 80,000 servants and 72 wives, over which stands a dome decorated with pearls, aquamarine, and ruby, as wide as the distance from Al-Jabiyah [a Damascus suburb] to Sana'a [Yemen].'"
7. Riane Eisler, *Tomorrow's Children* (Boulder, Colorado: Westview Press, 2000).
8. Riane Eisler, *The Power of Partnership: Seven Relations that will Change Your Life* (Novato, California: New World Library, 2003).
9. Riane Eisler, *The Real Wealth of Nations: Creating a Caring Economics* (Oakland, California: Berrett-Koehler Publishers, 2008).
10. See www.caringeconomy.org, www.saiv.org, and www.rianeeisler.com.

CHAPTER 7

DAKINIS DANCING THROUGH SPACE AND TIME, INTO OUR BODIES AND MINDS

Miranda Shaw

My contribution to women's spirituality was set in motion by paintings I encountered in college. During my sophomore year, I attended an exhibition of Tibetan scroll paintings and was mesmerized by the female images I saw in the art. Raised Methodist, exposed mainly to European art, I was captivated by the dynamic female figures dancing on the earth and in the clouds, ablaze with physical and spiritual vitality. Their lithe, unclad bodies were draped with flower garlands, delicate bone ornaments, and rainbow scarves set aloft by their movements. Most riveting was their direct, piercing gaze, conveying immense focus and inner mastery. They radiated passion, power, and freedom.

I felt compelled to find out who they were and what kind of women could have inspired such vibrant imagery. My quest for understanding set the course of my academic and professional life to the present day. Focusing on the period when this imagery first appeared in art and text, namely, in the Tantric Buddhism of 8th-12th century India, my journey led me through art history, religious studies, and Sanskrit and Tibetan language training. I traversed South Asia to explore regions and historical records where the tradition took shape and consult with living practitioners in current settings.

The figures I sought to understand are known as "dakinis." The term encompasses women and female divinities in the realm of Tantric practice. The Sanskrit word *ḍākinī* derives from a verb meaning "to fly," so it can be translated most literally as "a female who flies," elaborated in Tibetan as *mkha'-'gro-ma*, "female who moves in the sky" or "female who travels in space."[1] Flight has many layers and nuances of meaning as a central metaphor for the nature and spiritual attainments of the *dakini*. It signifies a soaring spirit, freedom from worldly and social constraints, and sense of elation. Flight also evokes an elevated view that encompasses a broad range of perspectives while holding none to be ultimately true. Sky, or space, is the natural element and home of the dakini. Just as space is a subtle essence pervading all, her mind traverses many realms, easily moving wherever she casts her attention. She understands that space permeates all realities, rendering all phenomena porous and fleeting. She revels in the illusory nature of reality and loves to soar in the open expanse of creativity, riding the currents of magical fluidity. In essence, her flight is the freedom that comes from knowing ultimate reality.

Both women and Goddesses are called dakinis, for there is not a clear dividing-line between the two. Divine dakinis—the Goddesses of the Tantric pantheon—represent qualities that women may awaken and express. My search also led me to human dakinis, the women of the early Tantric movement. The faintness of the trail made my historical discoveries all the more exhilarating as I gathered their stories and writings. In the 1980s, before Buddhist texts had begun to be digitized and available online, I searched through stacks of woodblock-printed manuscripts wrapped in cloth, in collections that had no card catalogues, and through the leaves of unbound volumes that had no indices. One search of many hours in a locked upper-story room at Harvard-Yenching Library yielded an anthology of "songs of realization" that women sang for each other at a Tantric feast, voiced spontaneously on the occasion to express their illumined wisdom and blissfulness. Holding the hand-inked folios in my hands gave me goose bumps, and the hair on my arms stood on end as I was electrified by a stream of energy—their words, their presence—reaching me across a span of a thousand years.

I encountered female teachers, masters, and leaders. Among them were luminaries whose teachings and practices shaped the tradition in profound ways. The female founders championed women and embraced the body, senses, and passions as sources of knowledge and power. The women's sense of worth and authority was rooted in their relationship to ultimate reality, not derived from an institution or male hierarchy. Their exemplars were divine dakinis, such as the female Buddha, Vajrayoginī, who embody the primordial wisdom of the female mind and sacredness of the female body. Theirs was a female-affirming metaphysics, positing that all the powers of the universe flow through and from women. The cosmos is born from the womb of infinite space and emptiness, understood as the womb of Vajrayoginī, Tantric Goddess and dakini supreme. Women and the earth are honored as sources of life, creative force, sustenance, and spiritual guidance.

I presented my findings in my book *Passionate Enlightenment*,[2] which met academic acclaim as an historical study and reached an international audience hungering for a life-affirming philosophy and embodied spirituality that honors women and sets forth a sacred role for intimate partnership and sexuality.

BUDDHIST GODDESSES OF INDIA, TIBET, AND NEPAL

I turned my attention next to the female deities who figured in the women's meditations and remain important in Tantric Buddhist practice. To place them in historical and cultural context, I examined the evolution of female divinity in the Buddhist pantheons of India and the Himalayas. Based on the limited information in print, I didn't expect to find a lot of material, but I discovered a wealth of sources and fascinating array of female deities, appearing among the earliest extant remains of the tradition and remaining prominent in their respective settings as objects of aspiration, artistry, personal practice, and communal celebration. The Buddhist stream of Goddess devotion rivaled and kept pace with the more fully documented traditions of Goddess worship in South Asia. Tantric dakinis rose with the tide of *Shakta* (female-centered) traditions that recognized Goddesses as universal source, cosmic mother, and liberator supreme.

I documented the development of the Indian pantheon in *Buddhist Goddesses of India*.[3] One of my current book manuscripts traces the ongoing evolution of the female pantheon as it was shaped by the distinctive cultures and Himalayan landscapes of Tibet and Nepal. A fuller picture comes into view when Goddesses are encountered in current worship, within a rich weave of local traditions, performance idioms, communal events, and active shrines, temples, and sacred sites. Goddesses have a dynamic presence in the religiosity of Tibet, as divinized female ancestors, female trance mediums channeling Goddesses, female masters recognized as incarnations of female deities, and protectors of sacred places and persons. The supreme guardian of Tibetan Buddhism and the Dalai Lamas is the fearsome Goddess Palden Lhamo. She has been a constant companion of the Dalai Lamas, safeguarding them throughout life, guiding them through dreams and divinations, and leading searchers to the next incarnation with visions on the surface of her oracular lake.[4]

Nepal boasts an uninterrupted tradition of Goddess worship from proto-historical times to the present. Goddesses are embedded in the landscape, inhabiting hilltops, rivers, and underground springs. They occupy major temple sites venerated as the power-generators of the Kathmandu Valley, established by kings to proclaim their divine sanction to rule, where the transforming powers of the Goddesses are channeled through devotion, ritual, and esoteric yogic practices.

WOMEN'S SPIRITUALITY

Women's spirituality gained momentum from the discovery of traditions in which deity is honored and envisioned as female, the earth is sacred, and women channel the holy elixir of life and spiritual blessings. When the maleness of God was no longer absolute, the foundation of patriarchal privilege crumbled, exposing gender roles as cultural constructs. We were freed to explore and esteem women's qualities. We claimed the authority of our experience and wisdom. We rejected the dualism that values the life and creations of the mind over the life and creations of the body. We exalt the role of mothering as exemplar and metaphor for nurture, bonding, and fierce protectiveness—of other women, children, the living earth. We glory in capacities once stigmatized, cherishing our capacity for bonding and empathy as an alternative and antidote for the greed, hatred, and violence that threaten our well-being and very survival.

Celebrating the female body is central to many strands of women's spirituality. Our body image is shaped by the fund of cultural images to which we are exposed. The legacy of theological hostility to female bodies surrounds us. Messages of shame bombard us in political discourse, public policy, visual media, and popular culture. We are presented with the *desacralized* female—female as objectified, judged on external appearance and usefulness to others. Rare the female in our culture who by adolescence does not experience insecurity at best, anguish and self-loathing at worst, about the "imperfection" of her body and hence of herself, diverting her energy from cultivating her talents and pursuing her dreams and destiny.

Because our psychological, emotional, and spiritual well-being are so closely entwined with our understanding and experience of our bodily being, the women's spirituality movement promotes embodied practices and restores the female body to the realm of the holy.

DANCING AS GODDESSES

My interests in Himalayan Goddesses and the sacredness of the female body converge in my current work on sacred dance. My graduate study was a disembodying period. The cerebral demands of doctoral work left me feeling like "a head on a stick," that is, all brain with a body there to prop it up. With that completed and *Passionate Enlightenment* in press, I took lessons in Bharat Natyam, an Indian classical dance style. This venture raised a new question about the Tantric iconography that had engaged me for more than a decade. That the dakinis are dancing I had known from the start. Now, as I assumed the core stance for Bharat Natyam—holding my torso upright, lowering my body with knees bent and splayed outward, and placing my hands on my hips, wrist to hip bone—I saw my pose mirrored in the paintings of dakinis lining my living room. When I found segments of my arm and leg motions, too, matched in the paintings, I realized there might be a Tantric dance tradition, launching me on my current project and book manuscript. It was not the presence of dancing as a visual motif but the exactitude of the postures that intimated a formal dance practice, or transmission of specific movements, rather than purely spontaneous outpourings of dance.

During my next research sojourn in Kathmandu, I encountered a Tantric Buddhist dance tradition known as Charya Nritya, meaning "dance as a spiritual discipline," practiced over the centuries as a meditative, yogic, and ritual art by members—male and female—of the lineages of Tantric priests known as Vajracharyas. There is scope and support for a dance practice in Tantra, on the view that bodily experience and sensory pleasures are not enemies of spiritual life and hence should not be deadened with self-denial but elevated to sublimity through music, dance, and song. My main teachers have been the late Ratna Kaji Vajracharya, an esteemed scholar and ritual master; his son Prajwal Ratna Vajracharya, who has devoted his life to his sacred dance heritage; and Helen Appell, one of the most accomplished practitioners of Charya dance in the world, who does dakini dances to divine perfection.[5]

Learning even basic movements, orienting myself to the dance style, changed my experience of my body. As awareness deepened into my limbs and torso, my body felt less dense and more diaphanous, less like a solid mass and more like a delicate lacing of radiant, pulsating tissues. Rather than a mind directing a body, attention to movement revealed a subtle interplay of intention, impulse, and expression flowing through every motion. Curving postures and circular motions fostered a more organic, less mechanistic sense of my body. The soft, fluidic movements and undulating spine further destabilized my sense of body as inert form, revealing and loosening patterns of rigidity, giving me a greater sense of vitality as suppressed energies were released. Slow, deliberate motions and pauses in the midst of movement called forth greater strength and balance. I never progressed to the more vigorous, dynamic dances.

After several years of periodic study and daily practice, I explored other dance forms and embraced dance as a path of transformation that integrates the bodily, mental, emotional, and spiritual levels of experience. I had discovered a resource, ever-ready at hand, for moving through problems and generating insights, stirring energy through areas of density and attuning to deeper layers of memory and motivation, driving my thoughts and behavior, and accessing the primal wisdom of my being that pulses so vividly in my bodily self.

Increased self-awareness is inherent in any dance practice, but Charya Nritya is directed to the Tantric goal of realizing one's innate divinity by unifying awareness and identity with the enlightened beings—the Buddhas, bodhisattvas, and dakinis —of the Tantric pantheon. A practitioner of Charya dance envisions herself to have the appearance, ornaments, and liberating powers of a given deity and invokes the spirit of the deity through the movements. An accompanying song describes and praises the deity on which the dance is based, while the movement quality and symbolic gestures of the dance convey the dynamic presence of the deity. Many Charya songs and dances are dedicated to divine *dakinis* and female Buddhas.

A woman who does a dance of a divine dakini, such as Vajrayoginī, understands the dakini to represent her own spiritual capacities. The dakinis provide a template of the qualities a woman can discover within herself. The iconography of a dakini—bodily color, ornaments, and other attributes—provides a visual and symbolic guide to the Tantric vision of female wholeness. Her vigorous movements display passionate intensity as she engages with all the energies of life. The five-pointed crown a dakini wears represents the five exalted states of wisdom a woman may attain, namely, fearless clarity, freedom from arrogance and insecurity, joyful discernment, all-accomplishing fervor, and spacious awareness. The curved blade and bowl of nectar she bears represent her ability to transform suffering into bliss. An elaborate filigree skirt adorns her hips with cascades of gleaming gold and pearls or carved bone beads. This adornment, dating from South Asian proto-history, becomes a potent talisman by absorbing the auspicious, creative forces concentrated in the womb and thighs, portal of life into the world.

The divine dakinis dance on a lotus throne, signifying spiritual purity, challenging a woman to claim her sovereignty and stand in her own authority and authenticity, with access to all the energy, insights, and creativity she could ever need—a source of blessings for herself and others, a font of wisdom and compassion, who soars in the blissful freedom of space, reveling in the magical power to shape her thoughts and transform reality, the power to liberate herself and others.

Through dance, the dakinis emerge from painted surface and sculpted form, traversing space and time to move and dance in our bodies and minds. In art and literature, dakinis are often found together, in female company, proclaiming that women must guide, encourage, inspire, and empower one another as we seek to bring forth the sacred treasures of the female heart, mind, and body—to join the eternal dance of the dakinis!

NOTES

1. On flight as a theme connecting Tantric dakinis with earlier divine females in Buddhist practice, see Miranda Shaw, "Magical Lovers, Sisters, and Mothers: Yakṣiṇī Sādhana in Tantric Buddhism," in *Breaking Boundaries with the Goddess: New Directions in the Study of Śāktism, Essays in Honor of Narendra Nath Bhattacharyya*, ed. Cynthia Hume and Rachel Fell McDermott (New Delhi: Manohar, 2008), 265–296.

2. Miranda Shaw, *Passionate Enlightenment: Women in Tantric Buddhism* (Princeton, New Jersey: Princeton University Press, 1994).

3. Miranda Shaw, *Buddhist Goddesses of India* (Princeton, New Jersey: Princeton University Press).

4. Miranda Shaw, "Palden Lhamo: Supreme Guardian Goddess of the Dalai Lamas," in *As Long As Space Endures: Essays on the Kālacakra Tantra in Honor of H. H. the Dalai Lama*, ed. Edward Arnold (Ithaca: Snow Lion, 2008), 155–170.

5. On Charya dance and its revelation outside Vajracharya circles, see Miranda Shaw, "Tantric Buddhist Dance of Nepal: From the Temple to the Stage and Back," in *Nepal: Nostalgia and Modernity*, ed. Deepak Shimkhada (Bombay: Marg Foundation, 2011), 101–110. See www.dancemandal.com for Charya dance at its US temple base in Portland, Oregon, and beyond.

CHAPTER 8

ADVENTURES SHE HAS BROUGHT MY WAY

Starr Goode

In 1968, I found the world where I belonged. I drove across the Bay Bridge and arrived in Berkeley, not so far away in miles from my home town, but in terms of political awareness, a distance of light years. In the atmosphere of that tumultuous year, with the assassinations of Martin Luther King and Robert Kennedy, the ongoing slaughter in Vietnam necessitating the military draft of students, I went to my first Consciousness Raising group. A simple but radical idea: young women sat in a circle and shared their lives, informed by the rising tide of the second wave of feminism. In that experience of sisterhood, we explored the social and psychological conditions of our experience down to its roots. Even at twenty, I discovered truths there that continue to shape me in one way or another, a foundation of values to last a lifetime.

In the next year, the campus became a combat zone of demonstrations over the War, People's Park, the near daily tear gas, the National Guard on street corners, curfews, mass arrests, a student shot to death. In these heady times, I met a woman from the CR group who knew another woman who had a printing press, and the three of us moved in together and started the first underground feminist newspaper, *It Ain't Me Babe*. Our inaugural issue came out on January 15, 1970. The cover article commenced with these words: "Sisters have united in Berkeley to defend our right to be treated as human beings." The accompanying photograph showed angry women with fists raised, marching in front of Harmon's Gym, demanding entrance to the Karate 1 class for men only. We wanted the opportunity to learn how to protect ourselves from male violence. What passion we had, what a totality of commitment to our vision of a better world! To quote the poet William Wordsworth about the beginnings of the French revolution: "Bliss it was in that dawn to be alive / But to be young was very heaven."

For many women, feminism remained a social struggle for liberation from the tyranny of patriarchy. For others like myself, the political movement incubated the seeds of a spiritual need for what we lacked—the Goddess, images and energies of a divine female. At the newspaper, even at the height of our insurgent activities in the outer playing fields of an unjust society, some of us began to awaken to the depths of a history that had been stolen from us. We regarded the medieval witches as our subversive sisters and organized protests against the sexist media, calling ourselves the Red Witches.

Perhaps our strongest reclamation of the past is a science fiction story we published about the Bene OE (Organic Energy), a cosmic order of priestesses who are out to save the universe from the deadly obstruction of male domination so that energy can flow naturally again. The priestesses gather in a circle for a ritual and partake of magic blue crystals so that they may hear the ageless wisdom of their ancient sisters.

We were ahead of our time, in light of the subsequent flowering of women's ritual circles and the emergence of feminist spirituality. For me, the Goddess was a process of revelation, a below-the-surface-presence that had always been with me, like a heartbeat I could sometimes hear but whose source I did not know. I became more conscious of Her when the word Goddess spontaneously kept recurring in my poetry, along with a lot of Goddess imagery. Many women reported having similar experiences. In this, we were attuned to the psychic event of our times: the Return of the Goddess. It was as if the Earth herself was forcing things up from the unconscious of the human race, erupting like a volcano in dreams, fantasies, symbols, creative images, ideas. All of this was to grab our attention to show us another way, all for the sheer survival of life.

Over the years, my work as a poet has appeared in numerous publications, such as *We'Moon, Squaw Valley Anthology, SageWoman, Return of the Great Goddess, From the Realm of the Ancestors.* In 1996, the book *Expanding Circles: Women, Art & Community* had a substantive essay with my Goddess-themed poetry: "A Gaia Hypothesis," "Water Movements," "Equinox," "The Mystery of Coming to Earth," and "Lady of Pazardzik." In collaboration with visual artists, my poetry was used in installations at the Orange County Center for Contemporary Art and at California State University, Northridge. The same year and closest to my heart, I was commissioned by the Los Angeles Metropolitan Transportation Authority to create a bookmark from my poem "Gossip" (women sharing the village news!).

On January 29, 1986, the cable TV series *The Goddess In Art* was born. I produced and moderated the show during the next five years. It was the first of its kind to explore the legacy of this oldest tradition in art. I interviewed scholars such as Marija Gimbutas, Riane Eisler, Elinor Gadon, and Miriam Robbins Dexter, whose work has done so much to uncover Her suppressed history. I talked with artists like Mayumi Oda, Christopher Castle, Ruth Ann Andersen, and Cheri Gaulke, whose creativity has been inspired by a radical re-imagining of the feminine to transform our ailing world. Other guests were visionary activists, witches, and shamanic healers: Starhawk, Vicki Noble, and Hallie Austen Iglehart. Some recurring themes in our conversations included the egalitarian civilization of Old Europe as model for a more hopeful future and how much the Goddess has become a part of modern consciousness. The TV series has been used in university courses throughout the country and is now housed in the permanent collection of the Getty Museum.[1]

Around the time of the start of the TV series, I had an experience that changed my life—I met Marija Gimbutas. I attended a lecture and heard her state that there was a time when people had lived in peace. This revolutionary knowledge overturned all my "education," which had insisted that violence and war were an indelible quintessence of human nature. One of the great figures of the twentieth century, Marija literally unearthed the past to gift us with our natural heritage. She gave the women's spirituality movement a foundation from which to rise.

When her cancer returned in 1989, my coven Nemesis did a healing ritual for Marija at her Topanga home. Outside in the summer night, our faces were painted black and white in the phases of the moon. Later, she asked, "Where did you learn this?" Part of the answer was, "From you!" When Nemesis appeared on the cover of *The LA Weekly* with the caption: "The Witches Next Door," Marija was thrilled. She held the newspaper and exclaimed, "For the last five hundred years they have tried to kill it out, but they cannot."

I had the privilege to coordinate two more rituals for Marija. In the fall of 1989, at a yurt overlooking the ocean, the Goddess community gathered to invoke the regenerating power of the Great Mother. We wanted to give something back to this woman who had given us so much. In the ritual, women and men placed their healing intentions for Marija into a bowl of holy water gathered from sacred sites around the world. Then at the center of the circle, twelve priestesses anointed their hands with the water and placed them on Marija's body. All the while, the outer circle chanted, raising energy. Afterwards, Marija danced out of the tent and into the night. Sadly, the next ritual was the last. A memorial celebration took place in the Topanga Mountains after she died in February 1994. Her daughters, friends, and extended Goddess community came together in a field with three trees. In those trees, we placed our blessings for the journey of Marija's spirit and for the influence of her work to flourish. We sent our prayers down through the roots and up through the branches, to travel out into the cosmos. We affirmed Marija as still alive in our hearts as a beloved ancestor. I would not allow the ritual to be filmed— it was a thing created for the eternity of that moment.

In September of 1988, Goddess Project LA (Charles Sherman, Nancy Ann Jones, and I) produced something that had not been done before: a Goddess Arts Festival! This month-long celebration of the sacred feminine in the arts had press coverage from the *Los Angeles Times* to smaller local newspapers. They called the festival "wildly successful," with descriptions like "September is Goddess Month in Los Angeles" and "Goddesses on Every Corner." Inspired by the oldest tradition in art, events to honor Her occurred almost daily: art openings, museum tours, poetry readings, lectures, video nights, performance art, TV shows, dance, radio programs, classes, and public rituals. All happenings were described in our calendar of events, the *Museletter*. Everyone was welcome.

Goddess Project LA also produced book events for *The Language of the Goddess*[2] and *The Civilization of the Goddess*.[3] *Language* debuted on Friday the 13th, October 1989, at the Santa Monica Bay Women's Club, an old building used by the suffragettes a century earlier. The gala evening featured a talk by Marija followed by the presentation to her of a beautiful handmade *Book of Tributes*. On the entire upper floor was a juried art exhibition addressing the theme of the Language of the Goddess.

The world premiere of *The Civilization of the Goddess* took place on November 8, 1991, in a church in Santa Monica. It was the only place where one could buy the book. A sense of history charged the air. The church was filled with flowers and art. The tickets sold out. The book sold out. People sat in the aisles—leaned against walls. Marija took the stage to a standing ovation from an audience of over a thousand people.

She gave the speech of a lifetime (later considering this the best talk she ever gave): "I spent thirty years reading thousands of books, visiting hundreds of museums, years supervising the dig at Achilleion, a decade of writing...my book is not a novel." It was her good fortune to live to see her work take on an unexpected relevance. The premiere was one of her last public talks, which she closed with these words, "I am extremely happy that the publishing of my books coincided with the resurrection of Mother Earth and with the need to bring spirituality into our beings."[4]

My current work centers around a subject which has absorbed my attention for over a quarter of a century—Sheela na gigs. Over the decades, I have traveled to Ireland and Great Britain to see the Sheelas and walk the land, lectured at universities across the country, and published numerous articles in journals and an encyclopedia. The capstone on these years of devotion is my forthcoming book, *Sheela na gig: Dark Goddess of Europe, In Pursuit of an Image*.[5] Nothing represents the necessity of re-imagining the female in Western culture more than the startling stone carving of the Sheela na gig displaying her large vulva on medieval churches.

The book has three parts: History, Meditations, Image, with over 150 photographs and drawings. The figure of the Sheela na gig is rooted in the soil of Europe, traceable back through Celtic influences to the classical figures of Baubo and the Gorgon Medusa, back to the earlier Neolithic Frog Goddess and finally to the vulvas drawn on Palaeolithic cave walls. But the image of a female displaying her sex is not an anomaly of Western religious art; it manifests as a reoccurring theme across time and space in non-European representations (see figure 5).

On every continent of the planet, expressions are found in the visual arts and in mythical narratives of Goddesses and Heroines parting their thighs to reveal sacred powers. So deep in our psyches is this ancient image, it seems as if the icon of the vulva is the original cosmological center of the human imagination.

One of the fundamental crises of our culture is a lack of connection to images that originate from the most vital, transformative part of ourselves. The image of the Sheela na gig embodies the numinous power of the Dark Goddess over the mysteries of death and life. Such primal energies challenge the efficient running of the oppressive machine of state. The Sheela symbolizes what most terrifies patriarchal society—the chaos of nature and female sexuality. Our fascination and need of the Sheelas is evidenced by the many contemporary scholars writing about her and artists reinventing the figure in their work (see figure 6).

No woman walking the earth ever looked like a Sheela na gig, with her hag qualities combined with the swollen lips of her fertile vulva half the size of her body (see figure 7).

Such a figure gives us an alternative sanctified image to dethrone the war-god now ruling our culture. The Sheela is part of the emergence of the Goddess spirituality movement, calling for us to look beyond the outworn images of patriarchy. She restores the stature of the feminine in this androcratic world. Striking in her originality, the Sheela na gig is an antidote to the war on women, the war on nature and the war on the imagination.

NOTES

1. The conversation continues with the entire *The Goddess In Art series* available for view online. Go to YouTube.com, enter in the search box: Starr Goode Goddess in Art TV Series

2. Marija Gimbutas, *The Language of the Goddess* (San Francisco: HarperSanFrancisco, 1989).

3. Marija Gimbutas, *The Civilization of the Goddess. The World of Old Europe,* Joan Marler, ed. (San Francisco: HarperSanFrancisco, 1991).

4. A documentary of the premiere, *Marija Gimbutas: Voice of the Goddess,* can be seen on YouTube.com; enter in the search box: Starr Goode Goddess in Art TV Series. A CD of Marija's talk is available from Opus Archives.

5. Starr Goode, *Sheela na gig, Dark Goddess of Europe: In Pursuit of an Image,* Forthcoming, Inner Traditions.

CHAPTER 9

CULTIVATING SACRED GROUND

Joan Marler

When I was five years old, my mother took me to a Baptist Sunday school, where I first heard the Garden of Eden story. I was shocked to learn that Eve, the first woman, was created as an afterthought by God out of Adam's rib and that she was responsible for all of the sorrows of the world. Eve had listened to the serpent and persuaded Adam to join her in eating the forbidden fruit from the tree of the Knowledge of Good and Evil. I was humiliated by the message that all females share the guilt of Eve's original sin. At the same time, this knowledge resolved my deep confusion about why my daddy was so mean to my mother and to me—why we were always being brutally punished. Suddenly I realized that my father—who was male, just like God—could kill us and it would never make up for our sin of being female. I began to pray every night to become Eve so I could somehow reverse the curse so that there would be no more pain and suffering in the world.

I grew up on the Mendocino coast of California, where my father was a fisherman. The briny power and savage beauty of the great Pacific Ocean eclipsed all human concerns in the swell and pulse of Her exquisite and all-consuming body. One year, when I was almost ten, She swallowed my little brother and none of our tears could bring him back. Afterwards, I spent most of my time alone in the redwood forest that seemed to go on forever, with its graceful cathedral of trees encircling the blackened remains of their ancient mothers. The great virgin redwoods, thousands of years old, had been clear-cut a century earlier, their enormous stumps deliberately burned. I would lie on the deep carpet of fragrant mulch blanketing the intertwined roots of these tall, stately daughter trees, gazing upward into their gently moving branches, feeling layers of anguish gradually softening. The life force of the Earth that regenerated the decimated redwood forest was the same resonating presence that sustained me as a ravaged child. This living sanctuary was more sacred to me than any church of the Father God.

The first artists, poets, and intellectuals began to appear in Mendocino during the early 1960s, in dramatic contrast to the local culture of loggers and fishermen. It was then that I found art, music, and most especially folk dance, which I seized with all of my youthful powers. From 1965-1969, I had the good fortune to study modern dance and the liberal arts at Mills, a woman's college in Oakland, California, where women are respected as intelligent human beings. This culturally rich environment was deeply nurturing for me, and I am grateful to my dear mother who worked very hard to make it possible for me to receive the education that she never had.

During the 1960s, great cultural and political forces were roiling and every edifice of Truth and Stability was being shaken. The zeitgeist of the time was change, transformation, cultural, spiritual and political freedom, and the rediscovery of meaning. At Mills, I was inspired by the pioneers of modern dance, especially Martha Graham and Doris Humphrey, who had stripped away all previous techniques to discover the primary impulse of movement for the creation of new, more essential forms of expression.

After graduating, I returned to the ocean and forest of Mendocino with one focus—to use dance as the path to discover the primary impulse and source of meaning within my own life. Miraculous events were unfolding in this intoxicating environment and almost immediately I was invited to live and teach in an exquisite dance studio in the woods.

One night, while studying Joseph Campbell's *Masks of God* series, I read for the first time that the Garden of Eden story was the retelling of a much earlier motif in which the woman, the tree, the serpent, and the garden formed an emblematic expression of the highest spiritual quest. I was absolutely stunned, as though an explosion had gone off within me. At that moment, I realized I was not wrong, as a small child, to yearn to become Eve—not the biblical Eve, but the one who is simultaneously the tree as axis mundi connecting earth and sky, the serpent of death and regeneration, and the garden as the matrix of all life. I asked myself: What ground am I standing on? The answer came in a flash: that my feet had been cut off and I was planted with my bloody stumps on the desiccated ground of the Punitive Father. At that moment, I knew I had to find the Sacred Ground under my own feet, and to recover this ancient female lineage within myself. That evening in 1970, I found the direction of the rest of my life. I shared this realization with my dance students and together we explored *being* the Tree of Life, the Serpent, the Primordial Woman, and discovering the Living Earth under our feet and within ourselves. I had no idea that anyone else was exploring these themes. Nevertheless, I was convinced that it was not only possible but utterly necessary to reclaim this sacred reality here and now and to manifest our wholeness in this way.

While women's spirituality had not yet constellated into a movement, some women, including myself, spontaneously began creating earth-based rituals and art in various media, expressing a female-centered, sacred sensibility. After moving to Sebastopol, marrying my sweetheart Dan, and becoming pregnant, I yearned for a circle of women to commune with me during the home birth of our daughter, Sorrel. So, in 1977 I gathered a group of friends and we practiced attending to each other in a sacred way, with no previous guidance or model, calling forth an ancient wisdom that seemed long buried and forgotten. My deep experience of being attended by women with a quietly sacred focus during the long hours of birth-giving intensified my recognition that it was within our powers to engender whatever is needed for personal and cultural transformation.

The publication in 1974 of Marija Gimbutas's pioneering text *The Gods and Goddesses of Old Europe 7000-3500 BC*[1] (republished in 1982 as *The Goddesses and Gods of Old Europe*) introduced the cultural symbolism of the earliest agrarian societies of Europe to the general public. My own response, a shock of recognition, was not unique when seeing Old European imagery for the first time: elegantly schematic sculptures— primarily female—often with animal masks, naked or wearing ceremonial costumes, bodies engraved with spirals and myriad signs and symbols. These images transmit the potent concept of the centrality of women in the ritual activities of the earliest horticulturalists of Europe. Moreover, the spirals, undulating serpentine lines, zigzag patterns, and circles within circles engraved or painted on their bodies and on the elegant Old European ceramics reflect a consciousness of the interconnection of all things. These designs are replicated to this day in the folkloric imagery and floor patterns of the traditional dances of Greece and the Balkans—the region that was Old Europe—which initially inspired my love of dance.

For twenty-eight years I had the pleasure of teaching "folk and ethnic dance" to adults of all ages through Santa Rosa Junior College. Our repertoire included many traditional dances with Old European roots. Their repeated patterns function as movement mantras evoking communal harmony with ourselves and with the Earth. I worked with my students to develop a kinesthetic awareness of how to move together as one living body while dancing in a circle and in serpentine lines, a potent antidote to our hyper-modern world.

In 1976, Merlin Stone's book, *When God Was a Woman,* appeared.[2] Its heretical title and well-documented contents spread far and wide on an electric current of revelation. Then in 1978, the very first "Great Goddess Re-Emerging" conference took place at the University of Santa Cruz. I immediately signed up and was ecstatic to hear each brilliant speaker—especially Carol P. Christ's keynote address, "Why Women Need the Goddess"—and to realize that I was part of a burgeoning movement that I had not known existed. That same year Susan Griffin presented her masterwork, *Woman and Nature, the Roaring Inside Her,*[3] followed by Naomi Goldenberg's *Changing of the Gods: Feminism and the End of Traditional Religions,*[4] joined by an increasing outpouring of brilliant works by Adrienne Rich, Audre Lorde, Robin Morgan, Marge Piercy, Judy Grahn, and other great women writers. *The Death of Nature* by Carolyn Merchant,[5] and anthologies such as *Womenspirit Rising,* edited by Carol P. Christ and Judith Plaskow,[6] and *The Politics of Women's Spirituality,* edited by Charlene Spretnak,[7] introduced transformational ideas that germinated within my mind and spirit. At the same time, I was paralyzed by a fear of expressing myself—an Inquisitional terror— as though if I managed to articulate the truth within me, I would surely be shot down. My head was filled with white noise and my mouth felt gagged, but I heard a voice from deep inside that said, "Here is your direction: Go into the eye of your greatest fear." Therefore, I drove down to Berkeley and volunteered as a programmer at KPFA FM, the mothership of free speech radio, to stand naked on the air in front of thousands of people and eventually to find my voice.

During the 1980s, I hosted "Voices of Vision," an hour-long program in the humanities featuring many of the pioneers of the Women's Spirituality movement, and for several years the writer and activist Penny Rossenwasser and I presented twelve hour marathons devoted to Women's Spirituality on KPFA. One of the interviews I conducted for radio and print was with the mythologist Joseph Campbell, who stated that if he had known about Marija Gimbutas's work earlier, he would have written much of his own work differently. Inspired by both Campbell and Gimbutas, I intensified my study of mythology and archaeology while working as a freelance writer and editor, which prepared me to finally meet and interview Marija Gimbutas. We immediately had an affinity, and in 1987 Marija invited me to work with her as the editor of her magnum opus, *The Civilization of the Goddess*,[8] a sister volume to *The Language of the Goddess*.[9]

While *The Language of the Goddess* introduces archaeomythology as a systematic, interdisciplinary study of Old European symbolism, *The Civilization of the Goddess* distills Marija's research on the peaceful, egalitarian societies of Old Europe and her Kurgan theory (the end of Old Europe) into one extraordinary volume. This work provides an indispensable key for understanding the long-lived, matristic roots of European civilization and the relatively late appearance of patriarchal socio-religious structures. Needless to say, the experience of working closely with Marija from 1987–1994 and absorbing her work gave me a complete spiritual, psychological, and intellectual chiropractic adjustment.

Marija Gimbutas modeled the highest level of scholarly achievement and uncompromising brilliance and rigor that continues to inspire me to this day. I yearned to know her life story, since an extended narrative did not yet exist, so I recorded numerous interviews with Marija, her family and colleagues in the US, and while traveling with her throughout Western and Eastern Europe—especially in Lithuania. This was followed by years of ongoing research. I later provided transcripts and other biographical material to Starhawk and Donna Read for use in their film "Signs Out of Time."

After *Civilization* appeared, Marija asked me to lecture for her when she was too ill to travel, which stimulated an intensive period of international presentations and scores of my own published articles inspired by her life and work.[10] During my first lecture tour of Germany, I mentioned to the artist, filmmaker, and author Luisa Francia that I felt Marija had hurled me into the unknown. She replied: "Typical initiation!" These journeys made it possible for me to meet and collaborate with vibrant communities of European women who were creating art, rituals, dance, and literature, combining feminist consciousness with female-centered spirituality. During the 1990s, I began teaching in the Women's Spirituality Program at the California Institute of Integral Studies (CIIS), at New College of California in San Francisco, and occasionally at Sonoma State University, where I earned a Master's degree in Archaeomythology.

Marija's death in 1994 was a tremendous loss to all of us. Her pioneering scholarship presents us with nothing less than a new origin story of Western civilization. Her work stimulated a dynamic flowering of new work in the arts, sciences, and humanities as reflected in the interdisciplinary anthology, *From the Realm of the Ancestors*,[11] which I compiled and edited in her honor. Conferences sponsored by CIIS in San Francisco, Pacifica Graduate Institute near Santa Barbara, and the Smithsonian Associates in Washington, D. C. took place in response to its publication.

It was clear that Marija's work had to continue. In 1997 the Indo-European scholars Miriam Robbins Dexter and Karlene Jones Bley edited an important collection of articles written by Marija from 1952 until 1993, *The Kurgan culture and the Indo-Europeanization of Europe*.[12] Miriam also edited and supplemented Marija's work-in-progress, published in 1999 as *The Living Goddesses*.[13] In the meantime, I organized an interdisciplinary conference of scholars in Greece, "Deepening the Disciplines" (1998), where we launched the Institute of Archaeomythology (IAM) in order to stimulate ongoing archaeomythological research in Marija's honor. The Institute officially became a 501(c)3 non-profit organization in 2003, and I continue to work as its Executive Director. IAM has since sponsored numerous international exhibitions, symposia, and other events on archaeomythological themes in collaboration with universities, academies, national museums, and other institutions located in the geographical area of Old Europe and beyond.[14] A notable focus of our ongoing investigations concerns the Old European signs and symbols, often engraved on female figurines, that Marija considered a "sacred script" (also referred to as the Old European/Danube script). In order to document our ongoing work, we began to produce the online *Journal of Archaeomythology,* as well as symposium proceedings, exhibition catalogues, and other scholarly texts (see, e.g., *The Danube Script: Neo-Eneolithic Writing in Southeastern Europe,*[15] and *Signs of Civilization: Neolithic Symbol System of Southeast Europe.*[16]

I eventually returned to graduate school to earn a doctorate in Philosophy and Religion at CIIS in San Francisco with an emphasis in Women's Spirituality. My dissertation discusses Marija Gimbutas's contributions to archaeology, deconstructs the backlash against her work, and presents my assessment of her significance and legacy. Portions of this work will be included in her completed biography.

The cultivation of sacred ground has taken many forms during the course of my life—metaphorically through dance, art, ritual, radio production, and scholarship, alone and in community; most tangibly by cultivating an organic garden for more than forty years around our little hand-built house. It is here, with my hands in the Living Earth, that I hear Marija affirming that Goddess is "all life in Nature," and the sacred realm is always here and now.

NOTES

1. Marija Gimbutas, *The Gods and Goddesses of Old Europe 7000-3500 BC* (Berkeley & Los Angeles: University of California Press, 1974).
2. Merlin Stone, *When God Was a Woman* (New York: Dial Press, 1976).
3. Susan Griffin, *Woman and Nature, the Roaring inside Her* (New York: Harper & Row, 1978).
4. Naomi Goldenberg, *Changing of the Gods: Feminism and the End of Traditional Religions* (Boston: Beacon Press, 1979).
5. Carolyn Merchant, *The Death of Nature: Ecology and the Scientific Revolution* (San Francisco: Harper & Row, 1980).
6. Carol P. Christ, and Judith Plaskow, eds. *Womenspirit Rising: A Feminist Reader in Religion* (San Francisco: Harper & Row, 1979).
7. Charlene Spretnak, ed. *The Politics of Women's Spirituality* (New York: Anchor Books, 1982).
8. Marija Gimbutas, *The Civilization of the Goddess. The World of Old Europe,* ed. Joan Marler. (San Francisco: HarperSanFrancisco, 1991).
9. Marija Gimbutas, *The Language of the Goddess.* (San Francisco: HarperSanFrancisco, 1989).
10. See, e.g., selected articles by Joan Marler: "Marija Gimbutas: Tribute to a Lithuanian Legend," in *Women in Transition: Voices from Lithuania,* ed. S. La Font (New York: SUNY Press, 1998); "Marijos Gimbutiene: Archeomitologinis Europos civilizacijos," *Liaudies Kultùra* (2000):7–17, Vilnius; "L'eredità di Marija Gimbutas: una ricerca archeomitologica sulle radici della civiltà europea," in *Le radici prime dell'Europa,* ed. G. Bocchi and M. Ceruti (Milano: Bruno Mondadori, 2001); "An Archaeomythological Investigation of the Gorgon," in *Treasures: Studies in Honor of Ivan Marazov* (Sofia: New Bulgarian University, 2002); "The Body of Woman as Sacred Metaphor," in *Il Mito e il Culto della Grande Dea,* Papers from the Myth and Cult of the Great Goddess conference, Bologna, Italy, 24-25, November, 2000 (Bologna: Associazione Armonie, 2003); "Der Mythos vom ewigen Patriarchat," in *Die Diskriminierung der Matriarchatsforschung. Eine moderne Hexenjagd* (Bern, Switzerland: Amalia, 2003); "Marija Gimbutas," in *Notable American Women* (Boston: Harvard University Press, 2004); "The Beginnings of Patriarchy in Europe: Reflections on the Kurgan Theory of Marija Gimbutas," in *The Rule of Mars: Readings on the Origins, History and Impact of Patriarchy,* ed. Cristina

Biaggi (Manchester: Knowledge, Ideas & Trends, 2005); "Die Ikonographie und soziale Struktur Alteuropas," in *Gesellschaft in Balance*. Collected papers from "Societies in Balance: World Congress on Matriarchal Studies," Luxemburg, Sept. 5-7, 2003, ed. Heide Goettner-Abendroth (Stuttgart: HAGIA / Kohlhammer, 2006); "The Iconography and Social Structure of Old Europe," in *Societies of Peace: Matriarchies Past, Present and Future,* ed. Heide Goettner-Abendroth (Toronto: Inanna, 2009).

11. Joan Marler, ed., *From the Realm of the Ancestors: An Anthology in Honor of Marija Gimbutas* (Manchester: Knowledge, Ideas & Trends, 1997).

12. Marija Gimbutas, *The Kurgan Culture and the Indo-Europeanization of Europe: Selected articles from 1952 to 1993*, ed. Miriam Robbins Dexter and Karlene Jones-Bley (Washington, DC: Institute for the Study of Man, 1997).

13. Marija Gimbutas, *The Living Goddesses*, edited and supplemented by Miriam Robbins Dexter. (Berkeley/Los Angeles: University of California Press, 1999).

14. See www.archaeomythology.org.

15. Joan Marler, ed., *The Danube Script: Neo-Eneolithic Writing in Southeastern Europe*. Exhibition catalogue. National Brukenthal Museum, Sibiu (Sebastopol: Institute of Archaeomythology, 2008).

16. Joan Marler and Miriam Robbins Dexter, eds., *Signs of Civilization: Neolithic Symbol System of Southeast Europe* (Sebastopol: Institute of Archaeomythology, 2009).

CHAPTER 10

The Journey of a Matriarchal Scholar in a Patriarchal World

Heide Goettner-Abendroth
*Translated from German by Karen Smith

My first encounter with religion was in the Evangelical Lutheran Church —the church I was born into. I found it impossible to relate to its sober work ethic and its powerful image of God the Father; its representation of the Last Judgement as a great punishment frightened me from childhood. In later years, I read much about the other major religions, hoping to overcome my exclusive exposure to Christianity, but since I found nothing to identify with I never got beyond the reading stage. I became an irresolute nihilist and found myself, as a young adult, with very little direction in the world.

Then, in Catholic folk-religion, I encountered the cult of Mary (similar to Goddess worship); its mythology appealed to me. Here I found a mystical background and a rich tradition that had otherwise long ago been buried. The discovery coincided with a major life crisis, and for a while the Roman Catholic Church became my church of choice. My experience of this church was intense, and so it happened that I kept painfully coming up against its limits—against the hard, pitiless dogmas that waited just beneath the beautiful mythological veil. As a young mother of three children, I became aware of the utter misogyny of this church.

So I turned away and followed a purely scientific worldview, one which had first emerged during my student years and which came into intellectual fullness in my own research and teaching at the university. I needed religion no longer, and I considered myself an enlightened, tolerant atheist. With calm rationality, I tried to understand my personal circumstances, to penetrate the society surrounding me, and to place myself at a critical distance from it.

But I had always been interested in mythology, which led me to the eye-opening experience of reading Robert Graves' *Greek Mythology*.[1] For the first time, I faced completely different ways of thinking, symbolism, and societal forms—which Graves clearly called "matriarchal."

Reclaiming the term "matriarchy" means to reclaim knowledge of societies that have been socially, economically, politically and culturally created by women. Matriarchies are perfectly balanced societies; that is, they are based on gender-equality, on a reciprocal economy of giving, and on consensus politics. This applies to the societal contribution of both sexes—and even though women are at the center, the principle of balance governs the societal functioning and freedom of both sexes. Matriarchal societies should emphatically not be regarded as mirror images of patriarchal ones—with dominating women instead of patriarchy's dominating men—as they have never needed patriarchy's hierarchical structures.

I was totally absorbed in a new world that I could immediately identify with. So it was Graves who gave me the impetus to investigate matriarchal societies more closely, especially those that still exist. I was completely swept up in this path, and during my university days in the '60s and '70s I unceasingly searched after matriarchal social forms in all their various expressions in the libraries. I was actually successful, as source texts did exist—but no one at the university would mention them. So I plodded on alone, working in parallel to my official studies and my training as a philosopher—and the more material I gathered, the more my amazement grew. My worldview was undergoing a radical makeover that I didn't dare to speak of—in fact, I was afraid people would think I was insane. But I had already decided I would bring this knowledge into the world, even if I was not sure how to do it.

Then came the Second Wave of the women's movement: prompted by this political surge from the United States, young German university women also became rebellious. They claimed their place in university hierarchies and founded feminist Women's Studies in Germany. As a young philosopher in the midst of all this, I presented, for the first time, my new insights on the matriarchal type of society. The women avidly grasped it. It was a time of great enthusiasm: we were radically politicized, and we felt we were creating a completely new culture. During this time, my first book on matriarchy was published. As I had not been sure whether to start with matriarchal social forms or matriarchal political economy, I began with religion and spirituality. In *The Goddess and her Heros* (1980; English translation 1995),[2] I followed the lead of Robert Graves but extended the analysis of matriarchal mythology to include India, Iran, Egypt and Northern Europe—all the while approaching the material, fascinating as it was, with scientific objectivity—as if all the various Goddesses I encountered had nothing to do with me.

Yet my calm equanimity was eroded by life's problems, and I found myself in a new, deep crisis in which my entire existence was on the line. During this time, since nothing was acceptable to me anymore, neither the known religions nor scientific enlightenment, as a result I experienced an inner strength that did not correspond to any officially accepted tradition. Although this epiphany brought me back to life again, I still could not identify it, though I gave it many Goddess names. But the naming itself was unimportant in light of the personal maturity and the peace beyond existing thought-systems, which I had found. In that way, the power of the Goddess—which I had written about at such a cool distance—swept over me, and this was my birth as a spiritual person.

However, I still felt very lonely on this path. Gradually, I met more and more women of my generation who had undergone similar life processes. They had the same desire to develop their spiritual power outside of the official religions, but they did not know how to do it. They asked me, but I did not know, either.

This gap drove me to use my knowledge of matriarchal mythology, symbolism and ritual to develop matriarchal rituals. The impetus—and the courage—came from Starhawk's book, *The Spiral Dance*,[3] and from Charlene Spretnak's impressive anthology, *The Politics of Women's Spirituality.*[4] But it was up to me develop the practice of the new "Matriarchal Mystery Festivals," a process that began spontaneously with a group of women artists in Switzerland. From that collaboration, the first versions of the festivals arose, which I referred to as our new "Matriarchal spirituality" (1983). In the German-speaking world (Germany, Switzerland and Austria), I was one of the first to initiate a spiritual practice for and with women—at that time most women were afraid to take part in a women's ritual. But every year new women came, wanting to celebrate the Matriarchal Mystery Festivals, and this spiritual work continued to develop over the next three decades until today. My sources for this always were my ever-deepening studies of the culture, symbolism, and spirituality of matriarchal peoples. To give the women a foundation upon which to build, I shared this knowledge in talks before and after the festivals.

In the German-speaking world, many women felt stimulated by this work, and gradually more and more circles developed, independently continuing to celebrate matriarchal festivals throughout the seasonal cycle of the year. Here too, a wider spiritual movement has now developed, although many women no longer know who started it. My path guided my own life forward, because my task was not only to be a spiritual teacher. Modern Matriarchal Studies, which I was about to create, also had a claim on my time and energy. Because of these studies, I left the university to pursue them. I had no desire to keep devoting my time to patriarchal philosophy, nor to ruin my life striving for a career in its institutions. And because so many women were interested in matriarchal studies, I realized how necessary this work is in today's world.

This change of direction was even more radical in that I left my marriage at this time and stood alone, depending only on myself. At that moment, in founding the HAGIA International Academy (1986), I accomplished what the university would not allow: dedicating myself to research and teaching on matriarchal societies, and further developing matriarchal spirituality for women.

From the beginning, both these elements were part and parcel of the Academy, and the twin focus gave it a structure of its own. The two elements fundamentally belong together, as matriarchal cultures are profoundly spiritual. It is not possible to understand these societies without understanding something about spirituality—and, to my shock, this was the problem I saw with many anthropologists. With the founding of the Academy, I put all my eggs in one basket, as it were—the divorce had left me with nothing but the house for the Academy, and there was no money. It was a leap into the unknown, and I had no idea if I would manage to survive. However, enough women came to the Academy to allow me to keep it going, as well as to support myself and my adolescent children (although my organizational responsibilities too often pre-empted my research). An incredible amount of energy had filled me ever since I had, in my own way, left the patriarchy; this enabled me to somehow prevail in the various crises that threatened the Academy's existence. And in addition, the ongoing solidarity of many women has kept the Academy open until this day.

My matriarchal research then drew me to travels around the world, made possible by the Academy HAGIA. There were study trips to follow the traces of matriarchal cultures: in Germany, as well as in Europe and on other continents. A high point was the study and research trip to the matriarchal Mosuo people in southwestern China (1993), in which I put my matriarchal theory to the test. I considered it to be validated, and I wrote a book on this very exciting anthropological voyage: *Matriarchat in Südchina,* 1998.[5] In the meantime, part of my main work, *Das Matriarchat,*[6] had been published; further books appeared; and one of my favourite projects was realized: three books on the great Goddess myths of Sumer, Egypt, Greece, Central Europe and the Alps, as interpreted through the lens of matriarchal theory.[7]

These travels gave me contacts all over the world, and I longed to put together a conference that would gather the many people who had dedicated themselves to the theme of matriarchy. As they were mostly unknown to each other, I felt it was necessary for them to meet to strengthen this new field of modern Matriarchal Studies. For a long while, it was no more than a wish, as I lacked the financial resources for such an ambitious event. But from time to time I would mention the idea to my students, and so it happened that, after a while, one of them put me in touch with the minister for women's affairs of Luxembourg, who was willing to lend her support to such a conference. The news came in a phone call, and it hit me like a lightning bolt. At first I was uncertain whether I should do it, because, once again, my research would suffer, but in the end, I did it.

The whole thing got bigger and bigger until the First World Congress on Matriarchal Studies took place in Luxembourg in 2003. This was not exactly something I had ever envisioned, but when a woman is led by the Goddess of inspiration, things like this can happen. The conference was a great success, and it provided the opportunity for me to get in contact with women from the Women's Spirituality movement in the United States—some of whom, like Joan Marler and Lucia Birnbaum, I had known since first participating in Joan's "Institute of Archaeomythology," in 1998. At the end of the Luxembourg conference, Genevieve Vaughan came up to me with a big smile on her face, and she handed me her book on the gift economy, *For-Giving*.[8] Soon after, she wrote to me of her interest in bringing modern Matriarchal Studies to the United States, suggesting that together, she and I should organize a second, similar conference. This came as a second lightning strike, as I had not considered a follow-up. After the first conference, I wanted to get right back to my research and writing, but that was not to be. Thus the Second World Congress on Matriarchal Studies was held in 2005, in Texas; there, we brought together a variety of indigenous researchers and presenters from still existing matriarchal societies. These people were also meeting each other for the first time and recognizing that their own matriarchal ways of living were not isolated, backward traditions to be overcome, but that they had existed worldwide, and still did—and that western women regarded them as a highly valuable heritage of humanity. They demonstrate that there is another way of living, besides the one practiced in patriarchy, and that we can learn from it. This knowledge constitutes a new paradigm that we desperately need, a new vision of overcoming patriarchy everywhere. This overarching intention made both of the Matriarchy conferences into events that were also political—although mainstream media fastidiously avoided publicizing it. At the most recent conference on modern Matriarchal Studies and Matriarchal Politics in Switzerland, in 2011, we made visible the political principles embedded in the paradigm of matriarchal studies. That was too much for the Swiss mainstream media, who made every effort to ridicule and defame me, as conference leader, as well as the other speakers and the audience.

Nevertheless, modern Matriarchal Studies will not be stopped—and the same goes for its deep connection to matriarchal spirituality. The conferences brought it to the world stage, and now my main work on matriarchal societies has been translated into English, Italian and Spanish. More and more people are coming to understand how profoundly this perspective invalidates and overrides patriarchal economic, social, political and cultural structures—and does so radically, as only a new paradigm of society and history can. It is becoming clear that this shift is necessary for creating a better world, so Matriarchal Studies has developed at the right time and place in this new millennium.

Of course, I cannot predict where it will lead me in the years to come, or which of the Goddess's lightning bolts might hit me next. I plan to develop modern Matriarchal Studies further, especially as regards its anthropological and historical aspects. I will also be developing a sharper, more precise formulation of the principles of Matriarchal Politics, and I will bring this out into the world. I also want to write a book on the Matriarchal Mystery Festivals that will present the meaning and practice of more than 30 years of this form of spirituality. And of course, I'll do my best to ensure the prosperity of the Academy HAGIA, along with everything else that matters to me, such as training women as instructors of modern Matriarchal Studies and as priestesses of the Matriarchal Mystery Festivals. But I have often experienced how my own plans are only one part of the whole process, so I will remain open for what wants to happen and what I am called to.

NOTES

1. Robert Graves, *The Greek Myths*, (Baltimore, Maryland: Penguin Books, 1955).
2. Heide Goettner-Abendroth, *The Goddess and her Heros*, German Edition 1980. Trans. Lilian Friedberg and Heide Goettner-Abendroth (Stow, MA: Anthony Publishing Co,1995).
3. Starhawk, *The Spiral Dance. A Rebirth of the Ancient Religion of the Great Goddess* (New York: Harper and Row, 1979).
4. Charlene Spretnak, *The Politics of Women's Spirituality* (New York: Anchor/Doubleday, 1982).
5. Heide Goettner-Abendroth, *Matriarchat in Südchina* (Stuttgart: Kohlhammer Verlag, 1998).
6. Heide Goettner-Abendroth, *Das Matriarchat* I and II.1 and II.2. (Stuttgart: Kohlhammer,1988-2000).
7. Heide Goettner-Abendroth, *Inanna—Gilgamesch—Isis—Rhea. Die großen Göttinnenmythen Sumers, Ägyptens und Griechenlands* (Königstein/Taunus: Ulrike Helmer Verlag, 2004). Heide Goettner-Abendroth, *Fee Morgane—Der heilige Gral. Die großen Göttinnenmythen des keltischen Raumes* (Königstein/Taunus: Ulrike Helmer Verlag, 2005). Heide Goettner-Abendroth, *Frau Holle—Das Feenvolk der Dolomiten. Die großen Göttinnenmythen Mitteleuropas und der Alpen* (Königstein/Taunus: Ulrike Helmer Verlag, 2005).
8. Genevieve Vaughan, *For-Giving: A Feminist Criticism of Exchange* (Austin, Texas: Plain View Press, 1977).

PART II

INDIGENOUS MIND
AND MOTHER EARTH

CHAPTER 11

STILL CRAZY AFTER ALL THESE TEARS

Luisah Teish

The wind blows leaves across the parking lot as women, children, and men enter the meeting room downstairs, the theater upstairs, or the lobby on the ground floor of the building anywhere we happen to be anytime. They are smudged at the door, meet and greet each other, receive stones, candles and flowers, then seat themselves on pillows, chairs, and parental laps. The chitchat stops as the primal heartbeat of humanity, the African drum, calls the village together. We sing ourselves into community. Caressed by the undulating beat, we sway and swoon in our seats until the drum fades and the house lights go out.

KINDRED SPIRITS CALL

Out of the warm dark silence comes the sound of the Shofar blown by a towering figure of a woman, a daughter of the Shekinah. Her horn announces, "let the ritual begin."

A Black Muslim sister, wrapped in her choice of veils, recites a prayer for peace. We are transported to the Tower overlooking the rising sun. A manila-colored woman from the Philippines recites a prayer in Tagalog on behalf of the hungry, the homeless, and the disabled. Lava flows and sizzles as Madame Pele dances across the floor to an ancient Hawaiian chant. The scent of her flowers, the flow of her hair and her skirt leave us breathless on an imaginary beach basking in the noonday sun.

Dressed in beads and feathers, a Native American elder calls the Thunderbird, the Wolf, and the Salmon as our people did long before Columbus came and the Buffalo went away. The ancestors are called to the circle in Yoruba, Spanish and Creole.

BACK TO THE FUTURE

On these nights we call the deities and the ancestors, the animals and the plants, the stars, and the stones of every continent, culture, and era to come be with us. In this room, in this sacred space, we are "kindred spirits," people who respect our earth, our cultures, our ancestors, and ourselves. We stand together; we pray, play, and struggle together. We trust each other and are political because we are spiritual. Our spirituality informs our political struggles, our years of high-risk living, loving, laughter, and tears. We have traveled over the mountains and through the forests, around the globe, to arrive at this common place: to inner and outer sacred space.

For me the journey began with a childhood dream, a whispering on the wind, a sense that I had come to earth to be someone with something to do. That recognition developed in spite of the perpetual gynophobia of the Catholic Church, a backdrop of late-'50s racism in the segregated South, and the pro-macho sexism of mid-sixties counter-culture.

The predominance of the "isms" put me in a peculiar position. The conflicts were multi-layered. In the late '50s–mid '60s my work was in the Black Community; I spent most of my time attending meetings, participating in demonstrations, and performing dance-dramas to heighten awareness and raise money for various defense funds.

Even though I was involved in a struggle for freedom, that struggle was undermined by the patriarchy and cultural limitations based on race and class. I was required to deny my multi-racial heritage, and to tolerate insults and superior attitudes from many of the men I worked with. Christianity had been "the religion" of the Civil Rights Movement and Islam was supposed to be the empowering alternative. But neither of these empowered me as a woman.

I came to realize that these "isms" stood in the way of my soul's purpose for being here, and I resolved to do something about it all. So I began by questioning the nuns and the Judeo-Christian Bible, by challenging segregation in the church, and by struggling to understand male to female relationships. In a Consciousness-Raising '70s moment I realized that "Eve was Framed." She had been accused of bringing all evil into the world, and because of her I was "destined" to share that burden. I realized that my own future and that of generations to come depended on changing the impact this mythology and its images had on the lives of real women, particularly women of color.

It was a time of great stirring in the Black Community. During those early years most women of color, and especially Black American women, did not find a connection to the Women's Movement. We perceived it as a mostly middle-class movement that did not address our concerns. There was some whispering of an alternative way of knowing, of stepping outside Orthodox religion and exploring nature and spirit. But all the available information was about Greco-Roman, Celtic, or Middle Eastern Goddesses.

So I began to look for "She Who Looked Like Me." I investigated and joined the Fahamme Temple of Amun-Ra, a Black Egyptian temple, and I was initiated to Isis, Hathor and Osiris. I looked for the meaning of folk beliefs I'd grown up with in Louisiana, and that quest for understanding led to the Loas of Haiti and the Orishas of West Africa. What a great discovery! I found the sacred myths of the African Goddesses: Yemonja, the Great Mother of the Ocean, Oya, the Queen of the Winds of Change, and my personal Goddess, Oshun, the beautiful and generous Goddess of Love. I learned that these Goddesses reflected the collective stories of generations of powerful women who walked the earth as daughters of nature.

This information inspired me beyond reason, wrapped me in the mystery of the Divine Feminine, and made me crazy with faith, drunk on the possibility of paradise in this garden, this sacred place.

Timidly, I wrote a letter to the editor of Plexus, a local women's newspaper. I asked if anyone was interested in learning about the African Goddesses, and I offered to have tea and talk about them. I got a call from the Berkeley Women's Center, inviting me to hold a session at their facility. I accepted and arrived with six tea bags and a few notes.

And far beyond my hopes and expectations, I walked into a room of about thirty crazy women who wanted to know the Goddesses, and to address them with love and reverence. These women were African-American, Euro-American, Latin, Asian, and Native American. They were midwives, artists, workers, and mothers. We were a beautiful bouquet of flowers.

Then I became active in the Women's Spirituality Movement. We worked together for many years, performing rituals, and staging demonstrations. We wrote articles addressing issues such as healings after rape, alternatives for battered women, defending women's sexual and reproductive rights, and combating violent pornography. The early '80s felt like progress.

THE FUTURE SHOCK

I made a commitment to Oshun that I would wrap my head in the cloth of power, honor my ancestors, and promote female power proudly in the world. To that end, I received initiations in Africa and the Caribbean, performed in Europe, and sat around firesides with indigenous clan mothers all over the world. I wrote *Jambalaya: The Natural Woman's Book of Personal Charms and Practical Rituals,*[1] in order to share what I had learned.

In the midst of all this joy there came the shock and sorrow of the '90s. Big money and media mania engineered particular shifts in popular thought and culture. Many of those shifts encouraged institutional corruption and represented the loss of rights earned through blood and tears in the past.

A Black Republican man led the parade against affirmative action in California, surprisingly. To this day I still can't comprehend just what a black republican is! The death of affirmative action was a crime and an insult to the memory of Dr. Martin Luther King, Fannie Lou Hamer, and the many people who died on the front lines fighting for our civil rights. The ancestors turned over in their graves.

The book, *The Bell Curve,* declared that black students were inherently inferior, a theory that had been disproved decades ago. Its publication and popularity announced that the same evil of educational racism, such as I had experienced in the segregated south, would rise again.

My concern for the minds of our children went off the charts when I attended a Black History celebration at a mid-western college and found that Sankofa and Malcolm X had been replaced by the Nutty Professor as the feature film for Black history month.

And hard-core gangsta-rappers, costumed in prison garb, scratched "Black classical music" albums to create curse-ridden declarations of woman-hatred, the background music to drive-by shootings. I watched children, whom I had delivered and taught, graduate into the penitentiary instead of the university. Some died of crack overdoses and I buried them. This wiped the smile off my face.

Rastafarian dreadlocks, a specifically Afro-Caribbean spiritual hairstyle, became the measure of a black woman's blackness; yet they can (like the natural wig of the sixties) be purchased on silk strings at weaving salons, and some sisters refrained from performing spiritual head cleansings for fear of getting their hair wet. Soon, even flaxen haired white women began to wear "locks." At that point I no longer understood it; the symbolism was lost to me.

For sure, sweat popped out of my scalp when I experienced a complete break with reality in the person of a white republican woman in a hot tub at my gym. She was fresh out of the military, and she informed me, emphatically, that slavery happened because black people needed "a masochistic experience" and that "the Jewish holocaust never really happened!" I asked her, "What happened to the belief that none of us are free until all of us are free?" She said all that allness was passé to a post-modern woman. I inhaled, smelled tar and feathers, and saw a modern Ku Klux Klan mother sitting in hot water with me. I thought she was crazy.

As we approached the end of somebody's millennium (not mine), the whole post-modern world seemed to be going crazy to me.

The Womanspirit Movement of the past decades had reclaimed a beautiful herstory and culture. But now I saw our contribution being usurped by exploitative and disrespectful cultural kleptocrats. Recovered Goddess images and indigenous body adornments such as Maori Moko, African nose rings, and Native American eagle feathers, usually awarded after a "rite of passage," became the purchased property of New Age dilettantes, so-called "modern primitives," and gothic vampires.

And finally my heart was broken when pagan priestesses who had been my "sisters-in-struggle" in the Women's Spirituality Movement referred to African spirituality in the negative, and now chose the "Dark Goddess" as the scapegoat for their "sexual need" to sport whips, collars, and chains, the symbols of the slave-seller, the slave-master, and the plantation overseer. It was "their right" and I shouldn't be upset about it; it was only history. I heard bloodhounds baying in the distance as the Promise Keepers, a conservative Christian men's international organization, promised to keep everyone in their "proper place."

I bought into the idea of being a" trailblazer." A trailblazer is very different from a "token." Whereas the token finds security in being the only one of its kind in a group, the trailblazer works from the inside, to change the group into something that is more suitable for more of its own kind to enter. I thought that the best way to insure a future for women of color in the Women's Spirituality Movement was to teach the coming generations. So I helped to establish Women's Spiritual Education as a legitimate subject in colleges and universities. And I fought against tokenism by keeping a list of books, organizations and works of art that reflected the cultures of colored women. For several years I enjoyed watching women blossom under the moonlight of Eco-spiritual knowledge. We read the works of writers like Merlin Stone, Paula Gunn Allen, and Octavia Butler. I taught courses on the Elements of Magic, Women's Rites of Passage, and Eco-spiritual Ritual. Whenever an administrator claimed that there was no one "qualified" to teach a subject, I handed them a list of names and phone numbers. I am proud to say that some of my students are involved in cutting edge research and community activism.

However, that joy has been overshadowed by the intellectual elitism of "the academy" and invasions by Corporate Conquistadors. The Women's Wisdom Council, with its gift of embodied experience, has slowly been replaced by the "Bored of Talking Heads." Women of Color pay outrageous prices and endure micro-aggressions in order to receive a doctorate in "delusional revisionism" from institutions claiming to be alternative. All this occurs on a backdrop of economic exploitation, cultural appropriation, and misguided information.

I have to ask: "Women, where are we now?"

Crazy with grief, now, I sometimes run off the road and take refuge in the forest, hoping to rest somewhere in an easy chair. But if I open my email, read the paper, or turn on the TV, I am again confronted with the unrest of war, gender violence, ecological destruction, epidemic, abject poverty, human trafficking, witch-burnings, and untimely death.

Sometimes I hide in the bushes and cry, and I try to forget that I came here with a soul-purpose, with somewhere to go and something to do.

KINDRED LOST AND FOUND

In the midst of all these tears, the drum sounds and ancestral figures rumble in the bush. They rise up from under rocks; they come dancing from behind the trees: Damballah, Maria Lionza, and Ayelala. They bring my kindred spirits out of the shadows.

At first I did not recognize them in their multi-colored skins and spiritual traditions. But they dare to walk out of the shadows with me, to accompany me on the road back to a spiritually empowered place.

Now we take deep breaths as we enter this smoke-filled room. The herbs and flowers we smudge with come from Equatorial rainforests where ancient trees, like us, have been burned by big business.

We hold our children on our laps, remembering those of us who stand in food stamp lines, duck bullets as we enter women's clinics, and run with our children from violent husbands and wives. We play the sacred drums and sing songs of freedom. Our voices ring louder than racial slurs, gender-class clichés, and politically correct half-truths.

We stand in a circle, hold hands, and call our ancestors from every direction, in every language. We dance for joy, for kinship, for peace. We dance for faith renewed. And we are happy to find each other—we who are still so crazy after all these tears.

NOTES

1. Luisah Teish, *Jambalaya: The Natural Woman's Book of Personal Charms and Practical Rituals* (San Francisco: HarperOne, 1985).

CHAPTER 12

ANCIENT WISDOM, SUSTAINING HARMONY

Brooke Medicine Eagle

HOW AND WHEN

I first awakened to the Women's Spirituality Movement in the early 1970's, while I was in the San Francisco bay area doing doctoral work. The fires of that awakening time were burning bright there and called powerfully to me (see figure 8).

I was working with the ancient knowledge to be found in my Native American background, and one of the most powerful aspects of that wisdom was the power and primacy of the Feminine. It figured in primary people's wisdom in many ways, the two following being the ones that lighted up the most for me personally.

THE TWO WISDOMS

The feminine aspect of life is often seen as a bowl, filled with all the possibilities that exist through all time—past to future. Like the sky above us, filled with stars, it is eternally there, a constant and everlasting richness from which life births itself in all forms. It is thus, in philosophical terms, first cause: the primary, original energy. In Lakota, this primary feminine is referred to as *wakan.* Then comes *skan,* the masculine aspect—brilliant, fast and brief—striking like a bolt of lightning into the sky of possibilities, combining with a "star" of energy there to bring something into material reality. In our own bodies, it is shown when a sperm disturbs and awakens an egg, which then eventually produces a baby in the physical world. I was deeply moved by this understanding of Feminine primacy, rejoicing in the cultures which recognized and respected this understanding and, as well, honored the supreme magic done by women in the creation of the species. My traditional vision quests were conducted under the hoop of the Buffalo Hat Lodge: a sacred altar which represents the nurturing and renewing power of the feminine. My sharing with the world had this at its base.

Along with that came the wisdom and power of women's moon-time (menstrual) mysteries. Learning from my elders these profound teachings and their implications—for women's health, as well as their lives of spirit and service to All Our Relations—I was moved to bring this potent information to light in the larger world of women. Harmonizing and empowering our bodies in concert with the pull of Grandmother Moon, and accomplishing the spiritual charge of becoming visionary leaders, have been worthy goals. I actually got in trouble with some militant feminists when I reminded everyone that feminine power didn't mean putting in a tampon and acting like a guy. There is much more power and magic in the deep feminine practices than that, and we all need to find that kind of understanding and depth, because hardly anyone has been given the menstrual and feminine mysteries. We are certainly still in process.

WHAT HAS BEEN ACCOMPLISHED BY THE WOMEN'S SPIRITUALITY MOVEMENT

I see a fuller and freer expression of women and their remarkable gifts at every level. Some women are even willing to take up the mantle of elected political positions, choosing to work in that arena to ensure that the feminine nurturing and renewing consciousness is represented there. Sexual expression is more open and healthy at almost every level. Same sex marriages are becoming more commonplace and accepted. And personally, I'm very interested in the work on extended female orgasm: the vitality and enriched relationships it seems to engender for both women and men. More awareness is being created regarding natural, healthful, youthful living. Women healers, nutritionists and cooks are helping us live better through nourishing food, joyous exercise, and quieting meditations. We are bringing ourselves back into more meaningful togetherness among women, where our mothers tended to get isolated in single family homes, with no quilting circles or spiritual gatherings to draw them together. This movement into connection and cooperation is central to our happiness and empowerment. Moon-lodge/ red tent wisdom and practices are coming into more and more women's lives around the world. Women are beginning to honor their health and spirits by taking time off during their menstruating days, and they are reaping the vision and wisdom which is often downloaded to them in these sweet and quiet retreat times.

WHAT I AM DOING TODAY

My guidance told me in the early days that I was to work for the Mother Earth, and that in these times of world crisis, it would be most powerfully done through working with the human family in order that they might learn to live in sustaining harmony. A strong part of this is what I called Embodying Spirit, with a focus on bringing spirit awake and alive within us here on Mother Earth in our "earth robes" (bodies).

Whatever the subject of my teaching—which ranged from native ways and ceremony to ecological living, from Permaculture to aboriginal skills, from psychological understanding to healing the body, and more—the underlying theme was always coming into harmony in order to sustain life on this sweet Earth (see figure 9).

This theme of sustaining harmony continues to be the essence of my work, yet in different ways than being on the road eleven months a year, teaching internationally. For the last ten years, I have moved off the larger teaching circuit to "put the teachings of harmony on the ground." With partners and helpers, I have focused my energy on the creation and development of homesteads, gardens, orchards and retreat sanctuaries with special attention to pure and flowing water. I have been called an EarthKeeper and feel myself coming more fully into that vocational expression. The larger framework of what I am doing at this moment is opening to transition, transformation, and renewal of self and service to the world as I move from years of being full-time in quiet backcountry gardens to traveling the world teaching and sharing again. I have always been supremely aware of the importance of the physical: how the state of our bodies affects our lives at every level. Having access to clean, healthy, nurturing food is a baseline, and it has been powerful to grow and share that kind of food. My family were always gardeners and produced much of our food on the ranches where I grew up, yet my life on the road for thirty-five years did not allow me to actively participate in that part of life. It has been empowering, as well as instructive, to start from scratch on a lovely piece of land, and to create home, outbuildings, gardens and orchard there. The growing and processing of nourishing food became my life and literally took over my days. My FlowerSong gardens were extensive, no-turn, heavily mulched and intensely productive; and eighty-five trees gave me their fruit! With the amazingly large amount of production came the challenge of processing and storing that much food. It was wonderful to have young people join me to help with all aspects of the work and to learn from experience how to do it on their own. During that time, I also realized my love of ecological building and creating natural beauty: waterfalls and pools and flowers and radiant gardens as well as simple and workable living spaces. I have lived far in the back country and often been sad that few people ever came to behold the exquisite beauty I have created; then I came to the realization that the high vibration engendered there made a powerful and positive difference on Earth, no matter how few or many saw it with their eyes. I was making manifest my Dawn Star[1] name, *Chalise (sha 'lease)* which means a chalice overflowing with light and love. The *FlowerSong* property was even shaped like a chalice, with terraces coming up from a central pool! I was learning to create beauty and love for all beings in the circle of life and to lift the quality of vibration. All life forms there were held in a protective circle of love created by dedicating it to the Goddess, with menstrual blood on the four corners. (It became obvious that *Chalise* was remarkably different from my Medicine Eagle name, which indicates one who picks up the Dawn Star's loving light in the East and carries it across the sky for all to see—a more yang assignment that had been mine for previous decades.) Working with the exquisite productivity of the land helped awaken a deeper understanding of my work; it is about a flowering of life on Earth, and I call it "Blossoming." That blossoming comes through love as a central principle. To give the reader some history, the charge of the passing Piscean Age has been to "Walk the Path With Heart," learning to place the creative, nourishing and regenerating power of love at the center of our Earth walk. With love in place with its generative, nurturing, supportive and blessed energy, our essential selves feel free (down to the DNA level) to open and blossom into all they can be. We can then move into the Aquarian Age and create a golden time on Earth.

And the teachings go further. Modern science is showing us that the physical heart is actually a potent brain and, in fact, the most beneficial and harmonious one, with the normal brain being an excellent executive assistant to make real the heart's intuitive wisdom. In addition, the sacred/spiritual heart is the home of Creation's loving wholeness and our own individual purpose. A heart of love not only makes us healthier and happier, but wiser and more positively powerful in our world. Through its support we can truly blossom our gifts fully into a world acutely in need of our very best. And it is understood that as more and more of us live from our hearts, there is a spiraling synergy which uplifts and restores ourselves and the world, with more ease and grace than we previously thought possible.

White Buffalo Woman's principle of holiness—wholeness, healing, cooperation, sharing, caring—is awakening and transforming the world and our knowledge of how to manifest that which truly works for all our relations. This quality of manifesting is also a part of my work and teaching. I have also been awakened to the role of one I call Dawn Star Woman—Mary Magdalene—who might be considered the high Goddess of this time, holding the feminine aspects of love in place so our human family can learn to function gracefully with them. Soon I will be working with my friend Ani Williams to guide groups to visit, and awaken to new empowered service, at the Magdalene sites in Europe.

Another aspect of my current work is creating in myself and others a youthful and healthy longevity. In my major vision quest on Bear Butte in South Dakota, I was given a very clear message that now is the time for women to step forward, to balance the negative masculine which is so rampant and damaging. I see a beautiful vision of retreat sanctuaries where powerful, but worn and exhausted, women can come for healing, teaching, nurturing, and support at all levels—in order that they can step back out into the world in the leadership roles we are being called to assume. Learning how to nourish ourselves through knowledge of nutrition, hormonal balance, relationship, energy sourcing, moon-time practices, youthing, and more will enable Feminine leadership to more and more positively transform the world in a way of honoring and good relationship for all. Modern science reminds us that women garner supportive energy and satisfaction in their lives when working in cooperative groups, especially with other women. These healing sanctuaries may take on the aura of Goddess temples as in days of old. We will build them around springs made sacred to protect the vital waters of life, and to hold and transmit the energy of love, peace, beauty, nurturing, and renewal for the upliftment of all.

MY MOST RECENT WORK

I have recently given stewardship of my exquisite FlowerSong place to another so that I may again move in the larger world with my teaching. Yet I am in a very vulnerable and open place between the past ways of being/working and this new phase which has yet to unfold and solidify; I step into foreign lands to learn and share—initially to South America to deepen into the ancient wisdom there as well as modern healing ways practiced by American and other ex-patriates who had committed the AMA-defined "sin" of doing incredible healing and charging little for it! Then I go on to Europe to explore the spiritual traditions and sacred places so abundant there. The whole Earth is again my home, and I am casting myself on the love of the world!! Even though I am in the Moon-Pause, elders' wisdom lodge, it does not seem that retirement is an option for me, though I am at the age the statistics say is the average life span of women. Having been told that I will live to 127, I still have lots of time to do something good and useful on this sweet Earth. Maybe I'm really just getting started!! I look forward to joining my sisters of all ages in this dance of an awakening and golden time.

NOTES

1. Christ light of the Americas.

CHAPTER 13

EARTH HEALING, EARTH ACTION

STARHAWK'S JOURNEY

Starhawk

BEGINNINGS

My involvement in the Women's Spirituality movement began with the Wiccan pagan occult movement in the late sixties. At age fifteen, I was reading Tarot cards at the Renaissance fair, and there was a booth full of Witches next to us. We got to know them and we were very intrigued by them but a little scared! In my first year of college at UCLA, an anthropology professor offered the option for students to do a project instead of a conventional paper, so a friend and I decided to teach a course on witchcraft through the experimental college there, where anyone could teach and anyone could take a course. We knew nothing whatsoever about the subject, but that didn't stop us. Although we had no idea what a coven was, we decided to start one, getting together, smoking marijuana, banging on sticks, drinking wine and generally having a good time. When we again encountered the Witches we had met at the Renaissance Fair, they told us that Wicca was a real spiritual tradition—focusing on the Goddess—and one that went back to a time before Christianity. For me, it was a revelation to even think that there *could* be a Goddess. I had grown up Jewish, with a strong attraction to religion, going to Hebrew school after regular school, and having a Bat Mitzvah. I even went to Israel on a Hebrew High School *ulpan* Summer in Israel program. However, my own actual spiritual experiences had not taken place in the temple, but in nature, so Goddess religion lit up for me as something I had actually experienced, a religious tradition where I could take leadership and responsibility.

INTRODUCTION TO FEMINISM

Several years later, probably about 1970-'71, while travelling with my boyfriend, I got the flu in Frankfort and spent the day in a youth hostel reading Kate Millett's *Sexual Politics*.[1] The book brought a whole other kind of revelation, addressing aspects of my experience that I'd never really made conscious. I was a student in the art department at UCLA, and I realized that although 70% of the undergraduates were women, in the graduate program it was reversed and 70% of the students were men. On the faculty there was only one woman, and she taught weaving. Nobody had ever talked about this or identified it as an issue before we started talking about feminism. I went to the Venice Women's Center down on Venice Boulevard for my first consciousness-raising meeting. The Center had just formed and in this heyday of antiauthoritarian feminist egalitarianism, they were choosing the new directors of the center by having everyone put her name in a hat. I walked out of that meeting as one of the directors of the Women's Center.

At this time, consciousness-raising came into being. We talked about so many different things, even spirituality, and occasionally we did rituals together.

I always felt an urge to bring together Witchcraft and feminism, but most of the feminist movement at that time thought all religion was the opiate of the people and very patriarchal. One day, driving down Lincoln

Boulevard in Venice, I saw a sign that said, "Feminist Wicca" and I nearly crashed the car! I pulled over and ran in and there was Z Budapest. She invited me to a ritual with a large group of women practicing Dianic Wicca: women only, sort of lesbian-oriented. I went to a couple of her rituals and really felt like my mind had been opened to the possibility that, yes, one really could talk about this and bring things together. However, my life changed radically; I broke up with the guy I had been living with, dropped out of graduate school, and traveled for a year with a bicycle and a backpack. I spent the winter in New York trying to publish a novel I had written in graduate school that had won a writing award at UCLA. During that time, I had some very powerful dreams saying, "You belong on the West Coast. You are not a New York person." I moved to San Francisco and began researching and writing *The Spiral Dance*.[2]

ORIGINS OF RECLAIMING

In the Bay Area I found quite a large, active Pagan community—much larger and less insular than in the LA area. I became deeply involved and found people to teach me; before long I was teaching myself. I helped to found Reclaiming, which drew on Wiccan and pagan roots plus activism; we encouraged people to engage with the world rather than withdraw from the world.

I had always been an activist. In high school I was arrested for protesting against the Vietnam War. Later, I participated in Take Back the Night marches and anti-nuclear organizing, which I wrote about in *Dreaming the Dark*.[3] We protested at the nuclear reactor in Diablo Canyon, forming Pagan groups doing rituals on the blockade line, in the back-country and in jail, weaving together our activism and spirituality.

When the *Spiral Dance* came out in 1979, HarperSanFrancisco offered to throw a book party, so we decided to use that as an excuse to create a huge public ritual at Fort Mason, a public space in San Francisco. We called the ritual "The Spiral Dance." In 2014, we had the thirty-fifth anniversary of the Spiral Dance.

We did not really formally think of ourselves as a group then. But I had a women's coven and my coven-sister Diane Baker and I decided to teach a six-week class, based on the elements of air, fire, water and earth and their relationship to magic and Goddess traditions. We co-taught and modeled shared teaching. Rituals were a component of the class, and each week we would turn over part of the ritual to the students. By the last class, the students created the ritual for themselves. The group loved it, and they wanted another class. We kept coming up with classes, recruiting some of our first group of students into student teaching, and before we knew it we had an organization. We called our classes things like "reclaiming our magic" or "reclaiming the Goddess," and we ended up calling the organization itself Reclaiming.

First it was just five or six of us who were in the coven together, and then it expanded. In September, 1981, we all went down to Diablo Canyon to blockade. We were having another Spiral Dance in October, and other people stepped up to organize it. By the time we came back, we had become a collective. At Diablo Canyon we had learned skills: how to organize affinity groups, work with consensus, and facilitate meetings. We modeled Reclaiming on the structure of those anti-nuclear actions. It was organized around small groups who sent representatives to what we called "spokescouncils." Decisions were made by consensus; instead of top-down, we were organized from the bottom up.

In the late eighties, we were asked to do week-long intensives: Witch Camps, in Vancouver and the Mid-West. Some of us started traveling. I never wanted to be the only person making decisions, preferring the early feminist approach to collectivity and shared power. I felt that it would be a burden to be the "spiritual authority." But we gradually outgrew our informal collective structure where all the decision-makers lived close together in San Francisco. By the mid-Nineties, we had people organizing and teaching in many areas of the US, Canada and Europe.

Reclaiming went through a major restructuring process, dissolving the original collective and writing our Principles of Unity, and reorganizing on a more decentralized model. At that point, we started thinking of Reclaiming not so much as a collective but as a tradition. Since then, we have been constantly juggling these questions of how to organize a very decentralized organization, and how to make collective decisions when we now have members all over the world and people are not physically together.

DEVELOPING RITUALS

We started doing rituals from the beginning, back when I was first studying the Craft and had no idea what we were doing. We would do a ritual and then we would critique it, "How did that work? Did anything happen? Were there parts where we were bored? Were there parts where we really felt emotionally moved?" And through that process we started to develop our ritual techniques, our technology. It was ten years later, in 1989, when I started drumming. We were organizing the tenth anniversary of *The Spiral Dance*. I had been teaching and doing workshops in Europe in the mid-'80s, and I didn't really drum very well. When I came into contact with some incredible African drummers, who were so powerful, I thought to myself, "I have to learn to drum!"

Back in the United States, I found Mary Ellen Donald, who was teaching Middle Eastern drumming in the Bay Area, and I started taking lessons with her. She also started drumming for us at our big Spiral Dances, and she still continues to do that every year. More than just playing the drum, it turned out to be a wonderful introduction to the whole culture of Middle Eastern music, and to the heritage and the traditions around it. Many of us from Reclaiming started taking lessons from her, or studying African drumming or samba or other forms. A lot of people at the time also studied with Layne Redmond; she was a wonderful teacher and drummer, bringing to us the traditions of the hand drum and the tambourine. Over the years, our basic level of drumming improved considerably.

Drumming was an outward reflection of our increasing ability to understand and move energy in ritual. We used meditation techniques, dance and movement, song and chant, and many inner techniques. Some of them we learned from teachers; some we developed ourselves. Perhaps most important, we became more and more aware of the need to have a clear intention for the ritual, an intention that is simple and succinct and tells us why we are doing the ceremony and what is at stake. With a clear intention, we can focus the acts and the imagery around a central thread and the ritual gains emotional power.

PAGAN RITUAL AND NONVIOLENT PROTEST

I was exposed to nonviolence as a philosophy early in the antiwar movement but it was when we became involved in the Diablo Canyon blockade that we became immersed in the practice of nonviolence in a clear, direct way. Nonviolence fit with my Goddess belief that we are all sacred beings. I can speak to a person as a sacred being even if that being is engaged in awful behavior. I do not have to demonize people. Nonviolence also fits my personal skill set. I am far better at things like staying calm in a crisis, talking to people and offering empathy, than I am at things like aiming, throwing rocks, and hitting anything.

And I felt again and again that nonviolent direct action gives us a tremendously powerful way to organize—a most effective strategy. When people are organizing nonviolently they do not need a security culture or need to be paranoid about who knows their plans. So, we can actually invite people into our movement, mobilizing them and bringing them in on a larger scale.

I have had opportunities to work with people in a lot of different places, training them for actions, working with different groups and movements. I have trained people who were going into military zones in Palestine, to try to negotiate with the Israelis, and others who were going into some very intense actions in the global justice movement, protests against the

World Trade Organization or the Free Trade Area of the Americas or the G8, where people were severely beaten and even killed. I have trained people from a wide diversity of political backgrounds, from people who were Gandhian pacifists to the hard-core, masked anarchists of the black bloc who were only reluctantly willing to take any training at all.

I understand the anger and the frustrations of some people who advocate for militant actions or even violence. I would not call myself a strict pacifist, not like my husband, David Miller, who was the first person to burn his draft card during the Vietnam War. He is a strict, no-violence pacifist, whereas I feel that if I had been alive in Europe during World War II, I probably would have been part of the Resistance. I do not think that the Resistance could have been a pacifist resistance once the Nazis came into power.

But I do believe that non-violent direct action is a powerful tool for our times today, and one that I am not willing to abandon lightly. For me, nonviolence goes very much with Goddess spirituality. What we say in Goddess traditions is, "Thou art Goddess." The Goddess is immanent; She is embodied in every human being and so it fits to say, "Yes, I prefer to talk to that Goddess part in you and help you understand that you have choices that you may not realize you have," rather than taking a gun and shooting you.

WHAT I AM WORKING ON NOW

I am working on a lot of things now. I am working with Reclaiming; I am helping to organize rituals such as the Spiral Dance, our big Halloween ritual, each year. This year I taught at two Witch Camps, but I no longer teach at every Reclaiming Witch Camp. I teach a lot of Permaculture[4] courses, which we call Earth Activist Trainings, that have grounding in spirit and so may incorporate some of what we teach in Reclaiming, but they also have a focus on organizing and activism and teach all of the permaculture tools and principles and techniques. I love doing that because I feel that permaculture is the practical aspect of the idea that the earth is sacred. Spirituality gives people a grounding for their personal sustainability, and ways to connect and create some of the cultural aspects needed for a long-lasting culture that can support regenerative earth-healing practices. Permaculture teaches us what those practices are and grounds us in ethics and principles that guide us. The organizing and the activism address the question of how to actually bring about these changes in the world around us.

Because I direct the permaculture program, I spend a lot of time fundraising. We offer a lot of scholarships and work trade for activists. We have been offering diversity scholarships for people of color who are working for environmental and social justice. I also write; I have just finished writing a sequel to *The Fifth Sacred Thing*,[5] and we have been working very hard to have both stories made into a movie or brought to television. I wrote a screenplay, as well as a TV pilot. In the last year or so I have not participated as much in street activism and trainings as I did for a while, just because I have spent so much time writing and working in permaculture, but I still do activist trainings and organizing as well.

I have a ranch that we are developing into a permaculture model for carbon-sequestering ranching. We are working on creating systems that can help pull carbon out of the atmosphere and put it back into the ground. I spend a fair amount of time walking with the sheep, planting trees, harvesting herbs, and being with the land.

I think this is an interesting moment for the Women's Spirituality movement. This year we have lost some of the real founders of the movement.[6] We are reaching the age where the first wave of us is getting older, and I think that it is going to be a crucial time in the next few years; I hope that younger people will step up and take leadership. There were three of us who had books that came out in the 1970s: Margot Adler, Merlin Stone, and I. I am the only one left. I am not that old yet: I am only sixty-three, but time is passing.

Notes

1. Kate Millett, *Sexual Politics* (Chicago, Illinois: University of Illinois Press, 2000).
2. Starhawk, *The Spiral Dance. A Rebirth of the Ancient Religion of the Great Goddess.* (New York: Harper and Row, 1979).
3. Starhawk, *Dreaming the Dark*, 6th Edition (Boston: Beacon Press, 1982).
4. Permaculture is a system of ecological design that was originally developed by two Australians, Bill Mollison and David Holmgren. The term was created as a way of expressing "permanent agriculture." Now it has come to mean "permanent culture" that can be sustained, since it refers to more than agriculture. It has since become a global movement; it is based on the idea that if one observes nature and understands nature's principles and applies them, then it will be possible to create systems that will meet our human needs while actually regenerating the environment around us, instead of destroying it. It draws upon indigenous wisdom and tradition wisdom, weaving them together with science and systems theory. It has a lot of very helpful ways of approaching land use, urban planning, energy systems, food systems, and bioremediation.
5. Starhawk, *The Fifth Sacred Thing* (New York: Bantam, 1994).
6. See the Dedication in this book.

.

CHAPTER 14

SPIRIT'REALITY, IN THE SPIRIT OF WE'MOON

Musawa

We'Moon is the creative expression of women's experience of spirituality (spirit'reality). *We'Moon: Gaia Rhythms for Womyn*[1] (co-founded by me in community with lesbians on land in France in 1980) is an astrological moon calendar/datebook full of art and writing inspired by multi-cultural earth-based women's spirituality—with space for women to record their daily activities alongside the movements of heavenly bodies. It is a handbook in natural rhythm, through which the sacred threads of one's life story are woven day after day as they are lived.

In the Spirit of We'Moon is also the title of the Anthology: *Celebrating 30 years of We'Moon Art and Writing.*[2]

"The Mother Tongue speaks to each one in the native language of her own inner voice. It is unique to each individual and culture: the first language we learn from our mothers, in the dialect of their own individual life experiences. And it is as universal as the language of Mother Nature."

So begins the Introduction to the We'Moon Anthology, which has just become available as an I-Book: Mother Tongue Ink's first venture into the world of electronic publishing.

I am grateful to have had very little exposure to established religions in this lifetime; that might have interfered with the natural unfolding of spirit'reality in my own experience. The only thing I remember about Sunday School was the time our teacher played "telephone" with us, and when the message whispered in each child's ear came back around to where it started—much changed from the original meaning—the teacher said: "That is how the Bible was written" (!)

Most of what I know about women's spirituality, I learned as a child, naturally, in the sacred realm of spontaneous play. Since I grew up in a non-religious family, when I wanted to know what "prayer" meant, I asked our black housekeeper, who said it is "doing something beautiful for God," to which I responded, "you mean like this?" as I circled my arms up around my head and down to the side, three times, in the gesture of the Nile River Goddess. That is my sacred sign to this day. Three was always my special number (rivaled by my older sister's favorite number, two). We made crosses of phosphorescent tape on the headboards of our beds—that were barely visible until we shined our flashlights on them after the lights went out—and then proceeded to converse with God "whoever you are," proving the closeness of our relationship by whose loudly whispered prayers lasted the longest before falling asleep under the glow of our phosphorescent crosses.

Although I have been initiated into various spiritual traditions, Nature remains my primary teacher. I was fortunate to be able to spend my summers growing up in the woods on a lake in Northern Michigan, free to roam in nature all day with two girl cousins my age, in the safety of a large extended family all around. We had a secret sanctuary the boys could never find ("for girls only," it was my first women's land), because it was simply a grove of trees by a creek, whereas the tree fort the boys built was easy to spot. I learned to meditate by lying still under the low canopy of ferns, silently witnessing the world inside and all around me for hours on end, invisible to the world of people passing on the path nearby.

I have a ritual I have done at the beginning and end of every Michigan summer for as long as I can remember: I swim out to where the lake drops off into the deep, alternating forward and backward summersaults to the four directions over the blue line, and then dive as deep as I can go and still come back up for breath— triumphantly bursting into the air, by circling my arms up above my head, three times, in honor of life returning with each new breath. I have known this place as "my spirit growing ground" for over seventy years now, and I am glad to be able to re-visit it, time and again. When my mother died a few years ago, my life partner and I, and our dog, swam out to the blue line with her ashes in a vase, and we dove down deep to release her mater-real remains to flow out, spiraling into infinity.

The first ritual I ever participated in outside with a group of women was at Cabbage Lane Women's Land in southern Oregon, where we tied knots to hang on trees across the valley that we were trying to save from being clear-cut. I loved that it was so fun and relaxed and not at all churchy—we could laugh and hoot and holler and that was part of our magical work. We hooted to the Spotted Owl to come, to preserve their old growth habitat—and we howled to the coyotes, who sang a loud chorus back to us each time. It was a thrilling response from the wild— brought home to me up close and personal, when a coyote accompanied me at a respectful distance all the way up the valley to the tipi where I was sleeping that night.

Most rituals, ceremonies, and sacred spaces I have experienced over the years consisted primarily of creating a cauldron for the interplay of natural elements that support opening to the spontaneous experience of Spirit'reality flowing through. On lesbian women's lands, it is more a way of life than a strict spiritual practice. Like the sisterhoods of old, we live together on the land in community. We honor the earth as sacred, share in some daily life practices, alone or together, and do ceremony around the natural cycles. Unlike most traditional religious sisterhoods, however, our spirit'reality includes honoring our bodies, our feelings, our sexuality, our individual beliefs and needs, our similarities and differences. We value the freedom to live our love in a life style of our own choosing, to be at home in expressing our spirit'reality, in a relaxed and creative way; we are generally eclectic in our beliefs and practices. We tend to see ourselves as a women's school of life in community with earth rather than as a disciplined women's wisdom or mystery school based on a particular established tradition. Love of women and the earth is our common root, and we live and work in direct connection with the elements, the directions, the cycles, seasons, the plants and animals, the earth, moon, sun and stars, the weather and ways of nature— including our own human nature.

The circle is our basic sacred form. We often pass the rattle around and sing our "heart songs," while others join in or listen with undivided attention to how Spirit comes through each woman in turn. Circle songs may come up spontaneously, as guidance in ceremony or in the events of everyday life—songs like "you can't hurry the Goddess, She's always right on time". . .or "cheer up, my sisters, live in the moment, we'll understand it all by and by," when that is the wisdom that arises in a particular situation. My inner voice prompts me often to ask: "What is the Goddess teaching me now?" inviting mindfulness and spiritual reflection as I seek the growing edge/the blessing/the gift in any situation, no matter how challenging.

For me, women's spirituality is about the reality of Spirit, as experienced by women, here and now, in life on this earth. It is a contemporary rendering of an ancient indigenous wisdom tradition that has been carried on through the ages by people living close to the earth. Monica Sjöö and Barbara Mor named it most succinctly in the title of their ground-breaking book in the early days of contemporary Goddess research: *The*

Great Cosmic Mother: Rediscovering the Ancient Religion of the Earth.[3] The Gaia principle, in its description of the earth, is a modern scientific explanation of what ancient peoples have always known: that the Earth is a living organism, and all of creation is an expression of the Great Mother in Her myriad forms. The material (mater-real) world of form is not separate from the spiritual (spirit-real) realm but is an embodiment of it. The "book of nature" reveals the teachings of the living Goddess at work. Mother Nature is my primary teacher, my root guru, my Lama (which translates in Tibetan as "the path of the mother"). From ancient times until now, threaded throughout the Great Disconnects perpetrated by patriarchy and permeating its religions, the Divine Feminine lives! And the Great Mother is being re-membered and conceived anew in the hearts and minds of women today, as we learn to re-connect freely with Spirit: in rituals as in everyday life, in meditation as in nature, in political and planetary actions as in our personal life—in experiencing our ongoing relation to all our relations.

NOTES

1. For the 2015 calendar, see: *We moon 2015 Calendar: Gaia Rhythms for Women, Wild Card* (Escatada, Oregon: Mother Tongue Ink, 2014). http://www.amazon.com/We-moon-2015-Calendar-Rhythms/dp/189093142X/ref=sr_1_1?s=books&ie=UTF8&qid=1428003262&sr=1-1&keywords=we%27moon

2. *In the Spirit of We'Moon: Celebrating 30 Years, An Anthology of We'Moon Art and Writing* (Escatada, Oregon: Mother Tongue Ink, 2010).

3. Monica Sjöö and Barbara Mor, *The Great Cosmic Mother: Rediscovering the Religion of the Earth.* Second Edition (New York: HarperOne, 1987).

Chapter 15

Green Witch, High Priestess of the Goddess

Susun S. Weed

My father was Jewish, my mother, Catholic. I grew up in Dallas, where both of their religions were viewed with suspicion. So, I was sent to Baptist Sunday school with the neighborhood kids. And then, with my babysitters, I went to churches where there were Holy rollers and gospel singers. At home, there were Seder dinners and Christmas trees. At the age of eleven I was prepared for, and completed, my first communion.

My home and my life were a comparative religions course. No wonder I thought of myself as an atheist by the time I left home for UCLA at age sixteen.

What a fertile field I was for the cultivation of Zen. A deep bow of gratitude for the Zen teaching that there is no God—because everything is god.

When I turned twenty-eight, something stirred in me. Astrologers say it was my Saturn return. I knew it was time to rethink the ways of my life. What had I been doing since I left home? I had spent the last thirteen years actively seeking to attract and please men. I had numerous passionate affairs, and even got married and had a child. Was I happy? Was I fulfilled?

What would my life be like in thirteen years, when I would be forty-one, if I spent them actively seeking to attract and please women? I was already a feminist. "Why not take it one step further," I thought. "Why not make women the focus of your entire life?" And so I did...I fell in love in all possible ways with women.

Ah, but here's the catch. When you focus on other, on men, you can stand outside yourself: you can love what is different. But when you focus on same, on women, you fall down the rabbit hole: the spiraling vortex of mother love, mother lust, sister bonds, commitment and betrayal and commitment once again. You fall into the chaos of yourself.

Doing things full-bore, as I prefer, I chose to be a woman-loving-woman, a lesbian. Okay, not merely a lesbian, but a lesbian separatist. For seven years I was a woman who lived apart from men. I associated only with women, worked only for women, hired only women to work for me, listened only to music created and sung by women, and read only books written by women. I built a house with only women (1974), opened a women's center in Woodstock, New York (1975), opened a women's gathering space (Sojourner's) and organized programs there for more than a decade (1976-88), organized two Health and Wellness Conferences for Women (1977, 1978), bought land for a women's healing space with my two lovers (1978), drew cards for, and published, *The Amazon Tarot deck* (1979; at about the same time Vicki Noble and Karen Vogel were creating the Motherpeace deck), and had passionate affairs, but didn't get married or have any more children.

I foraged for mushrooms and planted vegetable gardens, milked my goats and made cheese, and single-parented my daughter. I also taught midwives and women who longed to go back-to-the-land the skills they needed. I taught my first stand-alone herbal medicine class in 1975 (and have taught herbal medicine classes ever since) .

During this time, I invited Z Budapest to speak at the Woodstock Women's Center. At the end of her talk, she asked if any woman present wished to be initiated as a Witch. I stood immediately and went to stand in front of her, to be joined in moments by two other women, one a current lover, one a past lover. We formed The Coven of the Warm November.

We read the *Feminist Book of Lights and Shadows*.[1] We read *Beyond God the Father*.[2] We read *Drawing Down the Moon*,[3] *When God Was a Woman*,[4] and *Positive Magic*.[5] We read and reread *The Book of Goddesses and Heroines*,[6] *Lost Goddesses of Early Greece*,[7] *Daughters of Copper Woman*,[8] *The Civilization of the Goddess*[9] and *The Language of the Goddess*,[10] *The Heart of the Goddess*,[11] *Goddesses in Everywoman*,[12] *The Storyteller's Goddess*,[13] and *The Women's Encyclopedia of Myths and Secrets*.[14] My comparative religions course resumed, in the Catskills this time, and with greatly expanded parameters. Now it included women.

I was a pagan, a woman of the earth. I gathered with other women in circles and covens. I met for seven years with a group as we trained ourselves to be priestesses of the Goddess. I claimed myself as a Witch. I welcomed the Triple Goddess into my life. I investigated The Golden Dawn, Aleistar Crowley, tarot, and Monica Sjöö,[15] even before her book was published.

What year was it that China invaded Tibet? Soon thereafter, Tibetans came to Woodstock and opened a monastery. My lover, Pauline Oliveros, was deeply involved there, and so I came to be as well. I saw the Goddess in yet another context. Every day, twice a day, the monastery praised the Goddess and sang to her: "Om Tara." On the walls of the monastery were thangkas of dakinis. There were women monks. I took teachings. I took initiations. I took refuge in the Buddha and the sangha. And I was initiated and named: "Goddess of Bliss."

And at the same time, I met a woman who adopted me into the Seneca Nation. While teaching at Omega Institute, I befriended an older woman in distress. She was upset because she was the only woman in a group of native men and they had not treated her well on the first of five days. I didn't suggest it out loud, but she must have read my mind, for by the time we parted that day, Grandmother Twylah Nitsch had decided to quit the Elder's Circle and teach women only in her circle under the oak. It was the beginning of a relationship between us that has lasted beyond her death.

She invited me to visit her at the Seneca Reservation near Buffalo. There she showed me a matrifocal, matrilineal culture with intense spiritual values that prohibits spiritual leaders. She fed me, taught me, and initiated me into the Wolf Clan of the Great Peaceful Nations. And I was named "Onada," the spirit of the leaves.

I opened the Wise Woman Center in 1980 and invited Z Budapest to teach there. At her workshop, she assigned Goddesses to each student, asked us to portray them theatrically, and critiqued our performances, sometimes asking us to do it over and over until we truly understood and expressed that Goddess.

The Wise Woman Center allowed me to reach out to women I admired and invite them to come closer. Over the next decades, we were thrilled by Max Dashú and the Hidden History Archives, Merlin Stone and *Ancient Mirrors of Womanhood*,[16] Vicki Noble, Karen Vogel, and the *Motherpeace* deck,[17] Rachael Pollack and Mary Greer and their deep tarot wisdom, Donna Wilshire,[18] Brooke Medicine Eagle,[19] Dyhani Wahoo, Grandmother Twylah, and many more.

It all came together for me. I saw the reweaving of the Healing Cloak of the Ancients. I am not a Jewish woman, nor a Catholic woman, not a Baptist, or a Buddhist, or a Pagan. I am, we are, Woman. I am, we are, All One. I am, you are, She. The Goddess lives in every woman. The Goddess lives in me. The Goddess lives in you. The Goddess who gives birth to us, the Earth Mother, the Goddess of a thousand names and a thousand faces, is coming soon to a location near you, no, in you. You are "it!"

Have you seen Her? She came, She has come, and She is still showing up. She was there (and so was I), at the First Goddess Conference (in Boston in the 1970's). She is there, and has been for time out of mind, at the Glastonbury Goddess Conference. She is there at Z Budapest's Goddess Fest in the redwoods of California, and She is there at Goddess Spirit Rising in Simi Valley, and at Red Tents and Goddess events all over this planet. She is there at your altar. She is showing up more and more in art and music and dance. Have you seen her?.

The Goddess movement—the reawakening of the Goddess spirit, the re-emergence of Priestesses—is not just a delight to me and those of us who were in the right time and place to nourish and support this movement, it is a blessing to every woman on the planet.

The Goddess movement emboldens women to see themselves as the Goddess and to act like Her. The Goddess movement empowers women to walk out of situations and relationships where they are not honored. The Goddess movement urges women to join hands with their sisters in great glee and great anger. The Goddess movement allows women to feel satisfied with their bodies, as they are, knowing that the Goddess is every shape and every size.

There are so many wonderful Goddess projects right now, and certainly more to come in the future. I have been blessed by being able to help in the past by: writing herbal notes for *We'Moon* ,[20] passing out Nancy Passmore's *Lunar Calendar*,[21] finding money to help finish *The Goddess Trilogy* movies (*The Burning Times*),[22] encouraging Lisa Levart as she worked on her exquisite book: *Goddess on Earth*,[23] writing for *Sage-Woman* magazine, publishing woman-centered books through Ash Tree Publishing, and presenting at Goddess Conference all over the world, especially ZB's *Goddess Fest.*

The Goddess blesses my day-to-day work of training shamanic herbal apprentices, each of whom must choose a Goddess archetype to work with. She gives me month-to-month joy with the moon lodge, where women gather to speak their truth. And She stands with me as I initiate green Witches, women choosing to set their feet on the path of the Goddess.

My Goddess archetype? Up until menopause, I was Artemis, the Goddess of the herbalist, the wild woman. Afterwards, I needed to identify with an older woman. Many see me as Baba Yaga, and this I will never deny, but my inner Goddess archetype wears a headband, with spikes. She is a Goddess with attitude: She is the Statue of Liberty. (And she's green, too.)

Who is your Goddess archetype? If you haven't called her, open your heart, seed a dream, start a journal. The Goddess is right at hand, waiting for your call

"The Goddess is alive and magic is afoot."

NOTES

1. Zsusanna Budapest, *The Feminist Book of Lights and Shadows,* ed. Helen Beardwoman (Venice, California: Luna Publications, 1975).
2. Mary Daly, *Beyond God the Father: Toward a Philosophy of Women's Liberation* (Boston: Beacon Press, 1973).
3. Margot Adler, *Drawing Down the Moon* (New York: Viking, 1979).
4. Merlin Stone, *When God Was a Woman* (New York: Barnes and Noble, 1976).
5. Marion Weinstein, *Positive Magic* (New York: Pocket Books, 1978).
6. Patricia Monaghan, *The Book of Goddesses and Heroines* (New York: Dutton, 1981).
7. Charlene Spretnak, *Lost Goddesses of Early Greece.* (Berkeley: Moon Books, 1978).
8. Anne Cameron, *Daughters of Copper Woman* (Madeira Park, BC, Canada: Harbour, 2002).
9. Marija Gimbutas, *The Civilization of the Goddess. The World of Old Europe* (San Francisco: HarperSanFrancisco, 1991).
10. Marija Gimbutas, *The Language of the Goddess.* (San Francisco: HarperSanFrancisco, 1989).
11. Hallie Austen Iglehart, *The Heart of the Goddess: Art, Myth and Meditations of the World's Sacred Feminine* (Berkeley: Wingbow/Bookpeople, 1990).
12. Jean Shinoda Bolen, *Goddesses in Everywoman: A New Psychology of Women* (New York: Harper & Row, 1984).
13. Carolyn McVickar Edwards, *The Storyteller's Goddess: Tales of the Goddess and Her Wisdom from Around the World* (San Francisco: HarperSanFrancisco, 1991).
14. Barbara Walker, The *Women's Encyclopedia of Myths and Secrets* (New York: HarperCollins, 1983).
15. Monica Sjöö and Barbara Mor, *The Great Cosmic Mother: Rediscovering the Religion of the Earth.* Second Edition (New York: HarperOne, 1987).
16. Merlin Stone, *Ancient Mirrors of Womanhood: A Treasury of Goddess and Heroine Lore from Around the World* (Boston: Beacon Press, 1990).
17. Vicki Noble and Karen Vogel, *The Motherpeace Tarot Deck* (Stamford, CT: US Games Systems, 1983).

18. Donna Wilshire, *Virgin, Mother, Crone: Myths and Mysteries of the Triple Goddess* (Rochester, Vermont: Inner Traditions, 1994).

19. Brooke Medicine Eagle, *Buffalo Woman Comes Singing* (New York: Ballantine Books, 1991). See Brooke Medicine Eagle in this volume.

20. We'Moon is a calendar and datebook for women, based upon lunar, solar, and astrological cycles. The founding editor is Musawa. See Musawa in this volume.

21. The Lunar Calendar is a unique way of tracking and visualizing time. The founding editor is Nancy Passmore. For the 2015 edition, see http://www.amazon.com/15-Lunar-Calendar-Dedicated-Goddess/dp/1877920258/ref=sr_1_3?ie=UTF8&qid=1426980571&sr=8-3&keywords=nancy+passmore+lunar+calendar.

22. See Donna Read in this volume.

23. Lisa Levart, *Goddess On Earth, Portraits of the Divine Feminine* (Nyack, New York: Lush Press, 2011).

CHAPTER 16

TRANSFORMATION FROM MIDWIFE TO PRIESTESS

Jane Hardwicke Collings

Born in the '50s, I was a relative late-comer to Women's Spirituality. I was initiated into the movement as a student midwife. When I was 26 years old, in 1983, I showed up to do my hospital midwifery training in a big city hospital in Sydney, Australia. I was a rebellious, wounded (yet I did not know that!) young woman, a reluctant yet compliant daughter of the patriarchy. Although the accomplishments and achievements of the Women's Spirituality movement had been many to that point, and were what I had enjoyed as a teen, although I did not realize it, one place that had not been touched by the awakened feminine was the hospital birth industry. Changes that looked like progress, such as fathers being "allowed" to be in the "labor ward," actually originated in the late '70s because women insisted they needed protection from enforced procedures that they did not want. Birth-giving "in the system" was an experience of disempowerment and trauma, as it mostly still is today. Women's health seems to be one of the last bastions of patriarchal control, and most women seem unaware of this. In terms of birth-giving, women are encouraged to hand over their power to those in control, be they midwives or doctors, and to trust the caregiver's decisions rather than their own inner knowing. Women and their partners are discouraged from taking responsibility for themselves and their decision making and to give the midwives and doctors the responsibility for the choices to be made (see figure 10).

Being part of birth-giving in the system as a student midwife, I saw institutionalized acts of violence performed on women and babies in the name of safety. Realizing my complicity in the damage being done by mostly unknowing protagonists, I wondered why women came back for more, why they returned next time to have the same or similar experiences—changes which resulted in disempowerment and trauma —over and over again. One could understand if the interventions were necessary to save lives or improve wellbeing, but most were routine and unnecessary. Could they not see what was going on? Anthropologists have taught us that whatever happens during a rite of passage, such as giving birth, is significant. It teaches us on a subliminal level, how our culture values the roles we are entering, in this case mothering, and therefore how to behave. And what birth-giving in the system was creating were mothers who were mostly unaware of their power, taught that experts knew more than they did about their bodies, and that they could not rely on their bodies—or on themselves—for birthing. This was the "Cult of the Expert," as my dear, departed teacher and mentor, Jeannine Pavarti Baker, named this situation. Now I understood: the women returned each time to the hospitals and the "care" that I saw was wounding them, because they had been led to believe through what had unfolded for them, that they needed these "experts" and "interventions" in order to have a "safe" birth, when actually the unnecessary interventions made the experience more dangerous. Once I realized that the midwives were serving this machine that was taking women's innate power from them, I ran away as fast as I could, and I discovered the world of homebirth.

In the homebirth world, I met my tribe, a tribe that I did not even know I was searching for. I met my Soul midwives, Maggie Lecky Thompson and Elaine Hodges Norling. At homebirths, I met a different kind of women who were awake—and aware of things that others had no idea about, including me.

The first books Maggie gave me to read were not about midwifery but the start of the basic education I needed. My unlearning, relearning process had begun. I thirstily drank *Positive Magic and Earth Magic*,[1] by Marion Weinstein, my introduction to the wisdom of cycles, and the Divine Feminine, the Goddess, all so inherent in birth-giving, which went on to be the basis of my work.

I learned a lot through my personal experiences of giving birth and then applied the lessons and gifts to my practice as a midwife. I learned in my experience of birthing Sam, my first child, that births do not necessarily happen the way one wants them to; rather they teach a woman what she needs to learn about herself on her soul's journey to wholeness this lifetime. Sam's birth was a caesarean instead of my planned homebirth. Through dealing with my grief around this, I realized how familiar that feeling was; this unraveled my whole life story, because I was "seeing" the "lessons" I had come for playing out. I later realized, as my understanding of all this deepened, the connection between all our rites of passage, the shamanic dimensions and the healing opportunities these give us, for all our relations!

These days, sometimes, women come to the realization of the awesome power of their bodies through giving birth, either by having an empowering natural, "normal" experience, unlikely these days, or by what is called a shadow awakening, when they try to make sense of their traumatic experience, by asking "why did this happen to me?" This postnatal time is an opportunity for intervention of the healing variety. By employing the power of the de-briefing process after birth, women can find the lessons their experience taught them and incorporate them into their lives, both as a healing for themselves and as the quality within that is called for as mothers of these new babes.

My second and third experiences of giving birth were Ellie and Jackson, both home vaginal births after caesarean, both sublime, informative, mindset-shattering, life-changing experiences. I learned through personal experience the connection between sexuality and birth and the spiritual and shamanic dimensions of pregnancy and birth. I learned that mothering is a sacred path and a daily spiritual practice. And I long for all my sisters to know this. In a modern industrial world, where mothering is so often "out-sourced," I pray that we will see the role of mother sanctified.

I worked as an independent midwife, often taking my children with me to births when they were little. I lived in the city and the country and I learned more and more from Mother Nature, meeting the Goddess in everything as I grew into myself. I have been an activist, have held positions on professional bodies, and have worked tirelessly to do what I could to help, to make a difference, to "be the change I wanted to see in the world." My work over the past few decades has included giving experiential workshops for women. I see myself working for the Goddess, and one of the ways I mean that is that I am working for the Earth: my teacher is Nature, the Earth.

As a midwife, a priestess serving at the birth altar, I so often saw how difficult it was to change the sequence of events unfolding in the moment. I could see long-held beliefs, attitudes and fears that women held playing out in their language, their choices, and their birth outcomes. I thought hard to figure out where to make the most effective interventions to effect change and healing. I know that how a woman gives birth is affected by her mindset—her beliefs, attitudes and fears—and that our mindsets are created by our previous rites of passage, inherited from our parents and our culture and learned through our experiences. I saw women showing up to the birth altar unaware of the power of their bodies, or the effects of their beliefs and fears.

One of my main focuses for intervention, on my mission to help heal the wounded feminine, is the menarche. I feel that the "design," the blueprint, is for young women to be welcomed to womanhood at their menarche by a circle of women, which becomes their community, learning about and knowing the power they hold as women. I believe that the menstrual cycle is such a great teacher for our lives, especially for birth-giving. When we flow with the needs and calls of our bodies during our bleeding times, we are then more able to hear the call of labor, to travel deep within, to that familiar dark quiet place, our womb temples. To this end, I teach mothers and pre-menarche girls about the menstrual cycle, teach teachers to teach this, conduct community ceremonies welcoming girls to womanhood, and hold maiden's circles.

Next on my list of how to help women reclaim their innate strength and power is to teach the spiritual practice of menstruation itself. There is so much opportunity inherent in the menstrual cycle for personal development, letting go of fears and "bad" habits and rebirth—a monthly renewal—so much so that I believe if it were common practice the world would be a very different place.

Another arm of my mission is to help the birth-workers to become aware of and deal with the unconscious agendas they bring to their work. When birth-workers bring consciousness and respect for the process, change can happen. The sacred when honored works its magic, touching all, healing all. If birth-workers do all they can in every circumstance to ensure a gentle birth, healing will occur. Birth workers need to work together to ensure gentle births, practicing deep respect for the newborn and the mother and newborn "bonding" phase. The first hour of a baby's life is so important, impacting the rest of its life; we know this, the scientific evidence is there, it is common sense, and yet it is hardly practiced. If it were, it would uncomplicate so many lives. My work with birth-workers focuses on what they bring to their work—their own stories, themes and patterns—helping them see the importance of the role they play in healing themselves, their clients and the Earth. As Jeannine Parvati Baker said, "Healing Birth is Healing the Earth."[2]

I founded, run, and teach at the School of Shamanic Midwifery, a women's mystery school designed to shift the paradigm. The main objective is to raise consciousness and help heal the wounded feminine and wounded masculine of our time. The focus is on reclaiming feminine wisdom through reconnection with women's mysteries, the wisdom of the cycles, the feminine way, and teaching women how to teach this by first experiencing it themselves. I travel the world, teaching and meeting women and men who care. The project that has my attention today is helping to heal the wounded feminine face of "eating disorders." With one of my apprentices, Kristan Lee Read, we have started a preventative project called the Maiden's School of Magic, and Project Pomegranate, a front line first aid offering for women deep in the process of disordered eating, working with the elements to reclaim their lives.

Another part of my mission in helping heal the wounded feminine is to reduce rivalry and competition among women, which only serves to divide us further. To help heal this competitiveness, I founded the Women's Mystery Teacher's Circle and e-journal, which strives to bring teachers and practitioners together to increase the power of the sisterhood, remembering that we are all students and all teachers. A combined approach, working together, all remembering that we are on the same team, helps us do the work we've all come to do.

If I were asked, of all the things I have done, which has made the most difference, I would say the School of Shamanic Midwifery and its role in healing the wounded feminine, and also, the collating and distributing of the Herstory, which I distributed as free printed street press and is now a free download on my website.[3] The Herstory is the story of the effects of the patriarchy on the feminine in our culture. I read this out as part of one of my workshops and it has a huge effect on everyone who hears it, especially if they are hearing it for the first time. Also my essay, featured in many publications, Introducing Maga, after Mother, before Crone, has been hugely influential.[4] It brings a whole new season, Autumn, to women's lives, and this has a liberating effect. And my work of connecting our experience of menarche and our experiences of giving birth, The Connection Between Menarche and Childbirth—from one rite to the next[5] has been helpful for women unraveling their life stories and seeing the themes and patterns as they show up at our rites of passage, our portals to transformation. This information helps women to unhook from unconscious behaviors that lead to undesired outcomes and enables choice, a greater self-awareness and often different outcomes.

I am one of the founders of the "Waratah Project–Exploring Menstruation and Menopause in a Positive and Contemporary Context," a new initiative to influence the way we collectively think about menstruation and menopause away from the old notions of shame and towards a more positive and woman-honoring way of understanding these universal aspects of female experience.

As a teacher of the Women's Mysteries, every day I meet women who desire the knowledge held within the Women's Spirituality Movement; there is a re-membering occurring. In my own life as a grandmother, I see a generation turned digital and this worries me. I long for the children to experience the wild, in all Her reality.

I see what I call the death throes of the patriarchy, the horrible heartless acts of violence and discrimination against women, men, children, the earth, and animals. And I hope a rebirth will come soon. I think that this will be hastened by further application of the tenets of the Women's Spirituality Movement, and that it can be seen in the Red Revolution that is rising, in the current Red Tent Movement (see figures 11 and 12).

I give thanks to those who walked before me, and I pledge to honor the sacred in all things.

Blessed Be.

Notes

1. Marion Weinstein, *Positive Magic* (Franklin Lakes, New Jersey: New Page Books, 2002). Marion Weinstein, *Earth Magic* (Custer, Washington: Phoenix Publishing, 1980).
2. http://www.birthkeeper.org/
3. Moonsong.com.au.
4. http://www.moonsong.com.au/evolution-of-the-triple-goddess/
5. http://www.moonsong.com.au/the-connection-between-menarche-and-childbirth-from-one-rite-to-the-next/.

CHAPTER 17

CONCEIVING AND NURTURING A POIESIS OF HER

A PaGaian Cosmology

Glenys Livingstone

It was 1974; I was pregnant, young, single and alone—away from family and community so no-one would know: the child would be given away. I had what I felt to be an epiphany as I sat in a church in Melbourne (as I often did then): "what if the Deity were female?" flashed through my mind. This possibility came from nowhere within my conscious experience, yet I knew in that instant that everything about my situation would be different if this were so. But I was not able to find a way to follow through with any change to the chosen path then, though I did try: there was no support for such an idea and its implications in my world at that time. When I became pregnant again—this time within a married context—I came to read Suzanne Arms' newly published *Immaculate Deception*,[1] and some seeds were sown: here was some resonance with a deep unspoken truth I had perceived, about the ultimate significance of carrying and birthing new life, though I did not yet make a conscious connection. I first heard the word "Goddess" a few years later in a circle held by Rosemary Radford Reuther at the Center for Women and Religion, associated with the Graduate Theological Union in Berkeley, where I had begun to study theology, in my passion to understand ultimate origins. Largely, it was the experience of motherhood that began to radicalize me and connect me to a larger community of women. I was also totally unprepared for it, and had believed myself to be inanimate—inert—as matter itself was said to be: it was an awakening. In the context of my studies, Adrienne Rich's *Of Woman Born*[2] helped me to make sense of my experience, and to see what I was participating in.

In another epiphany at about the same time, four Goddesses appeared in a dream, laughing at a man who had told me that, as a woman, it was not my place to be studying theology. I had felt vulnerable to his aggressive directive, but with this dream, the mirth of these Goddesses empowered me and clarified my vision: I realized that I was in good company in my quest. Then came the reading of Mary Daly's *Beyond God the Father*[3] that same year: that is where the journey out really began —the holy exodus from my zealous Christian framework. I understood at last the betrayal of myself within that framework, and within my everyday speech and actions. Mary Daly stripped everything right back in my inner landscape. It was Starhawk's book *The Spiral Dance*[4] that planted greenery again for me, and revealed other possible poetry with which I could be and grow, and I participated in her first class in 1980 in San Francisco. I invited Starhawk to be a speaker at the Graduate Theological Union that year; I still have my handwritten notes from my introduction of her that evening. My search now was for the story of the Primordial Mother and it was encouraged by the Jesuit supervisor of my Master's degree in Theology and Philosophy—himself passionate about "the Divine Mother," though within his context; and I had also been influenced earlier by process philosophy and theology, which enabled a larger picture of consciousness. Yet I knew that She whom I desired lay beyond the outposts, in the open fields, and I was jumping the fence. She was much more than a bubble in the fish tank; as any God religion might position Her, She was the open air itself, to which the bubble or air belongs and towards which it tends to rise. I was joining the nation of women with wings. I grounded my search/research in Marija Gimbutas' *The Gods and Goddesses of Old Europe*[5] as it was then titled: reading it at first in a library in rural Australia in 1979. It was not allowed out on loan as it was considered rare, and it had been brought in from a city library.

I had returned to Australia with my husband when he finished his theological studies and found employment there; I was pregnant again and passionate about that, too. In the Australian context at this time, I became involved with a collective founding a women's health center, and I began to write for a journal named *Magdalene*, published by women who were emerging out of a Christian paradigm. I also contributed to other feminist journals. I devoured Robin Morgan's poetry and books, and more of Mary Daly. When I later returned to Berkeley, I connected with Charlene Spretnak, whose book, *Lost Goddesses of Early Greece*[6] and perspective eventually became a significant basis of the first workshops and classes I taught: *Re-Storying Goddess*. These workshops were also initially inspired by a women's spirituality course taught by Marie Tulip at the Women's Academy in Sydney, using the book *Weaving the Visions*,[7] edited by Judith Plaskow and Carol P. Christ. My Re-Storying Goddess workshops and classes focused on the three aspects of Goddess, because I had been introduced to the Triple Goddess by a paper given to me and written by Batya Podos; and also, the workshops and classes focused on "re-storying our Gaian selves": the celebration of Her in seasonal ritual. It was here that I began to notice the power of celebrating the seasonal wheel, as a method of embodying Her: how the wheel had an energy of its own. In these early circles of women we made a start on re-storying these three qualities for ourselves; we in-formed each other in ceremonial storytelling, using my teachings and images of Her that most of us had not seen before. At the request of the women, I went on to develop an intense sequel series, *En-Trancing Goddess*. I was also an active participant in the Women-Church group in Sydney, contributing to the publication of a protest creed in The Sydney Morning Herald during a papal visit to Australia. We also co-created rituals, and I wrote for the collective's international journal. At that time, I wrote and produced a twelve part series for local radio: *Re-membering the Great Mother*.

All these women were my mothers—it is always reciprocal—and there were more mothers. Especially in early days, there was a strong component of what I call "lesbian-mind," or "Mother-mind:" learning to think from within my female bodymind. Indeed, it was largely the lesbian community and music that nurtured me, though I did not identify as lesbian. It was, and is, a return to Mother-mind, an integrity, that beckons and seeks me; and it took so long to re-create. One usually has to be broken first, and I was, but I found transformative power in the brokenness. Even now the journey is ever new, and it continues into knowledge of Her, contributing to a return to Mother-mind on a planetary scale.

In the fertile time period of the late '70s and early '80s I began piecing Her together, getting a sense of Her story. In 1980, I presented a paper, *Women and Religion: What's Happening* at a Women and Labor Conference in Melbourne. This was a pivotal point for me. I was blown out of the water (or into it) with the media response: page three of *The Age* in Melbourne read "Pressure from pews to find a female God;" page 17 of the *Sydney Morning Herald* read "The search for a Goddess;" and there was a full page interview in my region's local paper, which upset the Catholic Archdiocese that employed my husband. I had a dream in which I was an ancient woman on the plains; I had a spear, and my grey hair was being cut. The Mother's call became cataclysmic. I returned to Berkeley without husband and children, to complete my Master's Degree in Theology and Philosophy. All the stars fell from the sky; there were no guides for this.

I later wrote in my book *PaGaian Cosmology*[8] (2005:44):

> I am an inventor, a mythmaker, who has received/taken remnants of her indigenous religious heritage, and newly available parts, and spun and woven new threads, fabrics and stories. When I became bold enough to assume such a task – out of a sensed necessity, I

had long been encouraged by the words of Monique Wittig where she describes the attempt to remember an earlier mode of being, for which it is said "there are no words" and therefore perhaps "it does not exist." Wittig says, "Make an effort to remember. Or, failing that, invent." (see figure 13)[9]

Since these early times, so much has been accomplished by so many; Her verdancy has spread from meager green shoots to a jungle. Her womb has thickened; there is a rich placenta, a fertile network around the globe. There is still much to do, but there is a new crop of young women (and some men) with so much more as starting base. Currently, I am fully engaged with the passing on of the gynocentric cosmology that I have both authored and been authored by, nursing it through to the future. I am currently teaching apprentices who will be able to continue the ceremonies that I understand are essential to bringing Her forth: places/spaces for conversation with Her. I also teach this as a year-long course in on-line format for both Hemispheres. There is much writing that I am doing: new work as well as re-publishing old work that has found new ears. In recent years I contributed chapters to *She is Everywhere, Volume 3* (edited by Mary Saracino and Mary Beth Moser)[10] and *Goddesses in World Culture* (edited by Patricia Monaghan).[11] I am a featured contributor to and part of the collective of editors for the *Return to Mago* blog which was initiated by Dr. Helen Hwang. I am transferring a lot of my meditations and Poetic videos to formats for wider distribution. There are frequent invitations for me to be guest teacher, or priestess, to speak: it is news of Her that is being sought. I am understanding anew my own rich experience and giving it over, becoming the gift for those who come after me. Several years ago, I became a founding member of the Goddess Association in Australia, which holds an annual conference, with which I always engage significantly. In recent years —at the turning of the century and into the new millennium—I have facilitated constant practice, celebration and the embodiment of Her in the whole annual cycle of Seasonal ceremony at my place in the Blue Mountains of Australia, with an open community. My partner and I built ceremonial space for celebration of the Primordial Mother within these years, naming it MoonCourt (see figure 14).

MoonCourt is a semi-circular, open, womb-like space made of cob and recycled materials. It has three markers on the Eastern wall for the rising Sun of the Solstices and Equinoxes; the Winter Solstice window is yoni-shaped with a triple spiral in the center, the Equinox marker is a downward pointing triangle with artwork in it, and the Summer Solstice window is round. The floor is embedded with a brass spiral with forty markers along it, representing some moments of note in the Universe story as Western sciences have come to know it, and that we may be thankful for; there is a Cosmic Walk script that I wrote to go with it.[12] I describe the constant practice of the whole cycle of Her annual Creativity as "religious" because it is an act/acts of belonging, of expressing devotion. It has been, and is, a method of re-creating Her, bringing Her forth, in self, other and All. It is not merely "feminist discourse;" it is rather what I have termed "PaGaian concourse," a speaking *with* my Place, con-versing with Her, which becomes a Poiesis, the making of a world, within self, other and All. The times beckon humans into new territory, places where none have been before, and certainly a place

> ... wherein we humans no longer primarily or simply engage in more talk and analysis, but we dare to attend sincerely and primarily to the complexity of actual relationship with, and comprehension of, our embodied engagement with our Earth-Universe-Gaian context.[13]

I do not consider PaGaian Cosmology to be just a "theory," though it may be so in a scientific sense; that is, its practice has been verified sufficiently to be more than a hypothesis, able to be trusted as ground for further exploration. I consider PaGaian Cosmology a "doing," that is, it must be an action of ceremonial practice, of entering into ceremonial conversation with Her Creativity as it expresses itself in one's Place. The practice of the whole annual cycle is a template of wholeness; it forms a womb/mandala—a sacred site—that can grow a person, a community, into deeper truths. It is a placement of self and at the same time a recognition of self as a Place. Primarily, it is a practice of relationship with Place, as situated in particular bodymind, region of Earth and Cosmos. PaGaian Cosmology may be identified as an indigenous methodology that has been spun out of my own Western tradition, of Earth-based indigenous Goddess-focused practice and Western scientific research, wherein each being is recognized as a Place, wherein the primary referent is Place: land, cosmos, where we are. It grew out of my female experience in an androcentric context of alienation from myself as a place, my search for Her. I did learn of myself, my bodymind, as "Land"—primarily from lesbian music, poets and writers of the late '70s—that my bodymind was a place, a country, and then from French feminist philosophers, particularly Helene Cixous and Luce Irigaray. Then later this came to be situated within Earth and Cosmos by the Western scientific story of the Universe as told by Brian Swimme and Thomas Berry (see figure 15).[14]

At the turning into the new millennium, I was able to document this engagement in academic form, writing it into a doctoral thesis, making it useful for those who came after me, seeking to bring change to the defining of knowledge, breaking new ground for those wanting new/ancient methodologies and priorities. I have been able to publish this work, contextualize it for a more popular audience, and make it freely available on-line. It is still maturing, as it finds new hearts and minds, as well as new expression. My work of PaGaian Cosmology has a core sensibility, but its expression may be very diverse, and it has been so where it is practiced.

At its core, PaGaian Cosmology is a situating of self within the Creative Cosmological Dynamics, imaged and known of old as a triplicity that runs through the Cosmos, expressed cross-culturally in a myriad of ways, but within my own Western tradition often as triple spiral, triple goddess, three matrons, identified often as three qualities essential to the unfolding of the Cosmos and/or essential to never-ending renewal, and ongoing creativity. These three qualities have various guises and valences; they are not simple and univocal. They are fuzzy and poetic, yet identifiable just as the phases of moon are. I identify them in summary this way: She who creates the space to be (old creative one), she who is the urge to be (young differentiated one), and She who is this dynamic place of being (mother, flux of being); or (and in reverse order) She who is, She who will be, and she who returns us to the "great subject." My passion continues to be to enable sacred space, to do the work of growing Her in ceremony, where there is space for deep self, in deep community, expressing a deep truth.

Recently, I taught an on-line course with Dr. Helen Hwang: *Gaia and Mago, Rekindling Old Gynocentric Unity*, in preparation for the 2014 Mago Pilgrimage to Korea that we co-facilitated: the unveiling of Mago, the Great Goddess, the Primordial Mother, of East Asia. This pilgrimage to sacred sites, visiting with female shamanic practitioners, conferencing with feminist scholars and encouraging seekers and artists of female spirit contributes significantly to the rising global unveiling of Her, strengthening Her new shoots and networks.

NOTES

1. Suzanne Arms, *Immaculate Deception: a New Look at Women and Child-birth in America* (New York: Bantam Books, 1975).
2. Adrienne Rich, *Of Woman Born: Motherhood as Experience and Institution* (New York: Norton and Company, Inc., 1976).
3. Mary Daly, *Beyond God the Father* (Boston: Beacon Press, 1973.)
4. Starhawk, *The Spiral Dance: A Rebirth of the Ancient Religion of the Great Goddess* (New York: Harper and Row, 1979).
5. Marija Gimbutas, *The Gods and Goddesses of Old Europe* (Berkeley: University of California Press, 1974: re-published as *Goddesses and Gods of Old Europe*, 1982).
6. Charlene Spretnak, *Lost Goddesses of Early Greece* (Berkeley: Moon Books, 1978).
7. Judith Plaskow and Carol P. Christ, eds., *Weaving the Visions: New Patterns in Feminist Spirituality* (San Francisco: Harper and Row, 1989).
8. Glenys Livingstone, *PaGaian Cosmology: Re-inventing Earth-based Goddess Religion* (Lincoln, Nebraska: iUniverse, 2005), 44.
9. Monique Wittig, *Les Guerilleres* (New York: Avon Books, 1993), 89.
10. Glenys Livingstone, "Spelling and Re-Creating Her," in *She is Everywhere. Volume 3, ed.* Mary Saracino and Mary Beth Moser (Bloomington, Illinois: iUniverse Inc., 2012), 384-402.
11. Glenys Livingstone, "GAIA: Dynamic, Diverse, Source and Place of Being" in *Goddesses in World Culture*, ed. Patricia Monaghan (Santa Barbara, California: Praeger (ABS Clio), 2011), Volume 2, Chapter 10: 143-154.
12. My version of the Cosmic Walk is based on one created over time—initially by Miriam MacGillis, then contributed to by Ruth Rosenhek, and Liz Connor.
13. Glenys Livingstone, *PaGaian Cosmology,* 45.
14. Brian Swimme and Thomas Berry, *The Universe Story,* (New York: HarperCollins, 1992).

PART III

RITUAL AND CEREMONY

CHAPTER 18

LA STORY

Z Budapest

It was in the year 1971, when being poor was fashionable. We all wore threadbare jeans and t-shirts with slogans on them. The revolution was printed on our women's bosoms. Mine said, "Sisters give rides to Sisters," referring to hitchhiking. Our idea was that if women gave rides to other Sisters, there would be far less rape.

Sharon was one of us; we were a small group of women from all over the country who staffed the newborn L.A. Women's Center. Sharon rode a motorcycle, proudly revving it up every morning and riding to work on it. Not too many women rode big bikes like hers back then. We often thought about how unsafe that was for her, streaking between cars and buses on Hollywood Boulevard, but it was not traffic that brought her down.

Just before she turned off from Hollywood Boulevard at the corner of Whitley, four guys pulled her off her bike, dragged her into a house, gang raped her, and then left her unconscious on the sidewalk where the police found her. The rapists stole her bike as well. The police brought her to the hospital. The doctors patched her up. Back then, there was no rape kit to do. We got a phone call to pick up Sharon; her friend Dixie went to get her.

That April, the birds of the Hollywood Hills sang particularly creatively, and all the flowers that could were blooming full on. The scent was intoxicating, jasmine mixed in with wild flowers, orange blossoms, alyssum and roses. L.A. smelled like heaven—but it was not.

We sat on the floor in a circle. Sharon arrived, her face so badly beaten that both her eyes were swollen shut; her lips were bleeding. She could not sit down. We, the women she called Sisters, laid her gently on the floor with a pillow under her head. Her right arm was in a cast.

Dixie motioned to us not to bother her too much. She had some serious drugs in her. So we had a meeting of the Women's Center without her.

"What happened?" We all asked, and Dixie, who was a cab driver and rarely emotional, broke down sobbing.

"Some guys grabbed her and raped her. Beat her up, stole her bike, and dumped her on the sidewalk. It is horrible. She was almost home," Dixie sobbed.

Joan, from the Women's Center on Crenshaw, who was working on rape issues already, took a deep breath. "We have to do something. This must stop."

The statement was unbelievably bold. Stop rape. Walk without fear on our streets. Why, that is civilization!

Nancy, who was a nurse and saw her share of horrors, said, "Rape is as old as war. I see the women at my hospital all the time. Every day, destroyed lives. Insane." All I could say was, "All wars are wars on women."

I have seen my share of wars up close and personal. I was born into the middle and post-WWII era in Europe. I still have vivid images in my head of the *ostrom* (siege) and the bombings of our building: my home. One bomb just wiped out four floors from our building; our floor was pulverized. I grew up with famine and frequent change of residences according to where my mother could place me, mostly in the countryside where there was still food. I did not get to live with my mother until I was ten years old. Mom was always worried that I might become brain-damaged from lack of nourishment.

When I was a child, I watched Hungarian women dragged away to "peel potatoes," for the Russian soldiers, but they did not take the men. We all knew potatoes had nothing to do with it. It was the ancient rites of horny soldiers to rape the conquered female population, one of the perks men get when they sign up to be killers.

But now it was L.A. in springtime! We were not involved in any wars on our soil. But even now any man could decide to take the war perks anyway, just because he could; and men usually do it like soldiers, in groups, in gangs. Raping in groups (or not) has nothing to do with sex. It has to do with domination as observed by other males—and in addition that they would see each other's genitals in action. One could argue that they gang rape for the latent homosexual satisfaction of the male genitals exposed, a male bonding in the forbidden act of rape. It is pretty ugly there in the land of denial. They also share the forbidden joy of watching the suffering of the terrorized woman whom they have hunted down. Power over a girl: cowards.

When Sharon came to a couple of days later, more details were revealed.

"They called me dyke! I rode a bike. They hated me and called me a dirty dyke!"

"You could have been riding a pink unicorn and they would have hated you," Dixie added.

Sharon was in a cast for two months.

So what to do? What could we, as a small group of feminists, do? Joan was way ahead of us.

"I think we should make a vow, that each time we hear a woman cry for help, we go and see what is happening; help her in whatever way we can."

This took us a while to agree to, but it sounded okay. We would respond to cries for help: honorable enough. We all knew feminism eventually would have to show some verve, some backbone.

Joan started organizing the new "Anti-Rape Squad." We were the first members. We put up signs at the Women's Center. Meetings were set and kept. We printed more "Sisters give rides to Sisters" bumper stickers and put them on our cars. Our meetings grew. From the small numbers of just our friends, the meetings started growing into twenties and thirties.

Joan wrote articles on the topic, and we listened for cries in the air. None yet were heard. Hitchhiking women gratefully accepted rides from us—except the sex workers, who told us to get lost.

The Los Angeles media heard about us, and the LA Times wrote an article about what we were doing. Feminist papers interviewed us as well, and the Free Press. There were radio shows where we talked about rape, prevention ideas, like more lights on campuses and streets. I always suggested women carry the super-long Chinese hatpins that were sold as souvenirs on the Boulevard, to use as weapons. I wore one on my sleeve, on the outside of my jackets, and I demonstrated how it can be quickly pulled out and pushed into the attacker's belly, or eyes, or genitals.

Thank heaven it did not come to that, but I was packing hatpins, a totally legal weapon.

Once we got our name and contact phone out there, we started seeing the rape victims regularly. Joan had another idea. When they went to the police alone, the women were asked over and over again to repeat the horrors of their rape to each and every policeman who wanted to masturbate later to the story. This we could stop. We started accompanying the women to the police station to report the rapes. The tone of the police remarkably changed for the better when they were witnessed by four or five feminists in the room.

A woman would tell her story and then we would demand that that be all. However, nothing happened to the rapists. Nobody found them. Nobody really looked. To the police back then, rape charges were a waste of time. The rapists hardly ever went to jail.

I was determined to do something. I had just started the Susan B. Anthony Coven Number One. It was a coven full of start-up feminist witches who were political as much as spiritual, and one genetic witch, myself, who knew how to hex the guilty. After one of our meetings I suggested, "We should hex the rapists!"

The women were a little surprised, not knowing what that meant. "I will show it to you, but the most important tool we have is that we have a righteous cause. These men who rape women insulted the Goddess; back in the days before patriarchy, rapists were killed for that."

"You are going to kill them?" They asked.

"Of course not; I just cut their good luck to shreds. Criminals need good luck to get away with their crimes. I send the Fates, the Furies themselves, after them and they deal with them as the Fates would. I do not need to specify."

"Really? Would that not come back to us tenfold?"

"We just never attack the innocent. Then we are safe." I assured them.

"But how do we know who these rapists are?"

"We do not have to. The Great Mother knows who it was. I just say 'whosoever raped this woman'." The women began to like the idea.

"It is elegant." Dixie said. "You do not even have to be there. Wow!" Joan started liking this too. She was a nonreligious person, and as feminists we were hurt by religion so long and so often that she did not want any religion involved. But Witchcraft is a Craft, not a religion. It is a knowing. One moves energy in order to balance out injustice.

And so we gathered for the first time and created an altar with bones and some bloody tampaxes (for elimination). We wrote on a piece of parchment paper "whosoever violated Maxine" and we followed up three nights in a row. It took a different kind of discipline, but the cause was very important. We burned a black candle with the words written backwards; this made it a little creepy.

Then we waited.

Three days after our hex on this rapist, Maxine reported that the truck she thought belonged to her rapist was all banged up. It had been in a major accident.

A few weeks later the truck was repossessed. Maxine watched as the mail was accumulating on the porch of this man. Then his place was rented out. When she asked about the earlier resident, neighbors just said, "We do not know what has happened with him. He was in the hospital a long time."

One has to be satisfied with that. Maxine was never bothered again.

Postscript on this: As the awareness of our efforts for women grew, Joan managed to get us some funding, and with that we started the very first Rape Hotline, which was then followed by others in all major cities across the United States.

Next, we organized the very first Los Angeles "Take Back the Night" march for women to take to the streets and give voice to their own empowerment to stop violence against women. This "Take Back the Night" march was gloriously attended: ten thousand women and men together marched through Hollywood, chanting feminist slogans. We sang songs to the Goddess.

There was a crescent Moon. I will never forget it. I still have LA Mayor Bradley's Declaration of Appreciation as a reminder of that march.

As I was walking with the women and men, I prayed to the rising Moon.

We all come from the Goddess

And to her we shall return

Like a drop of rain

Flowing to the ocean.

Nowadays, awareness about the rape culture is massive. There is a feminist movement even in the Arab countries. Women have awakened and organized themselves. Each of us in her own location must figure out how to respond, from forming groups of women who go and beat up the violent men as in Africa, or jailing the offenders as in the United States, women are fighting back by standing up for each other.

Men need to speed up their evolution and both trust themselves as noble humans and trust their honorable women. Nobody is raised to be a rapist or to be violent. No woman 'invites" or "asks for it." What we ask for is equality and respect.

Killing and raping women is killing our future as a species. It is degrading our human security. A nation is only as strong as the women in it. Killing and raping young and old women are despicable acts. Men as a gender have put our species on a suicide track.

Recently, one of the most creative ways of fighting against the rape culture has been the Billion Women Rising, which occurred in many countries this past Valentine's day. Women performed and videotaped a choreographed dance, with rousing feminist music and words and a defiant, powerful, and clear message. Over a hundred countries posted their Billion Women Rising on UTUBE.

What women can do to stop rape:

1. Explode with indignation if somebody is speaking violently against a woman, no matter why.

2. Do not judge. Notice how the men do not criticize each other with quite the same sexualized intense energy.

3. When men trash your name, who will stand up for you? Talk is already action.

4. Live and dress as you want to. Do not believe it is at all your fault if you are attacked.

5. Try going places in public with a friend.

6. Carry a weapon. A small bottle of Easy Off oven cleaner removes disrespect with a few sprays into the face of the attacker.

What men can do to stop violence:

1. Stop looking at women as the "other." We are not. We are one species: the human race. Women as a gender deserve men's respect. Individuals can be disappointing, but our gender carries the burden of the human species. That is our very existence.

2. Do not try to trick women into situations where you can rape us. Do not tell lies about showing us stuff in your apartment.

3. Even if you have the opportunity to rape a woman, you do not, because you are a mother's child, and your mother's gender deserves your respect and gratitude.

4. Dating: There is no way you can have sex against the woman's wishes. "No" means "no."

5. Spending money on a woman does not entitle you to sex. She is not a hooker.

6. When a woman is friendly with you, she is not "asking for it." We are looking for love or friendship, not your "it."

In order to finish my L.A. story: one late night, around 2.40 am, we did hear an unmistakable cry for help. We also heard blows administered to somebody who called out:

"Help! Somebody help me! Stop hitting me!"

Since we, the original six members of the anti-rape squad, lived in the same apartment building, we flew out of our beds, in different modes of disarray, and we assembled in the courtyard. "Where are you? Who is it?"

We looked and then heard a car speeding away.

There on the sidewalk was a poor woman with her skirt all torn up; her face was bleeding and she was trembling. All six of us ran to her and helped her up. Marcy ran back in to the house to get some cloth and water to clean her up a little. Patty and Marcy offered to drive her to the hospital. When the water and cloths arrived, I began to clean up her face. She winced. She had some deep cuts.

Then something else happened.

My hand touched her skin: rough skin, familiar, an after-shave texture.

Whaaat? I stepped back.

"Joan!" I called. Joan came over.

"I think our first rescue of a woman is actually a man."

"It should not matter," Joan said.

The "man" was a very pretty one. Violence had been directed at her because she looked like a girl. Slightly less proud and a bit shaken, we helped the "sister" into Marcy's car and they left for the hospital. Then we all went back to bed. Our first actual rescue when responding to the cries of help in Hollywood was over. The Goddess must have had a good cosmic giggle. We are a lot more sophisticated now.

CHAPTER 19

SERVING THE MOTHER

Hallie Austen Iglehart

I first discovered the women's spirituality movement on what was known amongst hippies as the Kathmandu Trail—or rather, when I got off it. Escaping many years of academic studies, I spent 1970 driving overland and back from London to Kathmandu, living on a dollar a day. For six months, I lived in fundamentalist Muslim countries, met Tibetan refugees, and waited out the monsoon in a remote part of the Himalayas. My experiences in fundamentalist Muslim countries rocketed my feminist consciousness sky-high; living with the Tibetans and the mountains deepened my spiritual consciousness.

As I describe in the first chapter of my book *Womanspirit: A Guide to Women's Wisdom*,[1] I spent the next several years torn between my feminist and spiritual selves. I alternated between working in the feminist healthcare movement in the United States and living in places where I could better explore other cultures, as well as my own inner world.

My lifelong dream of living on the island of Crete, site of the last Goddess culture in Europe 2500 years ago, was fulfilled by a generous friend. Three of us lived in a tiny two-room house on a remote cliff above the Mediterranean. For three months, we did not get in a car and were miles from any electricity or plumbing. We literally drew our water from a well in an earthenware jar. I swam four times a day in the sea and wandered the ruins of a nearby Minoan palace.

The place opened me up psychically. One day, I felt a trio of ancient olive trees pulling me in. Sensing that merging with them might make me "crazy" by my society's standards, I used all my will to resist that pull. It was my first initiation with nature spirits; it took decades for me to integrate this experience of merging with Oneness (see figure 16).

In 1972, I returned to live with the Tibetans in Dharamsala, where I saw "miracles" happening that I would not have believed—had I not seen them with my own eyes—events which challenged my Ivy League-educated view of reality. In love with the Tibetans and their sophisticated psychology, I seriously considered becoming a Tibetan Buddhist nun. Yet I had read *The First Sex*[2] by Elizabeth Gould Davis on a train across Europe and could see the patriarchy in Tibetan Buddhism. And so, feeling torn, I returned once again to American culture and economy to work in the feminist movement. It was 1973.

I count myself fortunate that I landed in the midst of the creative and dynamic feminist community of the San Francisco Bay Area. My mentor, Anne Kent Rush, urged me to organize a group of women who might also be interested in my two passions. I called the class "Feminist Spirituality, Spiritual Feminism." Having never heard of such a thing, I hoped to find other women who might share my interests. I did—and was so excited to find others who also felt that emotions, the body and nature were sacred, that women had once been revered and that spirituality was nonhierarchical.

I wrote an article for Country Women magazine about our discoveries. And the rest, as they say, is herstory. I soon found out that there were even more of us, and I continued teaching, writing, organizing conferences and leading rituals both public and private, large and small, for another twenty years. That first class was the seed for my book *Womanspirit*, which offers feminist approaches to mythology, art, dreamwork, healing and ritual.

The feminist spirituality movement certainly saved my soul—and my sanity—and those of many others, it appears. Until 1974, I could find no place in the women's movement—focused as it was on reproductive rights, job equity etc., and often drawing on Marxist principles—for my inner self. Spirituality was considered a diversion from the "real" work. And in the meditation circles, ashrams and temples, revealing as the teachings were, overt and subtle sexism was rampant.

It took the feminist spirituality movement to expand, redefine and clarify the values and actions of feminism. As Native American author Jamake Highwater notes, from a cross-cultural perspective, what our culture calls masculine and feminine values makes no sense. These are human values, belonging to all people. However, as one of my friends pointed out, at least women might have a better idea of what the feminine is. And so, rather than looking for a bigger piece of the patriarchal pie, we worked to bring values into balance. This has contributed to making health care more holistic, our economy more sharing, our power dynamics more partnership-oriented, and men more able to participate in parenting.

By our research into times and cultures where God is/was a woman, we have helped sanctify women's bodies, both in the medical system and in sexual relationships. Rebecca Solnit writes that, since September 11, 2001, the number of women who have died from domestic violence exceeds the total number of people who died in the 9/11 attacks and the ensuing wars.[3] Yet I believe that we hear more about this now because the pus is oozing out of the wound and that previously invisible acts are now more visible. Women recognizing themselves as Goddesses and their vaginas as sacred *yonis* can only help to strengthen them to reject abuse. Indeed, between 1994 and 2012, domestic violence fell 67%.[4]

There is much to be done to unravel the imbalance of the past 5000 years, yet we have begun. And we have managed to mainstream many formerly radical ideas. I remember how hard I worked, writing and rewriting *Womanspirit* to get it accepted by a mainstream publisher. I had written it because I wanted to reach more people than I could in the groups in my living room in the mid-'70s. And I remember how excited I was when, in the early '80s, a church group asked to use a quote from *Womanspirit* for a calendar they were producing. Although my values were far from theirs, I was grateful that they were brave enough to incorporate as radical a statement (for them) as "We are all the creation makers and there is a new world awaiting our creation" (see figure 17).

Most recently, I was intrigued when Jaime, my 31-year-old niece, referred to the importance of ritual in the feminist movement. She grew up with my second book, *The Heart of the Goddess: Art, Myth and Meditations of the World's Sacred Feminine,*[5] and at age 11, asked me to come to Boston to lead a coming-of-age ceremony for her. I realize that for her and her tribe, feminism has a new meaning.

What am I doing today? Quite literally, today I am on my mother's farm, where I grew up in Maryland. My mother is eighty-seven years old, living alone on the farm where she hopes to spend the rest of her life, but with no close family nearby. I am doing all I can to make this possible, short of leaving my beloved San Francisco Bay Area and moving to the East Coast. And so, every month, I fly across 4 time zones. Being here for my mother—who has been such a supporter of my work, even writing a paper herself on the Great Goddess when she went back to college after her kids were grown—is the one non-negotiable in my life right now, even taking precedence over my ocean cleanup work, which I will describe shortly. What better way to serve the Mother than to care for my own mother?

So today I am helping my mother prepare for electric shock treatment to her heart. I just walked out to a distant field to see if the Fox had eaten the leftovers we placed out for her/him, a ritual we have performed for decades, sometimes three generations of us. I discovered an ancient precedent when *The Heart of the Goddess* was published in Japan in 2001. I traveled there to teach with artist-activist Mayumi Oda. When we visited the shrine to Benten, the Japanese Goddess of creativity, Mayumi showed me a small shrine in the back to the Fox God/dess. She said all Buddhist shrines in Japan honor their pre-Buddhist animist religion in this way; no shrine would be complete without the Fox. This helps me place the rituals I share with my mother in a much more ancient context.

Today I am working on the classes I will teach at my niece's month-long Utopia School in Queens, NY. "At last we will be able to work together!" she said when she invited me. Jaime is my spirit-child, spiritually, politically and creatively. She says that many people her age (thirty-one) and younger are interested in the Goddess and ritual, so that is what I will be teaching to twenty- and thirty-something artists and activists.

Today I am also working on the closing meditation I will lead for Bella Gaia, a large-scale multi-media event depicting the beauties and ravages of Mother Earth. One of the local producers had felt immobilized when she first saw the show, and she asked me to help people integrate their feelings and transform them into action, something I am passionate about. I find myself in a similar situation as the in late '70s, when we used ritual to close a national conference on violence against women and later, a Take Back The Night March, calling on women to channel their outrage to constructive action. Today my audience is quite different—or maybe not. The work for the Mother takes many forms.

The biggest thing I am currently working on—ocean cleanup—is quite different from my previous work. It took an extreme case of undiagnosed Lyme disease to change my focus. Soon after *The Heart of the Goddess* came out in 1990, I became completely incapacitated with a mysterious illness, losing my health, my work, my sexuality and my community. Rarely able to teach and certainly not able to travel and teach, and with writing out of the question, I discovered how identified I had been with my work; my ego was shattered. At 43, I did not know whether I was going to live or die. I mourned the fact that I could not be doing more to help heal the planet. For seven years, I was unable to walk, drive, read or write more than a few minutes a week. In retrospect, I think those years in the Underworld opened me up to serving the Mother in a different way.

As my health slowly returned, I found myself completely focused on the health of Gaia, minimizing my own impact on the Earth and working on behalf of our relatives in the Ocean. In 2000, by a series of synchronicities, I co-founded Seaflow: Protect Our Living Oceans. Our mission was to educate people about the then little-known military and industrial use of low-frequency active sonar and its destructive impact on marine life. Sometimes I wondered how I had come to find myself talking about underwater acoustics and decibels. The only way I could reconcile this radical diversion in my life was that this was just a different way of serving the Mother. Since all three Seaflow co-founders came from different spiritual perspectives, we integrated meditation, art and ritual into our activism. We were extremely successful, affecting policy locally, nationally and internationally. Some thought our success was because of this synthesis.

In 2010, horrified at the completely preventable deaths of about one million sea creatures yearly from our trash, and drawing on some ideas I had evolved over the decades of picking up trash on beaches, I founded All One Ocean: Caring For Our Ocean, One Beach At A Time. We set up Beach Clean-Up Stations, small wooden boxes permanently installed on waterfronts. The Stations are decorated with kids' art and casual informational signage about the impact and longevity of our purchases, especially plastic. Inside the box are repurposed coffee bean bags, which people can take to use to pick up the trash as they enjoy the beach, making it possible for every day to be beach cleanup day (see figure 18).

We now have fifteen stations in Northern California and Hawaii, with many more in process for waterfronts throughout the United States. Interestingly, I find younger volunteers and staff hungry for the kinds of grounding meditations and ritual that were so much a part of my earlier feminist spirituality teaching. I am happy for this integration, though sorry it is not a normal part of their lives. Yet I know that what I share with them influences the future of this nonprofit, as well as that of any other they might be part of in their long (to me) future ahead.

Though gratifying, much of the work is tedious and funding is an ongoing challenge. In the first year and a half, I worked alone. The idea of setting up Beach Clean-Up Stations was a simple one but had never been done before. I spent a long time practicing what I call Polite Patient Persistence with beach agencies, sometimes taking a year to get approval to set up a Station. I wondered how I had gotten from the Goddess to trash —all I could figure was that it was my latest assignment from the Mother.

In all of this, I have felt the hand of something much larger than myself. If I put a name to this presence, it is sometimes Yemaja, Yoruba Goddess of the oceans. When I am lucky, I get to go to an actual beach. Every time I lean over to pick up a scrap of Styrofoam or spend yet another hour on emails, it is an act of worship, a prayer in action for the whales, dolphins, birds, turtles, fish—and ourselves.

One of these days, I hope to get back to working on an article a friend has insisted that I write. I was telling her about recent occasions when I had followed my instincts and done something I wasn't supposed to do (played hooky from work to go to the beach, crashed a neighbor's kids' party, trespassed, etc.). In all of these instances, I serendipitously made contacts that had extremely beneficial consequences for my life and for All One Ocean—exponentially more so than if I had stayed my course, been more "disciplined," done what I was supposed to do—which often meant stay at my desk. One of these impulses led to my being quoted (and thus All One Ocean) on the front page of the San Francisco Sunday paper, another to meetings 3000 miles away with international organizations, another to being on the biggest stage of my life and an invitation for a four-city benefit for All One Ocean.

I've noticed that, since my illness and those seven years in the Under-world, and even more so since starting an intensive qigong practice, that, when I allow space in my life, synchronicity comes much more into play, leading me through doors I did not know existed. Maintaining this balance between fullness and spaciousness, being and doing, is one of the greatest challenges for me in this 21st century. It is an important part of maintaining my health and is perhaps the most radical work we can do.

As we have seen in the past, technology can serve either oppression or liberation. Information technology has greater potential for either cause and presents challenges of its own. Learning to stop checking off the to-do list and emptying my e-mail inbox is a daily practice for this recovering Protestant. As I allow myself freedom, quiet time and space to follow the more convoluted path of the Great Mysterious, the Beauty Way, the Tao, I feel I am truly serving the Mother. Perhaps ironically, I also find that I am accomplishing far more than I ever could have dreamed of or imagined.

NOTES

1. Hallie Austen Iglehart, *Womanspirit: A Guide to Women's Wisdom* (New York: Harper & Row, 1983).
2. Elizabeth Gould Davis, *The First Sex* (New York: Penguin, 1972).
3. Rebecca Solnit, "Men Explain Things To Me," *Haymarket* (2014): 23.
4. Margaret Talbot, "Matters of Privacy." *The New Yorker* (October 6, 2014).
5. Hallie Austen Iglehart, *The Heart of the Goddess: Art, Myth and Meditations of the World's Sacred Feminine* (Berkeley: Wingbow/Bookpeople, 1990).

CHAPTER 20

ON WEAVING A WEB
AROUND THE WORLD

Mama Donna Henes, Urban Shaman

NETWORKING

I love working and playing with groups of women. I was not in a college sorority, so my first experience was in the feminist consciousness-raising group that I joined in the late 1960s. And what an eye-opening, empowering experience that was. We were a very diverse group, brought together by our Bohemian, politically radicalized lifestyle. Our backgrounds could not have been more different: the Detroit ghetto, patrician Manhattan, an Israeli kibbutz, the suburbs of the Midwest. We were artists, academics, shop-girls, political activists. We were married, single, mothers, lesbians. And the more we talked, the more we shared, the more we realized that our upbringing and current status as women was virtually the same.

Our group stayed together for well over a decade. We shared each other's struggles, sorrows, and victories. We helped each other overcome obstacles and achieve goals. We saw each other through advanced degrees, first books, childbirth, divorce, love affairs, coming out, mental breakdowns, addiction, domestic abuse, illness, and death. These sisters taught me the true grit and loving power of women.

In 1971, I hitchhiked through Europe with my best friend, video-taping interviews with women in the nascent Women's Liberation movement in Holland, Belgium, France, Switzerland, and Italy. In addition to all of the pamphlets we collected, my reading material was *The Golden Notebook* by Doris Lessing,[1] the perfect accompaniment to our project. In 1978, I joined the performance group, Disband, comprised of women artists who could not play instruments. Our collaboration—fun, argumentative, and mutually respectful—produced many clever, ironic, prescient, and powerful songs of social commentary and feminist pride. Today, in our sixties, we are still invited to perform our wacky, but seriously serious material, from Seoul to Salzburg.

Back in those heady, happy, hippie days, I had a career as a sculptor. I created giant free-form multi-dimensional webs that were site-specific installations in galleries and on the grounds of museums, libraries, schools, and parks all across the United States and Canada.

With a half-century of perspective, I can now see that these web environments were an expression of the network of women around the world that I was connecting with. But at the time, those fiber structures were unconscious, instinctive, and spontaneous in their design and execution. I did not have a worked-out philosophy or rationale for their creation. They were almost like doodling—automatic and nonintellectual. My fingers did their thing without thinking.

While these disparate groups and networks of incredible women fed my soul, they tended to be more personal and political than spiritual in focus. So a deep comprehension of the symbolic, mythic, archetypal meaning of my webs did not come to me until later. In November, 1975, I had a profoundly "tranceformative" spiritual experience, which changed my life forever and cemented me on my path to the Feminine Divine.

This epiphany was precipitated by a gift from a friend who had just moved into a new house. In the attic she found, among other saved treasures of a woman's life, a woven silver, gossamer, web-like veil. She sent it to me, because it reminded her of my web sculptures. When I opened the package, I put it on my face and ran to look in the mirror, and shazaam! I had an instantaneous, powerfully profound vision of the divine energy of Spider Woman, the Native American creatrix of the peoples of the Southwestern United States and Northwestern Mexico: Grandmother Spider, She Who Wove the World.

What I "saw" was not a spider, nor a personage, but rather, a new way of seeing: an intuitive, all-encompassing, gestalt understanding of the concept of cosmic connectivity, the gut-level quantum knowledge that everything is inextricably interconnected, interrelated, and inter-dependent, the unforgettably vivid realization that the world is truly held together by a web! This was my assignment from the Universe. It launched my career as a "professional" shaman. Suddenly, I was able to put my woven webs into a spiritual context and they took on new, deeper meaning for me. I understood that it was my job to spin connection, to create a web around the world that would serve to unite people with each other and the cosmos. The month after my meeting with Spider Woman, I facilitated a public ritual on the Winter Solstice—"Reverence to Her: A Participatory Chant to Invoke the Female Forces of the Universe Present in All People."

FOLLOWING THE THREADS

Spider Woman led me to the Great Goddess, and I have been in Her thrall and doing Her bidding ever since. In 1976, I joined the editorial collective of *Heresies: A Journal of Feminism and Art,* and I worked for the next year and a half on producing the Great Goddess issue. After publication, many of my co-editors created a Goddess Group that still meets monthly nearly 40 years later. The members who have participated over the years have all been Mothers of the Women's Spirituality Movement. Our meetings are rich exchanges of research, information, inspiration, spiritual support, and sushi.

Many a seminal book has come out of our connection and devotion to each other and the Goddess. These include the books of Merlin Stone (*The Paradise Papers: The Suppression of Women's Rites;*[2] *When God Was a Woman;*[3] *Ancient Mirrors of Womanhood*[4]), Mimi Lobell (Architect of the Goddess Temple Mound), Cristina Biaggi (*In the Footsteps of the Goddess;*[5] *Habitations of the Great Goddess;*[6] *The Rule of Mars*[7]), Mary Beth Edelson (Goddess imagery exhibited in museums globally), Buffy Johnson (*Lady of the Beasts: The Goddess and Her Sacred Animals*),[8] Kay Turner (*Lady Unique Inclination of the Night;*[9] *Beautiful Necessity: The Art and Meaning of Women's Altars;*[10] *Transgressive Tales*),[11] Nancy Azara (*Spirit Taking Form: Making a Spiritual Practice of Making Art*),[12] and Donna Wilshire (*Virgin, Mother, Crone*).[13]

I had a ringside seat from which I not only observed but participated directly in the formation and development of the Women's Spirituality movement. My own shamanic Goddess-honoring work was shaped by these early conversations and connections as well as my own devotional evolution.

All of the important parts of my life—my feminist allegiance, my artwork, my writing, my ritual practice—finally came together in a complex weave of reverence for the Feminine Divine and commitment to Her earthy daughters.

SPIDER WOMAN ON THE WORLD WIDE WEB

When I was a child, I had a meditation retreat in the attic, where I built altars, composed what I would now call affirmations, and did my own quirky rituals. I have never strayed from that path and I still do very much the same inner personal work. By the mid 1970's my private spiritual practice and artwork took on a more public face. Like so many other flower children of the era, I had the goal of reaching out and making a change in the world.

My role as a shaman is that of a catalyst: organizing and instigating innovative systems for genuine interaction, celebration, and communion. My spiritual goal is to facilitate meaningful opportunities for identification, association, and affiliation, through which people can interrelate with each other, the entire universe, and their own deepest, best selves. Closest to my heart is the empowerment of women as midwives for the birth of a new way of living that honors Mother Earth and each other. To that end, I have facilitated hundreds of what I call "Celestially Auspicious Occasions," public, participatory ceremonial celebrations of the equinoxes, solstices, cross-quarter days and lunar cycles, over the past forty plus years. And I have published four books (*Dressing Our Wounds in Warm Clothes;*[14] *Celestially Auspicious Occasions: Seasons, Cycles and Celebrations;*[15] *Moon Watcher's Companion;*[16] and *The Queen of My Self: Stepping into Sovereignty in Midlife*),[17] as well as a quarterly journal, *Always in Season: Living in Sync with the Cycles.*

Ever since Spider Woman came to me, I have been a devotée and practitioner of cosmic connectivity. My commission and commitment in honor of that profound vision has been to weave the threads of hope and trust, to spin sanity, to tie the knots that bind us in mutual care and support. The ideal result of both my writing and my ritual practice is the weaving of an energetically joined conceptual web, a real communications network that connects us all at our cosmic center (see figure 19).

> It seems to me that all my creation is an effort to weave a web of connection with the world. I am always weaving it, because it was once broken.
>
> –Anais Nin

When people used to ask me what my religion was, I would always answer, "The Web." That was before the Internet. Now, "The Web" has an entirely different connotation, but it is a true expression of my shamanic intention. The Worldwide Web is indeed an energetic, conceptual web, a Global-One communications network with the awesome power to connect and unite us.

Being on the web, this virtual network, appeals to me enormously. What could be more natural? Being Spider Woman's protégée, I love the positive, proactive possibilities for grassroots exchange of information, inspiration, opinions, options, and actions that the web offers. The potential for outreach is unfathomable.

I take full advantage of the web's endless possibilities for participation and interaction. In addition to maintaining my own four websites, I write for several online publications, publish my own monthly Ezine, have three active Facebook pages, a LinkedIn and two Twitter accounts, and I participate in several women's spirituality email list serves, not to mention personal and professional email correspondence with hundreds of folks every week.

Mainly, I reach out to women, specifically women of a certain age with spiritual proclivities. My publication, *The Queen's Chronicles*, has more than 7000 subscribers in thirty-three countries. My column for Beliefnet.com, "Meaning, Moxie & Majesty for Midlife Women," reaches women from all over, and they, in turn, reach me. It is an active/interactive community with lots of comments and offerings of personal experiences and observations. The same is true for "The Queen of My Self" Facebook page. I can tell you, we Queens are everywhere!

These online contacts, friends, and communities span the globe and are fascinating, sympathetic, satisfying, and mutually beneficial. This virtual Queen's Court is a worldwide web of relationship and communion. Having these connections with so many amazing women has expanded my understanding of the importance of weaving a web. I now see the web as a structural support system—a safety net that can catch us in case we fall.

It is my goal and fervent prayer that as more and more woman around the world step into their sovereignty and claim their personal power, they will reach out and connect with other Self-directed, empowered women to create a formidable network of prodigious Queens.

If we, the mighty Queens, bring to bear all of the extraordinary experience, understanding, and acumen that we have earned, we can, together, restore balance and bring healing to a world that seems hell-bent on ruin. And we are just the women to do it. Are we not daughters of the Goddess? Do we not speak for Her when we step forward in our crowning glory in defense of all life and living? Have we not mastered the art of transformation and positive change, emerging as Queens, rulers by virtue of our virtue?

Personally, I do not think that it is a coincidence that just as the planet teeters on the very brink of total devastation, there comes along a generation of fiery, accomplished, clever, ambitious women at the height of our supremacy, to whip it back into shape. It is just a matter of connection. If we join together in a web of influence, the sheer enormity of our numbers means that we can actually achieve the critical mass necessary to make a real and lasting difference in the world. The future is in our very capable hands.

> If the first woman God ever made was strong enough to turn the world upside down all alone, together women ought to be able to turn it right-side up again.
>
> –Sojourner Truth.

NOTES

1. Doris Lessing, *The Golden Notebook* (United Kingdom: Michael Joseph, 1962).
2. Merlin Stone, *The Paradise Papers: The Suppression of* Women's *Rites* (London: Quartet, 1977).
3. Merlin Stone, *When God Was a Woman* (New York: Barnes and Noble, 1976).
4. Merlin Stone, *Ancient Mirrors of Womanhood* (Boston: Beacon Press, 1984).
5. Cristina Biaggi, ed., *In the Footsteps of the Goddess* (Manchester, CT: Knowledge Ideas & Trends, 2000).
6. Cristina Biaggi, *Habitations of the Great Goddess* (Manchester, Ct: Knowledge, Ideas & Trends, 1994).
7. Cristina Biaggi, ed., *The Rule of Mars: Readings on the Origins, History and Impact of Patriarchy* (Manchester, Ct: Knowledge, Ideas & Trends, 2005).
8. Buffy Johnson, *Lady of the Beasts: The Goddess and Her Sacred Animals* (New York: Harper & Row, 1988).
9. Kay Turner, ed., *Lady Unique Inclination of the Night.* (Journal)
10. Kay Turner, *Beautiful Necessity: The Art and Meaning of Women's Altars* (London: Thames & Hudson, 1999).
11. Kay Turner et al, eds., *Transgressive Tales: Queering the Grimms* (Detroit: Wayne State University Press, 2012).
12. Nancy Azara, *Spirit Taking Form: Making a Spiritual Practice of Making Art* (Newburyport, MA: Red Wheel/Weiser, 2002).
13. Donna Wilshire, *Virgin, Mother, Crone: Myths and Mysteries of the Triple Goddess* (Rochester, Vermont: Inner Traditions, 1994).
14. Donna Henes, *Dressing Our Wounds in Warm Clothes* (Los Angeles: Astro Artz, 1982).
15. Donna Henes, *Celestially Auspicious Occasions. Seasons, Cycles and Celebrations* (New York: Monarch Press, 1996).
16. Donna Henes, *Moon Watcher's Companion* (New York: Monarch Press, 2002).
17. Donna Henes, *The Queen of My Self: Stepping into Sovereignty in Midlife* (New York: Monarch Press, 2005).

Chapter 21

The Life of a Priestess

Kathy Jones

My personal journey with Goddess began in the late 1970s when we started a women's consciousness-raising circle here in Glastonbury, England. This was also the time of women's peace camps and protests at Greenham Common Airbase, against the installation of American nuclear cruise missiles in Britain. Women travelled to Greenham from all over Brigit's Isles, including from the small country town of Glastonbury, to protest against these deadly weapons. Out of these protests and the experiences we had at Greenham, great realizations came. One time I remember standing in the darkening woods outside the green chain-link fence with policemen, soldiers and razor wire on the inside, guarding silos of death, and a group of women on the outside holding candles and singing,

> You can't kill the Spirit
> She is like a mountain

Old and strong,
She goes on and on and on......

– Naomi Little Bear

This was the first time that I remember singing about Spirit as She. Before then, the Earth could be She—our Mother Earth—but Spirit had always been He/God. This was a moment of liberation for me. In singing on the earth in this desperate place, I experienced Spirit as She, in my body and heart, not in a relational way to He, but as Herself, as She, as Goddess.

As part of my own consciousness-raising, I began to read ancient Goddess tales from many different lands, translated from scrolls or tablets of clay, such as those about Demeter and Persephone, and Inanna and Ereshkigal. For the first time for me, they were alive, and I understood that they were filled with meaning, expressing hidden truths, and mythical realities. As I opened my heart and mind to Goddess, I heard Her speaking to me and I began to see/feel/sense/know Her in living visions.

I started writing sacred plays based on these ancient myths. I would see/envision a brief scene for a future drama, which was later enacted in reality. Recognizing the patriarchal bias within so many of the early stories, which were only written down in patriarchal times, I changed them to reflect an earlier, and a future, empowered place of Goddess within society, rewriting the myths and connecting them into the present. This was heresy to many, something sinful and dangerous that one just did not do, but we did it anyway.

Our group of players became Ariadne Productions, and together we discovered the amazing power of sacred drama and the ritual enactment of myth, to change hearts and minds, to bring transformation and healing to performers and audiences. It was a soul training for me, learning to act from vision, from the knowing within, which I recognized as Goddess speaking directly to me. In the coming years, I became a vision-holder for many community spiritual projects and ventures. I also learned to trust that everything that happened in the moment was happening just as it should, for the greater good of the whole. Challenges arise for a reason, and it is our creative choice to meet and resolve them as they come.

Through the 1980s and early '90s I wrote one or two community sacred dramas each year, sometimes writing with others, sometimes alone. I directed, produced and sometimes acted in our amazing performances in the Glastonbury Assembly Rooms, with casts of up to 50 local people: performers, artists, and musicians. I was called a man-hater and ball-breaker by some, for redressing the Goddess/God imbalance, and putting Her out there on stage for all to witness, but on the whole many people were profoundly moved and educated by these sacred dramas, which became legendary in our small town.

The early plays we did were about well-known Goddesses from different countries in the world, for example, Greece, Rome, India, Tibet, but not from Britain, because Britain was a Christian country and we did not have Goddesses. Of course, I realized that this was not true; Goddess is everywhere and She had to be in my land, too. I began to look for Her with my partner Mike, in Glastonbury where we live. At the time, nearly all the legends in Glastonbury itself were focused on male heroes: King Arthur, Lancelot, Joseph of Arimathea, Jesus. The women, apart from the meek St. Brigit, were bad women: Queen Guinevere, Morgen La Fey, and others who apparently betrayed men and women. The landscape itself was described as male and centered on a phallic Glastonbury Tor, although the rounded curves of the hill belied that attribution.

As soon as we began to look for Goddess in our own land, She revealed Herself to us in the contours of the Glastonbury landscape. We saw Her there outlined, as Swan Maiden, Lover, Great Mother, and Crone. Within days of looking for our indigenous British Goddesses, I had found 400 and more of Her names: Brighde, Artha, Rhiannon, Domnu, Ker, Banbha, Keridwen, Danu. They were there in myths and legends, in poetry and song, in the names of hills and rivers. She was everywhere, yet unseen, forgotten. In quick succession I researched, studied and wrote several Goddess books about Her, *The Goddess in Glastonbury* (now *In the*

Nature of Avalon),[1] *The Ancient British Goddess*,[2] and *Spinning the Wheel of Ana*.[3] In 1995, I was inspired to create, with Tyna Redpath, the first annual Glastonbury Goddess Conference. It was a wonderful gathering of Goddess women and men, with ceremony, talks, presentations, art and craftwork exhibitions, music, poetry, song, and dance. The Conference is held each year at Lammas, the festival of the abundant Mother Goddess, and it is a glorious celebration of Goddess spirituality and creativity. We are now in our twentieth successful year.[4]

In 1998, I began teaching the Priestess and Priest of Avalon Training in Glastonbury, first as a one year training, but now as a three-year, Three-Spiral training. The first two Spirals are taught by Priestess Erin McCauliff and the Third Spiral by me. The Calling to become a Priestess or Priest of Avalon, Priestess of the Goddess, is very strong for many people in the present time.

In 2000, while on a visit to Mount Olympus in Greece, Mike and I were walking around the ruins of another ancient Goddess Temple; only a few stones remained, and a pool of water. I was overwhelmed with grief and anger. Over the years we have visited the ruins of many Goddess Temples in many lands and here we were at another. In that moment I vowed that when I got home I would endeavor to create a Goddess Temple in Glastonbury—one that was alive and not in ruins.

When we got home, I called together a group of people to see if anyone would like to help create a living Goddess Temple. We rented a room in the Courtyard of the Glastonbury Experience, for a few days at Beltane. We decorated the room as a Goddess Temple with colorful materials. We made a shrine and placed one of the large Conference wicker Goddesses, made by sculptor Foosiya Miller, inside it. We held a beautiful celebration for Beltane with prayers, strawberries, and champagne, and we had a wonderful time. We held the space open for three days for people to come and pray, meditate, sing, dance, and express their devotion to Goddess. We received donations from people who came, and that helped pay for the room. When the three days were over, we took everything down.

We had such a good time that we decided to do it again at Litha, the summer solstice seasonal ceremony. We hired another room and created another Goddess Temple.

We continued to do this over the next eighteen months, creating Temple spaces for each of the eight seasonal festivals of the year. In 2001, a space became available to rent within the Courtyard and we took the plunge to set it up as a permanent Goddess Temple. With great excitement, we opened to the public at Imbolc, 2002. We registered ourselves as a formal Place of Worship, not realizing until a while later that this was, in fact, an herstoric event. We are the first and so far (in 2014) only formally registered indigenous British Goddess Temple in Brigit's Isles and Europe for perhaps 1500 years.

Our Temple is dedicated to the Lady of Avalon, Nolava of the Sacred Land. We welcome all who love the Goddess to come and spend time in this small but powerful space, which is open every day of the year from 12 noon–4.00 pm, and it is cared for by Temple Melissas: bee priestesses, who give their time to serve our Lady of Avalon. We are financed by donations of time, energy and money from our Melissas and Temple Madrons, who give the Temple regular monthly donations, as well as donations from visitors, and also from the Priestess Training courses we teach and all the Goddess events we put on.[5] In 2006, I published *Priestess of Avalon, Priestess of the Goddess: A Renewed Spiritual Path for the 21st Century*,[6] expressing my understanding of what it truly means in the present day to become a Priestess of the Goddess and of the sacred Isle of Avalon.

Soon so many people were coming to our public seasonal ceremonies that we were in serious need of a larger Temple space to accommodate all those wishing to participate. In 2008, we bought (with a mortgage) our larger Goddess Hall, located in Benedict Street, which we use for our seasonal ceremonies and for teaching. We decorated the Hall as another Goddess Temple, with glorious paintings and images, including a wonderful new mural of the ancient Isle of Avalon, on the front wall, by artist Jonathon Minshull (see figure 20).

Our Temple teachings now include several year-long priestess trainings, Goddess teachings and healing courses. We also hold regular New Moon Healings, Ceremonial Goddess Healing Days, Goddess Oracles, and Embodiments of Goddess.

In 2013, we set up our Goddess Temple Gifts shop in the Courtyard; this gives priestesses and Goddess artists and craftspeople the opportunity to earn their living from their Goddess-inspired work. It is a beautiful sacred space managed by artist Sue Quatermass. Profits from the shop go to support the Temple. (*www.goddesstemplegifts.co.uk*)

We are now looking for a larger Goddess Temple space to accommodate everything that we would like to include in our vision of what a modern-day Goddess Temple means: larger and smaller Temple spaces, shrines and oracle rooms, healing rooms, flowing water, spa facilities, healthy food café, sacred gardens—all we can dream, all offered in service to Her.

In my life I have many passions. My dharma, my karma, my life purpose is to bring Goddess back into human consciousness, to the best of my ability. I live my life in service to the Lady of Avalon as Her priestess. I am always exploring what that means, what the world of Goddess is, what the spiritual and mystical dimensions of the Sacred Isle of Avalon are. I am listening for Her inspiration in any moment, so that I can bring new awareness through. This is what excites me and motivates me. I have a passion to empower women and men to become who we truly are, fully embodied souls upon the earth, and to expand our understanding of what that means. I want to be free to be who I am and I want that freedom for everyone else, too.

One of my current passions is bringing the Vision of Motherworld into being. Motherworld is a society inspired by Goddess, where mothers, and the values of mothering—love, care and support for each other, and for our Mother Earth—are placed in the center of our lives, rather than being left out on the periphery: the reverse of what happens now.

This vision of Motherworld feels really important at the present time when everywhere we can see the destructive impact of patriarchy on our world. We are surrounded by the effects of dominant, power-over control and coercion, greed, destructive competition, violence, rape, child abuse, war, slavery, suffering, hunger, poverty, and pollution of Mother Earth and Her atmosphere. All these negative human expressions must be challenged, deconstructed, transformed, and healed.

The name "Motherworld" comes from Barbara Walker's novel "*Amazon,*"[7] which described an ancient fictional matriarchal society; but this is not a return to such a society. I see it as a forward movement to a new kind of mother-centered community, where all are valued, supported and appreciated just as a mother naturally loves and cares for all her children. Motherworld evokes a loving world where we are held safely in the Great Mother's embrace.

I have become aware, in my own life as a Priestess and Goddess-loving woman, of the wounded emotional and psychological patterns which are activated when we try to change the world. It seems that instead of dealing creatively with the negativities of the patriarchal world, we women are all too ready to attack and undermine each other. Like many other teachers and writers, I am questioning why this is so. Is it our internalized, patriarchal conditioning that is fighting for survival or are earlier memories competing for expression?

It is my belief that a large number of mostly women have incarnated at this time, to bring awareness of Goddess back into the world again. We are the same souls who were alive at the ending of Goddess cultures in ancient times. We have returned to bring Her back to human awareness. We have incarnated to serve Her once again, although Her Temples are now few and Her life-loving cultures are gone. We have to build everything again from the ground up, for Her.

As we incarnate, however, we also bring with us buried memories of the painful and shocking experiences we suffered when the Goddess Temples and cultures were attacked and destroyed by patriarchal forces. We have incarnated with the memories of those dreadful times carried in our soul-vehicles. Sometimes they emerge slowly as an awareness of having lived in other times and places, or they erupt suddenly as memories of being wounded, maimed, raped, and murdered. Many remember being burned or hung as a witch; many remember dying beside an altar of the Goddess.

We were not always the completely innocent victims of oppression. Sometimes we betrayed each other to save our own skins. We colluded with others to protect ourselves. We ran for our lives. We found ourselves alone, cast out of safety and sisterhood. We had to hide who we were. We fought each other then and we fight now when it is no longer necessary for our survival. In Motherworld, one of our first works is to love and support each other in taking responsibility for our individual karmic wounding, recognizing where these wounds come from in this life and previous lives.

In the present, the wounds from ancient times hidden within our unconscious minds can undermine all of our best endeavors to change how we act in the world. The unexpressed hurts are often projected unconsciously onto our Goddess sisters, our nearest and dearest. They affect our lives as Goddess-loving people, as Her priestesses who wish to stand proudly in Her name, but instead find ourselves hiding away. They affect the commitments we make to Goddess in the privacy of our own homes and how much we dare to show our love for Her in the world. They are wounds that prevent us from becoming truly empowered. There is no easy path to healing the wounds we carry, but we each begin by healing ourselves.

This healing journey is one of my current passions as I experience Shadow material being projected towards many teachers and visionaries within the Goddess movement in different countries, between many soul sisters on the path of Goddess. I want to help heal these wounds in our

Goddess communities, so that we can have a real and lasting impact on the world, changing everything for the better. Goddess is returning and we are all part of Her return.

May we all be blessed in Her love.

NOTES

1. Kathy Jones, *In the Nature of Avalon* (Riverside, California: Ariadne Pub-
    lications, 2007). See www.kathyjones.co.uk.
2. Kathy Jones, *The Ancient British Goddess* (Riverside, California: Ariadne
    Publications, 1991).
3. Kathy Jones, *Spinning the Wheel of Ana* (Riverside, California: Ariadne
    Publications, 1994).
4. See www.goddessconference.com.
5. http://www.goddesstemple.co.uk.
6. Kathy Jones, *Priestess of Avalon, Priestess of the Goddess: A Renewed Spiri-
    tual Path for the 21st Century* (Riverside, California: Ariadne Publications,
    2006.
7. Barbara Walker, *Amazon* (San Francisco, California: HarperSanFran-
    cisco, 1992).

CHAPTER 22

WHEN WE RE-DISCOVERED THE POWER OF WOMEN'S MYSTERIES

Ruth Barrett

I was born and raised in Los Angeles, in the mid-1950s. Like many women who evolved (emerged? bolted? escaped?) out of male-centered religious traditions in the late 1960s, there was no Goddess movement to "come into" yet. At that time, Los Angeles was also home to Marija Gimbutas, Deena Metzger, Starhawk, Shekhinah Mountainwater, Z Budapest, and many others who influenced the flowering Women's Spirituality and Goddess Movements. I was blessed to live there during the years when intersecting movements (second wave feminism, Goddess archaeology and research, ecology, and anti-war movements) created a catalyst for social change.

The best way to describe my personal journey is to say that it has been a process of coming into myself. My two brothers and I grew up playing and singing American and Israeli folk music with our parents. Thankfully, my parents were progressive Reconstructionist Jews who raised me with a deep appreciation for meaningful ritual in daily life and the importance of making my unique contribution to healing the world. My father was a cantor (clergy who sing the liturgy for religious services), and my mother a family therapist and author. They encouraged me to think critically and develop my own concept of "God."

Around the age of twelve I began writing poetry about "the Goddess." Late at night She would awaken me to take dictation, giving me words to write before I became fully conscious. I would read Her words in the morning and be mystified at their messages. They were always conveyed in poetic lyrical form. In those days, there was no support system for a young girl exploring her spirituality, and certainly none for the Divine as "She." As a young woman, where could I have gone to find others who felt the same? It never even occurred to me that there were others. I felt alone, like I was inventing my own religion.

In the late 1960's there were no organized groups, certainly not public ones. But soon women began gathering to share their experiences of living in a patriarchal society. They talked about equal pay for equal work, physical and sexual violence in the home and on the streets, reproductive freedom, and how to help end the war in Vietnam. The only books that had anything to do with the Goddess were *The White Goddess*[1] by Robert Graves, and some by Jungian writers like Ester Harding (*Women's Mysteries*)[2] and Erich Neumann (*The Great Mother*).[3]

Truthfully, as I look back, I believe She found me. I heard Her voice, and I answered Her call with my life. Her call to me has never wavered, and to this day, through all of life's joys and sorrows, She remains at the center, my guide and inspiration. Now that I have entered my Crone years, it is so clear to me that you cannot know you are a part of making a "movement" when it is in the early stages. Any pioneer is simply taking one inspired step at a time, moving and expanding, and taking the next needed step. It is only now, after many decades, that I can look back and see the entire path that lay before me, the identifiable path I helped create. In her own way, each of my sisters in this book has shared this journey with me, and together we danced our feet along this path to make a road for others to follow.

Part of what accompanied me down this Goddess road was my love of folk music. Folk music led me to the study of folklore, which led to the study of paganism and pre-Christian customs and beliefs. Being attracted to the so-called "supernatural" or magical ballads of old led me to years of collecting, comparing, and investigating their meanings. I started playing a folk instrument called a mountain dulcimer in 1971, so that I could accompany myself as I sang. Little did I know that I was becoming part of what is now described as the "dulcimer revival." The dulcimer is an American folk instrument from Appalachia. My style of playing was first inspired by Jean Richie, a Kentucky native. In 1974, dulcimer player and folklorist Holly Tannen taught me how to play the dulcimer for Renaissance music. In 1979, I met another mountain dulcimer player, Cyntia Smith, and we collaborated for twenty years, creating our own record company to make our original and traditional music available. We were among the first "out" pagan musicians to record Goddess-centered folk music. Neo-pagan culture was just beginning to form, and as more pagan and Wiccan folk felt safe to come out of the "broom closet," the more our budding culture began to flourish. Straddling the genres of pagan, women's, and folk music was never easy. It is still challenging today, because the music I love cannot be placed into just one category.

I was blessed to have two musical mentors. In the 1970s Frankie Armstrong, a British feminist activist and singer of traditional and original ballads, inspired me to sing powerfully in a lower register. We were both interested in singing traditional songs that were about strong, intelligent, or clever women who overcame difficult circumstances during the times they lived in. In the 1980s and 1990s, Kay Gardner (of blessed memory) was my mentor and friend. Kay was a muse-inspired composer and a pioneer in the field of healing with music. She encouraged me in my own song-writing, and she helped me to understand the healing power of music and its effect on the whole person.

By the mid-1970s, women who were fleeing "God the Father"[4] began finding and falling in love with themselves and one another, and the center of the universe shifted. A new world was revealed, experienced, and claimed. This new world was based on a new paradigm: seeing the world through the eyes of Her, the female of the species, as the primary reference for life. We tore off our muzzles and found our voices. We shouted, screamed, sang, cried, and spoke hidden and unexpected wisdom together. We removed our blinders and saw our beauty in all our wondrous diversity of color, shape, and size. We reclaimed the mirror as a sacred tool to see our reflections as a face of the Goddess, the divine Female. We kicked down the locked doors of our minds and started to comprehend, beyond deception and enculturation, ecstatic states of self-knowing.

For many of us, men and a male god were no longer the center of our personal and political universes. Suddenly, it occurred to us that even God was born from between our legs! We came home to ourselves, to Her. She saved our lives, and we saved Her. Although many "authorities" refused to acknowledge that the Goddess was worshiped long before "God the Father," once the lies, deceptions, and obstructions within ourselves dissolved, She poured out of us like a flood that had been held back for centuries. She filled us, inspiring our art, dances, music, poetry, scholarship, politics, sexuality, and personal empowerment.

In the beginning, we did not consciously understand the power that was being released in us, and back into the world: a power to heal our very souls. We were reviving and creating a once and future Goddess[5]-centered culture, and we could not hide from our birthright as sacred beings, once we knew who we were. Nor could we hide from our responsibility to Mother Earth.

We created sacred spaces in our gatherings and rituals to experience and affirm ourselves as sacred. We felt that we were coming home, returning to the sacred Female as center. Being in female-centered and Goddess-centered circles changed us, giving us a sacred space in which to heal, celebrate, and grow into an interdependent community of independent women. These experiences confirmed female identity and gave us tangible experiences of creating non-patriarchal reality.

It was not always easy, though. We learned that the legacy of patriarchal "power-over" enculturation was alive and well, and living within us. We hurt one another and healed with each other. We endeavored to work with power differently, sometimes falling on our faces in the efforts. In the early years, we did not ask what women did outside of our coven meetings, and some took Goddess names or names from nature. It was understood that we were initiating ourselves, apart from the dominant culture.

In 1970, I met my first teacher of Goddess spirituality, Shekinah Mountainwater, a brilliant and inspired teacher, song writer, and poet/musician, whose love of the Goddess and women fueled and directed her life. We were both working as performers at the Renaissance Pleasure Faire in Agoura, California. Our personal friendship developed and grew through our mutual love of the old songs, exploration of mythology, Jungian psychology, and Goddess spirituality. I was a student in Shekhinah's first teaching circle in 1975 and 1976, in her "moon hut" in the mountains of Santa Cruz, where a small group of women explored Goddess-centered spirituality and developed a pact of Sisterhood. Developing new ways of living, we chanted "MA" for the Mother and raised power to Her.

In 1977, after moving to Los Angeles, I met Z Budapest (see Z's piece in this book) at a production of "Rise of the Fates," at the former Women's Building. After our meeting, I began circling with the Susan B Anthony Coven #1, and I was initiated into the Coven soon thereafter. On Halloween night in 1980, when I was 26, Z ordained me as a High Priestess so that I could continue her ministry when she relocated to northern California with the coven name. Inheriting Z's ministry gave me the responsibility of continuing what she had started, although I developed the Dianic tradition in my own way. I borrowed Shekhinah's deeper seasonal and elemental correspondences that overlay the female life cycle and integrated them into the Dianic tradition where they had a welcome home in Dianic (exclusively female) Women's Mysteries.[6]

Because Z's priestessing and teaching style was, and is, largely improvisational, I focused on developing a magically sound foundation for magic and ritual practice that I could teach my students and community, and that could be passed on through their knowledge and skills to future generations of Dianic witches. I am proud to say that the classes and open community rituals I developed in collaboration with my sisters have consistently been offered for women and girls in Los Angeles since 1980. I deeply appreciate my first coven, Moonbirch Grove, Circle of Aradia, and Temple of Diana, Inc., for keeping the doors open for seekers looking to participate in Dianic spiritual community.

My passion as a Dianic elder is to teach ritual making and facilitation that honors and celebrates Women's Mysteries. This includes teaching magic that is sourced from our female bodies, and how our female bodies inform and shape our life experiences. In spite of the influence and tireless efforts of patriarchal culture to define us, we continue to heal from those influences, and to discover who we really are, or could be, without those influences that seek to disempower and control us. In my forty plus years of experience, I have learned that this process can take one's whole life-time, given that most of us are still inundated with sexist and disempowering messages on a daily basis.

Recent debates over sex and gender, who is a woman and who is not (and who gets to decide), feels sadly, to me, like another version of woman-hating that our Dianic tradition has always had to deal with. In the early years we were criticized, ostracized, and attacked for excluding males from our rites. Since our rites were never about male life experiences, this criticism seemed to be based on misinformation and ignorance. Now, however, the Dianic tradition is under attack because of its exclusion of transgender and transsexual individuals. Dianic tradition has always been about the life cycle and experiences of the female sex. It was never about individuals who "feel" they are women and/or acquire a female form through hormones and/or surgery. I did not expect that in my later years I would still need to defend our right to simply exist, or to gather with our sisters as we choose, or to practice our magic and rituals in peace.

Our female and Goddess-centered tradition, (as well as other forms of women's spirituality) was always about meeting the needs of females: those who were born female and raised and socialized as women in a world that dishonors the female blood mysteries, and who suffer the religious, economic, social, legal, and political consequences of their birth as females. We continue to explore and become conscious about how growing up in a patriarchal culture affects our daily lives, our female identity, and our self-perception, including the awareness of an epidemic of female self-hatred.

For Dianics, Women's Mysteries are the doors by which we come to know ourselves as Divine. From ancient times until today, our female mysteries are revealed as girls and women experience them together in circles, or alone under the moon. These Mysteries become known to us through revelatory experiences and our ability to create a connection to Goddess through our bodies. I describe the Dianic tradition as an "embodied" Women's Mystery tradition that is sourced from ancient roots, from the beginning of the beginning to this moment and beyond. Our intuitive knowledge, crafted into skills that can be taught and passed on to the next generation of daughters, is our Holy Book.

For the past fifteen years, I have focused especially on the magic inherent in the female body, as a sacred source of creativity, oracular inspiration, and power. Embodiment, as I define it, is experiencing the totality of being/knowing through the revelatory experiences of our female senses. To "embody" is to develop the skill of bringing into conscious awareness all of the sensory information our bodies provide, including inner and outer sight, sound, and "feelages" (taste, touch, vibration, temperature, weight, texture). This ability can help us come into deep resonance with another person, creature, or other sentient being. When women who are participating in ritual physically embody this spiritual experience, a fundamental intention of the Dianic tradition is realized: the female body is re-sanctified as a manifestation of the Goddess, the source from which all things emerge and return.

Since I retired from holding the center in a specific community, in 2012, I have been free to do more of what I love (teaching workshops and priestessing through my music, song, and chant). The old Celtic and English folksongs and ballads continue to be "portals" to other realms for me. I sing, enter into other realms, and hope that I may be a conduit for others to enter as well, while continuing to write songs, prayers, and invocations as She provides them to me. At the turn of the millennium, Falcon River (my brilliant and magically adept life-partner) and I co-created the Spiral Door Women's Mystery School of Magic and Ritual Arts (a national training program for women interested in going deeper into elemental magic, energetic and ritual skill development, and spiritual leadership). I love our Spiral Door program for the tools it gives our students to better their personal lives and spiritual communities. It is my passion to assist others in becoming great ritualists who can step into any ritual role, at any time, and be able to be present with what is needed in that moment with inspiration, grace, and humility.

I enjoy traveling to different communities, to teach or give concerts, going to those places where what I have to offer is needed, useful, and appreciated. Yet, with each passing of our foremothers, I become more aware of time left to me, and I take nothing for granted. The loss of my dear friend, brilliant poet and scholar, Patricia Monaghan, in 2012, leaves a tear in my heart and a rip in the tapestry of Goddess culture. Because of these types of experiences, I choose my projects based on the energy budget for a woman in her 60s. For this reason, my spiritual practice is more private now, communing under oak trees on our rural land, where we can watch the moon rise between the breasts of the southern California mountains. Still, since now I am a Crone and find that I can think forwards and backwards with greater flexibility, I remain open to the next call from the Goddess and bless Her for all She asks of me.

NOTES

1. Robert Graves, *The White Goddess* (New York: Noonday, 1976).
2. M. Esther Harding, *Woman's Mysteries* (New York: G. P. Putnam's Sons, 1971).
3. Erich Neumann, *The Great Mother: An Analysis of the Archetype.* Transl. Ralph Manheim. Bollingen Series XLVII (Princeton, New Jersey: Princeton University Press, 1955).
4. Mary Daly, *Beyond God the Father: Toward a Philosophy of Women's Liberation* (Boston: Beacon Press, 1993).
5. Elinor W. Gadon, *The Once and Future Goddess: A Sweeping Visual Chronicle of the Sacred Female and Her Reemergence in the Cultural Mythology of Our Time* (San Francisco: HarperSanFrancisco, 1989).
6. The Dianic tradition is a vibrantly creative and evolving Women's Mystery tradition, inclusive of all female women and girls. Our practices include celebrating and honoring the physical, emotional and other life cycle passages women share by having been born female. Contemporary Dianic tradition also recognizes the greater or lesser effects and influences of the dominant culture on every aspect of women's lives.

CHAPTER 23

THE TANTRIC DANCE OF FEMININE POWER IN THE FOURTH WAVE OF FEMINISM

Vajra Ma

My awakening to the reality of the Goddess came through direct experience in the body by way of moving meditation. This "bodyknowing," as I call it, was catalyzed in a combined context of a) my first exposure to Goddess studies, the scholarly research and critique that breaks the grip the patriarchal paradigm has on conceptual thinking, and b) the feminist spirituality that co-arose with that pioneering research. These three factors, Goddess studies, feminist spirituality and bodyknowing, worked synergistically in me and subsequently formed the "synergistic blend" that is the basis of my work. Bodyknowing, particularly subtle bodyknowing sourced from the womb, is what distinguishes my work and will continue to do so.

While Goddess studies and feminist spirituality are essential pillars of the women's spirituality movement, bodyknowing—direct knowledge through the body—is far less recognized and developed. I hold the vision for womb-sourced subtle bodyknowing to come to the fore of the women's spirituality movement because it is in the subtle body where internalized patriarchal conditioning resides and it is in the subtle body where this conditioning must be unraveled in order to restore the natural connections, sensitivities, and wisdom of women's bodies. My nearly thirty years of exploring the female subtle body (defined further below) convinces me that the full awakening and empowerment of women, individually, collectively, and globally, requires going beyond concept and scholarship and even beyond feminist spirituality, as physical as it may be with ritual, drumming, dance, singing and enactment, and venturing into conscious interaction with the finer energetic reality of the female body. This inner work is what will fully liberate women from patriarchal thinking and behavior and will break the cycle of passing it down to daughters and sons. Goddess studies and feminist spirituality show that the female body is the particular embodiment of the Great Goddess and Her guiding wisdom and bliss. Yet to fully realize this wisdom and bliss, women need to cultivate communion with their womb and subtle body.

Bodyknowing is crucial in women's spirituality and empowerment because it is most particularly woman's domain. Women have direct, visceral connection to reality through the monthly wisdom cycle of blood, life, death and rebirth, through the capacity to conceive, gestate, bear, and suckle life; and through the extensive subtle body neural network that connects womb, heart and third eye, and makes woman innately the seamless weave of physicality and spirituality. All these powers are unmatched by the male body. And this is why patriarchy targets women's bodies for control—and demonization.

Bodyknowing is "carnal knowledge." The fact that patriarchy targets women's bodies is precisely why the next wave of feminism, the fourth wave, must be the body. Bodyknowing exists beyond any paradigm of control, dogma or codification, and, once experienced, cannot be taken away. Bodyknowing is the nemesis of patriarchal control.

Bodyknowing arises from attunement with the body's language that gives a direct experience of reality. The body speaks through sensation, breath, sound, shape, movement, and emotion. Subtle bodyknowing is attunement to this language at a highly refined, detailed and nuanced level of frequencies and sensate awareness.

We all experience the subtle body when we experience a feeling or emotion, a warm flush of well-being when lovingly embraced, a quick stab of fear when in danger, a gut sense about something ("I had a feeling..."). Feelings and emotions and the sensations of which they consist convey information about our selves, others, and surroundings. I call this "knowing." However, the degree to which one is aware of this information or interacts with it varies greatly. Usually, these sensations and the knowing they carry remain generalized and are only felt in passing. Subtle bodyknowing, on the other hand, is the conscious, detailed feeling, participation, and interaction with subtle sensations as intelligent carriers of knowledge and wisdom. This is beyond cognitive thought; it is direct, holistic, spherical knowing. The moment one focuses keenly and receptively on subtle sensations, these sensations will "dance" inside, they will shape and re-shape, and if one approaches them with reverence and devotional intention they will lead into a realm where sensation and spiritual knowing conjoin. In other words, the subtle body is the portal to spiritual awakening and awareness. The wholeness of the female body and womb is that portal par excellence.

My own awakening to the Goddess came directly through the subtle body. My discovery started in 1986, at age 36, when I studied two forms of meditative movement, beginning with a Middle Eastern dance teacher, Gena Reno, who experimented with guiding women into holding more energy and higher frequencies in their bodies through "refined movement." Many times I felt high frequencies register as a pleasurable piercing or spinning in my head and body. I felt as if I were being expanded or stretched beyond anything I could explain in words. Gena started her classes by reading papers on "feminine knowledge," which included the "pleasure connection" and animal powers, particularly "serpent knowledge" of the body: Kundalini (Kuṇḍalinī). Each woman then had the opportunity to be witnessed as she moved sensually and spontaneously from the pleasure she felt by connecting internally with her vagina. During this time, Gena referred me to my first of many books on feminist spirituality, *The Great Cosmic Mother: Rediscovering the Religion of the Earth*, by Monica Sjöö and Barbara Mor.[1]

Overlapping in time, I studied Continuum[2] with Susan Harper, the close associate of Continuum founder Emilie Conrad. Susan's teaching opened for me a previously unfathomed inner world of detailed subtle sensations and exquisitely nuanced feelings. Eventually, I found myself having spontaneous experiences of various Goddesses.

My first subtle body experience of a specific "Goddess energy" came during what Continuum calls "exploring the wave." Susan had demonstrated various movements and positions we could take to repeatedly undulate the spine and soft tissue of the body. She encouraged us to make subtle vibratory sounds and feel their resonance in our body. As I did this, a spontaneous sequence of elongated vocal sounds that swelled and ebbed with the wave motions emerged: "Yeeaaaaaeeeyyy...maaaaaeeeeee... Yaaaaaahhhh." The sounds felt soothing, comforting and nourishing. I repeated them over and over. Gradually, the vowels became shorter: "Yeh-maaeee...yaaahh. Yeh-maaee-yah. Yeh-maee-yah..." until I realized I was sounding the name of the Yoruban Goddess of the Ocean: Yemaya! I was having direct experience of her oceanic essence and motherly love as I bathed in waves of sound, movement and pleasurable sensations. Once I cognized this, my feeling of being comforted and loved increased. This one direct experience is imprinted deeply in my body. I will forever have some measure of living relationship with Yemaya. She will never be merely abstract to me. This is the way it is with subtle bodyknowing.

This phenomenon of bodyknowing first, then mental recognition ("Oh, this is Yemaya") has become a pattern for me over the years. The body knows before the mind cognizes. It also knows what the mind cannot name or quantify at all.

Since these "Goddess energies" were not happening for other people in the Continuum classes, I realized that the cognitive information from my Goddess studies was important in awakening the bodyknowing encoded in Goddess mythology and iconography. The patriarchal paradigm-busting, compelling perspective in *The Great Cosmic Mother* had combined with the awakening of my direct bodyknowing to blow me wide open and set me unfalteringly on the path of exploring the wisdom and powers inherent in the female body. I wanted to experience more of this spontaneous, direct embodiment of Goddess, more of the synergy I was experiencing between 1) the sensual-sexual "feminine knowledge" of Gena's classes, 2) the knowledge encoded in Goddess myths and images, and 3) the infinite nuances of subtle sensation I was experiencing in my Continuum explorations. But no one offered such an integrated and mutually synergistic practice.

This is what, in the late 1980s, compelled me to call together my own "Goddess-Circles" of twenty or so women, where I shared teachings on Goddess myths and iconography, followed by a sacred dance circle. Each woman had the opportunity to come to the center of the circle and, starting from stillness and silence, be witnessed in her spontaneous movement and vocal expression while we amplified her expression by attuning to her with our drums, rattles and voices. As we did this, we tapped into the collective body-mind intelligence of "the female shamanic group," a term inspired by Vicki Noble's research.[3] These Goddess Circles activated bodyknowing and shamanic healing powers, but I knew there was much more and I hungered for it. What would happen if we collectively accessed the more potent, transformative powers of the *subtle* body? I experimented with giving classes that incorporated witnessed sensual solo dances as Gena had, but, to further develop subtle body

230 FOREMOTHERS OF WOMEN'S SPIRITUALITY MOVEMENT

awareness, I added a preliminary guided Continuum-like movement exploration.[4] These explorations departed from the biological, asexual orientation of Continuum to focus on movements that would stimulate the seamless weave of erotic and heart feelings inherent in the female body and on pleasure to cultivate receptivity to the body as sacred.

As I taught, I learned. What evolved was the subtle body moving meditation, The Tantric Dance of Feminine Power, and it was indeed distinct. The Dance continually revealed itself, its powers, manifestations, and phenomena, over an intense formative period, from 1992–1996.

At times, because I had no model for what I was doing, I felt like I was climbing a sheer cliff by my fingernails. In order to give women adjustments and refinements after each dance, to help them maintain sensitivity to subtle sensation while moving, as well as coordinate all the other factors of the Dance, I had to listen with my entire being, beyond cognitive thought. The understanding and words came as I spoke, not before. It was revelation, moment by moment, woman by woman, dance by dance. I did not invent this practice or piece it together from other forms; it revealed itself, slowly, over years, through my own dances and witnessing of thousands of dances. Eventually, there came a period where every week in class, my core group of ongoing students and I marveled, "That was powerful! We can't possibly experience something that powerful again next week." Yet we did, over and over, week after week. The Dance burst open like a rose in bloom, then another and another and another. And like a rose, it had to start each time from receptivity to the root—the womb.

When I had begun my studies in the '80s, there was little or no focus on the womb in the Women's Spirituality movement, other than relating the womb to women's blood mysteries. There were no teachings on accessing the womb and its wisdom at a subtle level, what that means, and what that could do or lead to. As I guided women, I learned that staying rooted in the womb increases our capacity to absorb greater concentrations of energy and power rather than letting them dissipate, and it allows the intelligence and power of the womb to permeate the heart and third eye chakras, and then the whole body. I learned that this womb-heart-third eye continuum creates a mutually alchemizing synergy which, when received in reverence and devotion, in turn generates a register of high frequencies in the body that catalyzes direct epiphanies of the Goddess. "Frequency" is no poetic expression but a concrete, tangible phenomenon. Every thought, notion, object, every bodily impulse, shape and feeling, every name, aspect and power of the Goddess and Her animal epiphanies has a frequency. Each such frequency contains and transmits information, if one will receive it. The nuances of knowledge in-form(ation) are infinite. Our experiences in The Dance therefore are not general or abstract, but specific and intensely personal. At the same time, because they contact the underlying reality of wisdom and bliss and nourish both ourselves and those witnessing, they are transpersonal.

What makes The Tantric Dance of Feminine Power so potent is that movement is combined with subtle body awareness. This combination increases bodyknowing and the creation of new neural pathways, not just doubly or triply, but exponentially. However, this coordination is extremely delicate because movement itself can so easily dominate one's attention and obliterate subtle sensate awareness. It takes refined continual calibration and simultaneous awareness of subtle sensation, movement, and shape to "catch" and "ride" a frequency so that it can permeate the body and consciousness, through womb, heart and third eye, with its information. When one absorbs this information with reverence and devotion, the body and consciousness are suffused with wisdom and bliss.

Naomi Wolf, in her 2012 book *Vagina: A New Biography*, gives a fresh perspective on women's empowerment that illuminates the womb-heart-third eye continuum. Her hypothesis, based in recent neuroscience, states, "female sexual pleasure empowers women biologically...and thus also psychologically, and politically..."[5] Neuroscience confirms "a powerful and important brain-vagina connection."[6] She illustrates over and over how the ubiquitous verbal (derogatory or demeaning language) and physical attacks on the vagina disrupt and negatively impact "the electric inward network extending from pelvis to brain" (which is much less extensive and complex in male bodies) and that this affects everything about a woman, her creativity, health, spirituality, self-esteem, and her capacity to thrive in work, home, politics, and relationships. This problem is huge, and, as Wolf points out, it has received virtually "no mainstream ink."[7]

This documents that women's empowerment is more physiological than has been generally realized. I recognize this "electric inward network extending from pelvis to brain" as the womb-heart-third eye continuum of female subtle bodyknowing. The disruption of this continuum is the physiological internalization of misogyny. This is why it is crucial to bring subtle bodyknowing to the fore of the women's spirituality movement.

One student recently described how this subtle womb-heart-third eye network directly affected her life. She had been a successful activist against corporate greed, but she had "burned out." She realized that for the health of her soul she needed to tend to her female embodiment, which, for her, was to create beauty and devotional art. In hindsight, she realized the burnout had come largely from "internalized patriarchy," which she described as repressing her sexuality and hiding and silencing herself in many ways, even though she was simultaneously visible and vocal as an activist. She told me The Tantric Dance of Feminine Power greatly helped her heal, to "take her seat of power" from which she was again able to actively effect social change. Her experience illustrates the very real correlation between a woman's subtle body neural network and her ability to act creatively and effectively in the world.

To end patriarchy, women need to address the misogyny internalized in their inner neural network. This is where the real transformation takes place. It is truly an "inside job."

Women have the ready capacity to feel and activate this womb-heart-third eye "inner electric network." When one does so with devotion, reverence, and deep feeling, the body is infused with spiritual awareness. Afflictive emotions are transmuted in the pleasure of the inner landscape. Internalized misogyny melts away and divine pride (self-esteem) can flourish. This is women's wisdom, beyond concepts and words. It is the wisdom encoded and wired into the female body that equips women individually and especially as a collective to be the natural spiritual authority and guide of humanity.[8]

Women have developed the crucial cognitive understanding to dismantle patriarchal concepts and have developed a degree of embodiment and practicum (ritual, drumming, dancing) but still need to cultivate full embodiment at the subtle, neural level. Women need to restore their wombs and subtle bodies as the cosmic enfoldment of wisdom, love, creativity, and bliss that they are, the embodiment of Goddess.

The next wave of feminism must now take women fully into the body. This is not "essentialism," which relegates women to biological limits. This is reality, physiological reality that liberates women into their inherent powers and wisdom, for their own sake and the sake of humanity. It is the reality of the original moon lodges, or red tents, from which women originally guided humanity with collective womb-sourced love and wisdom. This is what the fourth wave of feminism can bring and this is what humanity needs.

NOTES

1. Monica Sjöö and Barbara Mor, *The Great Cosmic Mother: Rediscovering the Religion of the Earth* (New York: HarperOne, 1987).
2. Continuum is the pioneering modality of the internal movement genre and is taught worldwide.
3. Vicki Noble, Personal Communication, February, 2015.
4. I first tried a classical Middle Eastern (belly) dance warm-up, but the technical-mental focus clashed with and did not prepare us for or activate subtle body awareness.
5. Naomi Wolf, *Vagina: A New Biography* (New York: Ecco, an Imprint of Harper-Collins Publishers, 2013), 2.
6. Ibid., 1.
7. Ibid., 79.
8. For a full discussion of woman's natural spiritual authority, see Vajra Ma, *From A Hidden Stream: The Natural Spiritual Authority of Woman* (Sunny Valley, Oregon: Shakti Moon Press, 2010). See the author's web site: www.GreatGoddess.org.

PART IV

ARTISTS AND ACTIVISTS

CHAPTER 24

A ROMANCE OF POETS

Judy Grahn

Women's Spirituality as a grassroots field was an inherent part of the Feminist Movement that began for me in late 1969 as a loosely held set of meetings and projects in an organization, Gay Women's Liberation, which I co-founded. This movement continued into the establishment of women-only (primarily lesbian-only) households. From the economic and collaborative foundation of these households we established public and protected space for women, and this meant we had our own educational spaces for poetry, performance, presentations, theater, meetings, and so on. Max Dashú was showing visual evidence of female deities and shamans by 1971, and by 1972 I was performing "She Who" poems— which have been described as "the Goddess as a verb." In 1973, I began my ecotopian novel, *Mundane's World.*

My poetry had spiritual content as early as 1967, when I wrote a sort of prayer, "Asking for Ruthie," with these lines: "sun cover her/earth make love to Ruthie/stake her to hot lunches in the wheat fields/make bunches of ravens fly out in formation/over her eyes..." *The Common Woman Poems* (1969) also have spiritual metaphors attached to the power of females—crow, thunderstorm, wine, a third eye, bread, the moon, and an oath of commitment to gender justice. A paraphrase of the seventh poem, "The common woman is as common as good bread and will rise," became a talisman of the movement from one end of the country to the other. Early in 1973, I wrote my first nine-part poem, "A Woman Is Talking to Death," with its stance of taking responsibility for self in relation to others.

A revolutionary romance of poets helped lead early phases of the mass Women's Movement: besides myself, Alta, Susan Griffin, Pat Parker, Willyce Kim, Adrienne Rich, Audre Lorde, Ntozake Shange, Gloria Anzaldua, Cherrie Moraga, Paula Gunn Allen and many others provided women-centered, revolutionary, transformative, ethical, erotic, spiritual, and liberatory inspiration to a broad spectrum of people. Love infused our writings, sparked our relationships, aroused our audiences. In the 1980s, I expanded from my earlier woman-centered work into book-length epics exploring a Goddess-fallible-human figure, beginning with "Helen of Troy." Continuing to research Her, I am constructing a poet-drawn archetype and mythological history that moves backward to the ancient Mesopotamian-area cultures that produced Inanna, Ishtar, and Astarte, and forward to Helena/Epinoia of the Gnostic Gospels and permutations by modern poets, especially Charles Gounod's *Faust,* and H.D.'s *Helen in Egypt.* I have written two of an expected four volumes, *The Queen of Wands*[1] and *The Queen of Swords.*[2] Currently, The Queen of Cups is teasing me.

I've given over a thousand public readings and presentations. About 2005, I began collaborating with musician-composer Anne Carol in putting some of my poetry to music and performing it. This is so much fun! Her chords and sounds provide a rich context that makes it easier for me to relax into expressing the poems. As always the arts are challenging yet satisfying to do; they are a direct conduit to spirit and very nourishing.

I began reclaiming and revising menstruation as a cultural subject in 1970, publishing my first article on menstruation and human cultural origins in Charlene Spretnak's *The Politics of Women's Spirituality: Essays by Founding Mothers of the Movement.*[3] For twenty years, I concentrated on demonstrating women's contributions to culture, gathering information from recorded menarche rites, very different in most of the nineteenth century world from the shame and hiding attached to the subject in my own and most other Christian families. And "why is this?" becomes an ongoing, intriguing question. Using a poetic sensibility and associative thinking, I constructed a framework of categories and terminology that I first called "Metaformic Theory" when testing it out, and now call "Metaformic Consciousness," a lived, embodied philosophy that is non-dualistic, equalizing, massively explanatory, transforming of consciousness, and on occasion, liberatory. The term "metaform" is a poetic one, a combination of metaphor and form; metaforms are elements of culture that can be shown to stem from menstrual and related rituals. Describing humans as distinctive "ritual beings," externalizing ideas into "metaforms," then brings all of nature into view as intelligent and conscious. In other words, the "missing link" of what has made humans so different from other creatures is that we are metaformic; the connection between menstrual cycles and lunar cycles pulled our consciousness outside of ourselves. In *Blood, Bread, and Roses: How Menstruation Created the World,*[4] I laid down a basic outline of the philosophy, and in Metaformia Journal (online) many of the ideas are extended. The best way to begin learning Metaformic Consciousness, however, is to take a class with me or another teacher, and do an application, a study of some aspect of your own culture, or one that interests you. Working with this material makes me exceedingly happy; it puts me in a place of both curiosity and fresh comprehension.

While going through Elinor Gadon's off-campus Women's Spirituality Ph.D. program at California Institute of Integral Studies in the late 1990s, I had the opportunity to compare Goddess rituals with menarche rituals in South India; this became the basis for my dissertation. Following graduation, I became director and then co-director of the Women's Spirituality Master's Program at New College of California, in San Francisco, continuing in this role of forming and guiding when the program moved to the Institute of Transpersonal Psychology in Palo Alto. Courses I taught in this program included Metaformic Theory and Consciousness, Creative Writing, Women's Sacred Texts, Archaeomythology, Spiritual Autobiography, Thesis Writing, and Erotic Literature of the Sacred Feminine. I am currently a free-lance professor.

I have had the privilege of taking presentations on Metaformic Consciousness to South India and England, with my colleague Dianne E. Jenett, and to Chile with my colleague Anya De Marie. Hopefully, I will be able to write a second book on the subject in the future.

My current projects include a collection of twenty stories surrounding true encounters with nonhuman beings—embodied and not. Some of this is a personalized eco-spiritual journey. Somewhere between "man alone on a cold dead planet" and "we are one with the cosmos" are the actual experiences we each have with nonhuman beings—from ways creatures signify meaning to us, to visitations from spirits, pre-cogging, receiving messages, engaging the mind/s of nature. Other projects include a comparison of the Book of Job text with ancient Mesopotamian texts, and a collection of my nine-part poems which explore subjects of women, gender, sexual orientation, class, race, "sanity," soldiering, social violence, and ethics. There are six of them; I am hoping to write as many as three more and publish them along with essays others have written that will help the poems be teachable. Then those last two book-length poems— ye gads! Wish me energy and focus!

NOTES

1. Judy Grahn, *The Queen of Wands* (Freedom, California: Crossing Press, 1982, 1983).
2. Judy Grahn, *The Queen of Swords* (Boston: Beacon Press, 1987, 1989).
3. Judy Grahn, "From Sacred Blood: Menstruation to the Curse and Beyond" in *The Politics of Women's Spirituality*, ed. Charlene Spretnak (New York: Anchor/Doubleday, 1982): 265-279.
4. Judy Grahn, *Blood, Bread, and Roses: How Menstruation Changed the World* (Boston: Beacon Press, 1993, 1994).

CHAPTER 25

LOVE OF THE GODDESS

Karen Vogel

My first conscious experience of the spirit realm was in 1968, when at the age of eighteen I found myself unconscious and near death for two days, with a fractured skull from a car accident. Surgery was planned to reduce the swelling around the brain that could cause irreparable damage or at the least a personality change. The swelling suddenly subsided without surgery, and I awoke feeling myself in a state of immense love like nothing I had ever experienced.

I recovered and went to college, where I began a periodic and profound relationship with psychedelics, giving me another glimpse into the spirit world and the realization that everything is alive, and I saw patterns and designs that would later inform my artwork. At the time, I had no wider context or language for these private experiences with the spirit world.

Before my entry into the Women's Spirituality Movement, I had already considered myself a feminist who broke down barriers and stereotypes, beginning in 1969, when I worked as a builder doing remodeling in New York City. I loved physical challenges and had already taken my place in the all-male domain of whitewater rafting at college, only to be turned down for employment when my river-running friends started a professional company, and I was told flat out that if I rowed a raft it would diminish their ability to impress female clients.

I refused to be told I could not do something because I was a woman and after my stint in the trades in New York City, I moved to Vermont with my building partner to construct a 3-bedroom house on raw land. Winter arrived, with occasional days when it was 35 degrees below zero, while we were still in the early stages of framing up the house.

I did not make any money, but I did learn how to design and build a house on raw land, a skill I took to New Mexico in 1972; there, I bought land and built my own house on a rough dirt road bordering the national forest. I lived there for two years with no electricity, running water or telephone; I thought the revolution was coming. Living simply and close to the earth was my preparation for the changes that seemed inevitable, and it also was a time for me to deeply bond with a place. The surrounding wild land was filled with an intensity of natural forces and wild animals, which on occasion I exquisitely amplified with psilocybin mushrooms.

The charm of my remote and beautiful life wore off and change in the world was more evolution than revolution. My revolution came when I fell in love with Judy Shirek and readily agreed to leave New Mexico with her and her 5-year-old daughter, to go to Berkeley, California, in order for Judy to return to teaching. Judy had gotten her PhD from the University of California, Berkeley and done postdoctoral work at Stanford in Physical Anthropology.

Once we arrived in Berkeley, I discovered that Judy's colleagues were powerful women anthropologists, ten years my senior; they had done fieldwork and research, asking questions such as: did women universally have less power than men and was it biologically preordained? I had studied anthropology at the University of Denver, and I resumed my studies at the University of California, Berkeley. In addition, Judy and her friends mentored me: an intensive training in feminist science.

After our time in Berkeley, the anthropology department at Colorado College hired Judy and we moved to Colorado Springs in the summer of 1975. Vicki Noble was living there, about to graduate from Colorado College. She knew we were coming, because she had heard that the anthropology department had just hired a feminist with a 5-year-old daughter. Vicki was the mother of two slightly older daughters and soon after our arrival we began trading childcare. I trace the how and when of my involvement in the Women's Spirituality Movement to the day Judy took her life in November of 1975.

Vicki and I bonded through that momentous event, going through a spiritual door to an initiation into one of life's big mysteries—death. After Judy's death and my subsequent partnering with Vicki, I went searching for a context and worldview that integrated all the threads of my life. That led me into the arms of the Goddess and a search for the roots of female oppression in the archaeological record.

Vicki and I, with her daughters, moved to Berkeley, where we took our academic background and recent spiritual experience with Judy's death to jump into the fertile developing Women's Spirituality Movement. There, I found many of the same questions being asked as in the feminist science world.

In the late seventies, I rode a creative wave of ritual and healing modalities. I delved into a study of what already existed in shamanic or animistic cultures, especially those that included Goddesses. My exploration involved creating, remembering, and inventing new events, art, and ways of doing ritual. The fluid nature of the Women's Spirituality Movement allowed for tremendous freedom. I chose to put aside careful scholarship in order to be more speculative, as well as to uncover and recover information that was ignored or hidden by the male-dominated academic world.

During this period of time I began to focus on developing my connection to the Goddess through studying Goddess art and cultures and experimenting with rituals and meditations to invoke Goddess energy. In one ritual meditation I found myself in the arms of the Goddess, surrounded by a quality of love that was infinitely vast and reminiscent of the love I had felt in my near death experience. From that day on, I felt that I was one of the Goddess's special children, a position not unique to me since I think she has room for anyone who seeks or falls into her embrace.

In the field of the Women's Spirituality Movement, I planted a seed that flowered into the cocreation of the Motherpeace tarot deck.[1] Vicki and I were able to blend our academic training with our drawing styles and shared spiritual perceptions into the deck we called Motherpeace. Our cocreation has become a fundamental tool and practice in the Women's Spirituality Movement and has rippled out to be widely used in the traditional or alternative healing movement, with over 300,000 decks in print.

The Women's Spirituality Movement has contributed many books, artwork and rituals that have gone a long way in profoundly healing a worldview that excluded women and Goddesses from a place at the spiritual table. Now I live in a world where it is taken for granted that women have spiritual power and that Goddesses are alive, which to me means that a revolution has occurred.

What I am doing now is a continuation of all the threads of my life, building, remodeling, fixing, tending a large habitat garden, studying anthropology and feminist science, writing, and making art. My artwork has been most widely seen in the Motherpeace deck but I'm not primarily a painter. I've been a woodcarver since childhood, returning again and again to express, through wood, my connection to the spirit world and my perception that everything is alive. I find both animate and inanimate objects to have spirits and personalities I relate to. I communicate with the animals around me and I have friendships with my tools and other objects in my life. When I pick up a tool to carve, we are familiar with each other and join together to bring out a certain spirit in the wood. Sometimes, I search for a particular piece of wood that can contain the spirit and form of a particular animal, Goddess or ancestor; at other times, the wood tells me what tools to use and what to carve. I have carved pumas, coyotes, snakes and faces of Goddesses and ancestors many times because these are the beings that are most a part of me and that I want to know better by bringing them alive through the wood (see figures 21–24).

Over the years, I have shown my woodcarvings and sold work that people have treasured as spiritual icons and sources of healing energy. When I am doing a carving, my intent is for a piece to be beautiful in a decorative sense and also be a part of someone's ritual life. As an example, I have been commissioned to carve specific animals and other symbolic allies to go around doorways as a kind of guardian passageway into a person's home. I have particularly savored the opportunity to have my woodcarvings be a part of large ritual performances. In recent years, I carved four wooden faces for the large freestanding Goddesses that I made of bamboo, fabric and beads. These were for the stage set in Jennifer Berezan's *Praises for the World* ritual performances in Oakland, California, that brought together music, dance, spoken word, and visual arts.

The Motherpeace deck continues in my life through readings and teaching. My training for this profession began when I was a child and I used to play a game in which I tried to stay awake as I dropped into dreaming. Once I learned how to become conscious in my dreams, I put the game aside. I returned to this skill as an adult when I worked on developing my intuition as part of my studies in Berkeley in the late seventies and early eighties. I took my ability as an intuitive into a practice of helping others through my Motherpeace tarot readings and teaching, as well as running the business that keeps the deck available. Since publishing the deck I have written two books: *The Motherpeace Tarot Guidebook*[2] (1995) and a novel, *Coyote Tails*[3] (2007), as well as an article originally written for ReVision (2003), called "Female Shamanism, Goddess Cultures and Psychedelics."[4]

In the past several years, I have a new cocreation, with Lisa Baiter, of the habitat garden at Ocean Song Farm and Wilderness Center in Sonoma County, California. In this case, I use the word cocreation advisedly because many other gardeners preceded us. In our work we strive to create a beautiful and healing space for humans as well as sanctuary and food for other animals. We encourage the plants that thrive in the particular conditions of each bed and tend them to provide nectar, seeds and insects for hummingbirds, butterflies, bees and other pollinators. The garden also provides food and nesting sites for birds, as well as food and shelter for rabbits, foxes, badgers and raccoons.

Tending a habitat garden is wonderful and relentless work, with specific seasonal demands and new things constantly needing attention. This past winter, when I was pruning the rambling assortment of fruit trees, I got to a plum tree with many long branches needing to be cut back. I saw that the tallest one was the favored perch of a hummingbird, so I left the perch although it made it appear that I forgot to finish pruning. Once the needs of the hummingbird passed and he no longer used his high perch, I cut the branch.

I started out as a builder and that continues to this day because I am the maintenance person at Ocean Song. It sounds vague and mundane to say I do maintenance, but in reality it is anything but dull. I am always problem-solving, using my skills in plumbing, electrical and carpentry to do a variety of ever-changing activities. Depending on what needs to be fixed or kept working, I build new structures or improve existing ones. Through a lot of time for trial and error, I have honed skills and gathered tools to transform what is broken or missing and find uses for something that is discarded or forgotten.

The kind of shaman, elder and maintenance person I want to be is one who is useful to my community, with the wisdom and insight to help others.

Originally, I studied Physical Anthropology because I wanted to go into the field and study apes and monkeys and leave my species. Recently, I did a carving that I call "Forgiving Humans;" it depicts a salmon and the Goddess of Forgiveness—She who forgives our human follies. The Navajo have a word, ch'ééná, that translates as sadness for something that will never come back. I sought solace for that sadness and found a Goddess to help my grieving. She helps and revitalizes me and my love of the earth, including our human follies: a tall order for any Goddess (see figure 25).

NOTES

1. Vicki Noble and Karen Vogel, *The Motherpeace Tarot Deck* (Stamford, CT: US Games Systems, 1983).
2. Karen Vogel, *The Motherpeace Tarot Guidebook* (Stamford, CT: United States Games Systems, 1995).
3. Karen Vogel, *Coyote Tails* (Occidental, California: Motherpeace Tarot, 2007).
4. Karen Vogel, "Female Shamanism, Goddess Cultures and Psychedelics." *ReVision: A Journal of Consciousness and Transformation.* Women and Entheogens, ed. Mary Gomes. (Winter, 2003, Volume 25 Number 3), 18-28.

CHAPTER 26

EARLY ARTISTIC WORK INSPIRED BY MY ACTIVISM IN THE 1970S

Cristina Biaggi

In the early 1970s, I began to discover that society and its old mores were changing rapidly. The tightly woven social structure of the 1950s was dissolving and in its place there gradually appeared greater social and gender flexibility. The new wave of the feminist movement was in full swing, the civil rights movement was underway, and the sexual revolution was contributing to more gender equality.

It was at this point that I began involving myself with art created by women artists who were part of the feminist and civil rights movements. I started examining ideas about the imperative need for gender equality, looking at how the oppression of women under patriarchy had affected women's creativity. It was as if a whole set of belief systems, by which we had lived until now, were being shattered and were about to be swept away.

During the late 1970s and early 1980s, I created a series of crucifixions in the triptych, a common form for church altarpieces during the Middle Ages and the Renaissance consisting of three panels: the central panel and two wings. The outer wings of such triptychs were typically hinged to the central panel so that they could be closed during certain high holidays, such as the period of Lent before Easter. The central panel of the triptych was considered the most sacred part. It featured either Jesus on the Cross or the Virgin Mary during the various important events of her life (such as the Annunciation, the birth of Jesus, etc.). On the wings of the triptych, saints, or oftentimes the donors who had commissioned the work, were depicted. Instead of painting my triptych, I use collage to make them more contemporary; I created them with collage (modern) on a wood background (Medieval).

In my first triptych, I depicted a female Christ on the cross and used, as my model, my partner at the time, Virginia Dare. I actually photographed her nude except for the *de riguer* loincloth. If one looks closely at Virginia's body in the photograph, one will notice that under her left breast is a large scar akin to a crater. Shortly before the photograph was taken, Virginia had undergone an operation to remove a very large melanoma from which she had almost died. Around Virginia is a billowing nimbus of folded and crushed white tissue paper, which serves to heighten her sacredness. She is portrayed with her head bowed, a crown of thorns on her head. Around her I placed images of angels and saints from some of the late Medieval Italian and Flemish painters, which I was teaching in my art history class, and in which I was deeply immersed at the time. Two images of Joan of Arc, one of my heroines, can be seen on the bottom right. On the wings of the triptych I depicted a combination of angels, saints, and donors who are gazing with great concern, pity and compassion at the female Jesus on the Cross. The message seems to be that Woman has been, so-to-speak, on the cross since the advent of Patriarchy five thousand years ago. I created a total of four black and white collages and one colored collage using this triptych form (see figure 26).

In the second crucifixion, the female Christ (Virginia) is depicted totally nude, unashamed of her beautiful body and yet vulnerable. In this version, she is here depicted as the Goddess in her full physical glory and yet she is still on the cross. Joan of Arc (Ingrid Bergman in the movie *Joan of Arc*, in which she starred) stands vigilant and expectant at her feet and the nimbus of crushed white tissue paper surrounding her face and figure is continued throughout the central panel and on the wings, serving to unify the participants/spectators/devotees with the mystery of her anguish and exaltation (see figure 27).

In the third crucifixion, Virginia/Christ is depicted in negative form (the photograph's negative has been printed so that she appears dark, as a Black Goddess). Black and white curving ribbon-like shapes emanate from her head and body, spilling onto the participants below like accents of power. In this crucifixion, the central figure (Virginia/Christ) appears not as a victim but as an inspirational force. Inspired by her, the participants are depicted with black and white flames of power emanating from their heads, echoing her much larger, fully realized waves of energy (see figure 28).

In my fourth crucifixion, I depicted a black woman on the cross. Black women were the most victimized during the time of slavery and women of color are still the ones who suffer most around the world, bearing the brunt of all the evils of war and unstable economies. What black women suffered under slavery and are still suffering all over the world cannot be conceived or computed. Again, the figure is surrounded by black and white lines that emanate like slashes from the white aura around her form, and they spill from her body onto the participants/acolytes below. In this version I have included members of my family whom I photographed looking at and participating in the mystery on the cross (see figure 29).

The fifth and final crucifixion is called the Animal Crucifixion. This was particularly difficult and agonizing to create. My new partner at the time, Pat Walsh, and I had become immersed in the Animal rights/ Liberation movement. In fact, we had created a video called, *What is an Animal?* in which we interviewed a number of people who were to become luminaries in the Animal Rights Movement: Ingrid Newkirk, Alex Pacheco and Dan Matthews of PETA, the late Cleveland Amory, founder of the Fund for Animals, Betsy Lewis, founder of Lifeline for Wildlife, as well as others.

The central figure in this piece is the macaque monkey known as Domician (one of the Silver Spring Monkeys), being tortured "for the benefit of science." Flanking and below him are other monkeys, dogs, cats, pigs, rabbits and other animals being tortured for "the benefit of science." Red is the predominant color because what is happening is virulent and violent and bloody and we human beings are the cause of it. On the wings of the triptych are photographs, which I took of dogs (including my own), cats and other animals who are looking at the central figure, knowing they may be next (see figure 30).

From the original Animal Crucifixion, which measured two and a half feet square, I had a huge fourteen foot by twelve foot cloth banner created and framed to carry in a big 1989 Animal Rights demonstration in Washington, D.C.. It emphasized our objection to the Department of Health's treatment of monkeys, contributing to a protest that launched PETA and led to the first U.S. Supreme Court victory for animals used in experiments (see figure 31).

The '70s and '80s were heady and inspiring times full of new and transformative ideas. The Women's Rights Movement was in full swing at that point, partly inspired by the Civil Rights Movement of the sixties, as was the Anti-Nuclear Movement (which was actually started when the U.S. dropped the atomic bomb on Hiroshima, Japan). New ideas were emerging at a rapid rate and were being discussed, written and argued about. Original new art, overwhelmingly by women, was being created constantly. I reacted to what was happening around me as an activist and my activism translated into a body of artistic and written work that reflected those transformative times.

Currently, I am working on three things. I have finished writing my fourth book, *Art and Activism*, which is about my activism and the art it inspired from the seventies to the present; I am trying to find a publisher for the book because the publisher who published my first three books went out of business.

Secondly, I am working on large, commissioned abstract collages and collages in general. I just finished a piece which measures 22 feet in length and 7 feet high; it is destined to be installed in a beautiful private home in a canyon in Arizona.

Finally, I am continuing to create sculpted portraits of animals and people, work I have been doing for the past thirty years; these are also commissioned pieces. I just completed the portrait of a dressage horse and am now finishing the portrait of an especially beautiful eleven year old girl. As I mentioned, lately I have not created political art because of other commitments, but I'm sure that I'll be once again inspired to do so when the need arises—perhaps when Hillary Clinton runs for president.

Chapter 27

A Beginning but No Ending

Donna Read

My entry into the world of women's spirituality is as vivid now as it was in 1982 when I was walking in the woods in the Laurentian mountains near my home in Montreal. I had stopped to drink from the stream running nearby. I looked up at the scene around me and experienced a profound feeling like no other before, a connection of spirit within me and the spirits all around. In that quiet glade I resolved to tell stories that don't get told, to give voice to the voiceless through film. The next day at work my boss handed me Starhawk's *The Spiral Dance*[1] and asked me to begin research on a new film project about Witches. That was the beginning of a new life path for me, one I have happily traveled for over thirty years now.

By today's standards it would be unheard of to be handed a film project without even asking for it, but the National Film Board of Canada was an agency of the government and funding was generous. It was also the only place in Canada to learn filmmaking by an apprentice system, which unfortunately favored the male gender by significant odds. Women were typically hired as script "girls," prop "girls," secretaries and assistants.

I was working as a free-lance director/editor with Studio D, formed in 1974, the International Year of The Woman, to make films for women, about women, by women. In Studio D we were producers, directors, camerawomen, sound-women, and editors. It was revolutionary in the male-dominated, bureaucratic NFB and it was resented, dare I say, feared. I was very fortunate to be part of a hub where women were exploring new dimensions of feminist thinking and creativity, making films the other studios of the NFB avoided. Almost all of us had come from different backgrounds; none of us had much experience.

My background was typical of the times; I grew up in the fifties, in Toronto, graduating from Ryerson's Radio and Television Arts Program in 1960. Then I did what I was brought up to do: I got married, had two babies, and "kept the house" just like my mother and grandmother before me. I watched with envy while my husband and several other graduates hired by the Film Board shaped their careers, travelled to interesting places, and got the opportunity to make their own films. There were no opportunities for me, a thirty year old housewife with no resumé.

The first film I cut, "November," was done at night because I had to sneak into a NFB cutting room when nobody was around. I received no salary and had to fight for an editing credit when the film was released, but nevertheless I was happy. I still love editing films.

But something was happening, women were speaking out, and Studio D was listening. Betty Friedan's book, *The Feminine Mystique*,[2] opened a whole new world of possibilities for many; we met in little groups we called "consciousness raising groups;" and we talked about our lives, our hopes and dreams, like never before. We encouraged one another as we battled a system clearly designed to keep women "in their place." Sisterhood became more than just a word.

I often feel gratitude these days, when I remember just how difficult it was to even ask questions. We all stand on the shoulders of those women who came out in the sixties and seventies, who took a risk, who were laughed at and ridiculed for their thinking. What gave that movement substance and sustaining power, in my opinion, was the emerging story of our origins being told by women scholars. Merlin Stone's *When God Was A Woman*[3] was passed around feminist circles and empowerment became a word we cherished. I did not realize it at the time, but tapping into a different kind of energy together, remembering our ancestors, doing our own rituals on the full moon or solstice, even simply holding hands, was powerful. In my memory, our conversations together, around the table, over tea, were enhanced considerably.

Studio D films were akin to pouring gasoline on an already substantial fire. Keeping in mind that this was before television broadcasts and digital movies, these films could only be seen on a big screen. It took effort to get out of the house, but women were on the move, they were making themselves visible, and NFB screenings were the catalyst for changing awareness on many, many levels. In movie theaters all over North America, screenings of Studio D films provided a place to meet, to exchange ideas, to have the conversations desperately needing to happen: conversations about pornography, child abuse, incest—subjects avoided by the male establishment. Studio D films opened a window on the lives of women existing in a patriarchal system they were born to change.

The emerging women's spirituality movement motivated a number of films from Studio D. "Half the Kingdom" dealt with the changes in Judaism. "Behind the Veil, the History of Nuns" was a hit, in no small part due to an early sequence in Part One, where the story of the Goddess in Ireland was interwoven with shots of Newgrange and Kildare. Women responded enthusiastically and they demanded to know more. There was a groundswell of interest in those pre-patriarchal times and Studio D answered the call.

"Goddess Remembered" was released in 1989 and it went right to the heart of the women's spirituality movement, revealing major Goddess sites especially in Europe: Silbury Hill, Carnac, Avebury, Malta, Crete, Delphi, and showing images of ancient Goddesses and Gods, temples, symbols, art, and pottery. The Great Goddess of antiquity was on the screen for all to see for the first time. Women loved it; men were not so happy, especially the men in the NFB, but what could they do in the face of such demand?

"The Burning Times" generated much more fear, both within and without the NFB. I was moved from office to office, producer to producer, cutting room to cutting room. Someone scribbled "devil worshiper" on my door. The Government of Canada was presented with a suit for libel from the Catholic Human Rights League, claiming that we had misrepresented the Church in our assessment of the events leading to the massive burnings of women in the 13th-16th centuries. There was a debate, a commission, and "The Burning Times" was finally released, based on artistic merit.

If "Goddess Remembered" was a window to a world we were proud of, "The Burning Times" produced what might now be called post-traumatic stress. Over the years, I spoke with hundreds of women who had a visceral reaction to "The Burning Times," something that produced dreams and discomfort. I took part in many conversations while women articulated their feelings about this chapter in our recent history that had been virtually ignored. Often we came up with our fears and how we are still battling the same issues: abortion, health care, equal rights, equal pay, child care, authority issues, laws that are clearly stacked against us, to name a few.

"Full Circle," the last film in the series, was an important conclusion, showing how the ideas and the values of Goddess spirituality were currently practiced. We were refused finishing money, although the film was shot. Word went out through women's groups and institutes all over Canada, and letters as well as money started to pour in to the Board. It fell right into their lap and the film was reluctantly finished with as little support from the NFB as possible. "Full Circle" was never distributed like "Goddess Remembered" and "The Burning Times;" even now it is one of the only films in the NFB library not to be digitized for public viewing.

Over the years, I travelled through North America extensively with these films; I saw first-hand how the women's spirituality movement gave power to the political, depth to the environmental, and equanimity to the civil rights movements gaining ground at the same time.

Looking back, it seems that it was a pivotal moment when we questioned the gender of God Himself and the hierarchy of the "divine." Sometimes it feels like that vision has been dimmed, that Sisterhood is an old fashioned word, but I don't accept that. The women at the dinner table in "Goddess Remembered" are today our elders. The vision they had then has not dimmed with time; it is shining out in ways we couldn't have imagined all those years ago.

I left the NFB in the mid-nineties; Studio D was closed in 1996. The interest subjects related to women and spirituality followed me out the door. I was approached by a group of women to make a film about the archaeologist, Dr. Marija Gimbutas. Her research, the scientific data she collected, provided proof of the existence of a time and place she called "Old Europe." Her books, *The Gods and Goddesses of Old Europe*[4] and *The Civilization of The Goddess*,[5] had been controversial among her colleagues but warmly embraced by feminist scholars who were also researching and writing about the pre-patriarchal eras.

There was a definite intention within the women's movement to share this important knowledge of our past; the response we received for "Signs Out of Time," from Australia to Ireland, and all over North America, was overwhelming. Contributions large and small enabled us to continue working on a film neither sponsor nor distributor was interested in. It took ten years, and by the time it was delivered to our donors, I couldn't help but see that this film was a true measure of the weight women's spirituality carried in the hearts and minds of many, not just women but the whole culture. The Goddess was no longer a joke, no longer a conversation stopper, no longer just a pretty face. Looking back, it was quite a change in consciousness we manifested.

The principles of permaculture design to me are a practical application of Goddess spirituality, one that sees the interconnections I know exist.[6] Researching and filming "Permaculture -The Growing Edge" put me in touch with what I felt was a coming together of all the different issues we had struggled with. It was a pleasure to interview men and women dedicated to sustainability, creating not only communities of plants and bushes, chickens and goats, but communities of people who cooperate with each other and attempt to work through their issues transparently and with respect.

I am grateful my work path and my spiritual path are still intertwined; today I find myself working with some of the women of "Candomblé," the oldest spiritual tradition of Africa.[7] I can't help but see resonance when African-American women come upon the lore and stories of the Orixás, the Goddesses and Gods of their ancestors. Candomblé is an oral tradition; the elders I interviewed are the carriers of that religion which has been passed on generation after generation in spite of unimaginable suppression. I was warmly welcomed in their "terreiros," or temples, and I was comfortable in their rituals; there was something uplifting about seeing a tradition with a direct line to the past, and something satisfying to experience the persistence of spirit through time.

Working with these elders, these "Mãe de Santos," has given me a sense of how quickly information and ideas can spread these days. Mãe Filhinha was one hundred and eight years old when I interviewed her; her Father had been a slave, and there I was recording their story to be shared with many, many others. I feel a sense of completion in this last work.

Everyone's story is important and I am grateful to have been part of the Story of Women, to join with my sisters, my ancestors, and all those who also walk "The Good Road." I am grateful to be able to share what I learned, about a time before now when we all knew the earth is alive just as we are.

NOTES

1. Starhawk, *The Spiral Dance. A Rebirth of the Ancient Religion of the Great Goddess* (New York: Harper and Row, 1979).
2. Betty Friedan, *The Feminine Mystique* (New York: W.W.Norton & Co, 1963).
3. Merlin Stone, *When God Was A Woman* (New York: Barnes and Noble, 1976).
4. Marija Gimbutas, *The Gods and Goddesses of Old Europe, 6500-3500 BC: myths and cult images* (Los Angeles: University of California Press, 1974).
5. Marija Gimbutas, *The Civilization of The Goddess. The World of Old Europe,* Joan Marler, ed. (San Francisco: HarperSanFrancisco, 1991),
6. On *Permaculture*, see Bill Mollison, *Permaculture: A Designer's Manual* (Tasmania, Australia: Tagari Publications, 1988).
7. On *Candomblé*, see Ruth Landes, *The City of Women* (University of New Mexico Press, 1994).

CHAPTER 28

MY MUSES:
GLINDA THE GOOD,
MERLIN STONE, AND
MARIJA GIMBUTAS

Mary Mackey

Because I am a novelist and poet, my work forms a single, continuous, creative whole which springs from everything I have read, experienced, and imagined. To explain what I am working on at present and how deeply that work is imbued with Women's Spirituality, I need to invite you to accompany me on a journey through my involvement with Women's Spirituality and introduce you to my muses.

Right now, I am writing a Prequel to *The Earthsong Trilogy,* three novels about the Goddess-worshiping cultures of Old Europe (e.g. *The Year The*

Horses Came,[1] *The Horses At the Gate,*[2] *The Fires of Spring).*[3] All three of the novels in *The Earthsong Trilogy* were inspired by the research of Professor Marija Gimbutas. The Prequel to *The Earthsong Trilogy,* which is titled *The Village of Bones: Sabalah's Tale,* is also based on Professor Gimbutas's work. It tells the story of a young priestess and visionary named Sabalah who flees from the Black Sea to the Coast of Brittany to save her daughter Marrah from the coming invasion of Old Europe by patriarchal Sky-God worshiping nomads known as 'Beastmen."

I envision *The Village of Bones: Sabalah's Tale* as the first in a new series of novels about Old Europe. Forming a continuum with the novels of *The Earthsong Trilogy,* it will recreate the pre-invasion, earth-centered, Goddess-worshiping cultures in all their beauty, mystery, ritual, and complexity.

To put this another way: for over twenty years, ever since 1993 when *The Year The Horses Came* was first published, a single great story has been unfolding in my mind: the story of a time and place where the Goddess Earth was worshipped by people who had never known organized warfare or genocide. They honored women, children and elders and saw the Earth as the body of the Goddess. But there is another story, one that has been growing in my mind and my imagination much longer than twenty years.

My involvement with Women's Spirituality first began over sixty years ago as I sat on my mother's lap, listening to her read from the *OZ Books.* Thanks to these books, I first learned about Glinda The Good, a good witch who defied all the stereotypes of evil witches. I later learned that L. Frank Baum, author of the OZ series, had been married to Maud Gage, daughter of Matilda Joslyn Gage, the famous women's suffrage and radical feminist activist. Glinda, a power sorceress, was my first Goddess. As I grew from child to woman, I carried the talisman of Glinda The Good Witch in my mind and heart as I struggled to survive in an America that was deeply hostile to the idea that anything divine could be female.

In the mid-to-late 1960s and early 1970s, I became involved, first in the Civil Rights Movement, then in the Anti-Vietnam-War Movement. Rebelling against the male domination of both, I joined the emerging Women's Movement which is now generally known as Second Wave Feminism. By that time, I had also found my vocation as a poet and novelist. Thus, as Women's Spirituality blossomed all around me in a thousand ways, I began to incorporate it into my work, composing chants, hexes, and spells for the women's guerilla theater group W.I.T.C.H., creating poems about Goddesses, and writing my first novel, *Immersion*,[4] in which a woman who is redefining her sexual identity merges with the rainforests of Costa Rica in a single, ecstatic, spiritual whole, essentially becoming a Goddess.

By the mid-1970s, I had danced in women's moon circles on a commune, gone to women's healing ceremonies, and met some of the foremothers of Women's Spirituality, including Charlene Spretnak; Susan Griffin; Mara Keller; Judy Grahn; and Jeanne Tetrault and Sherry Thomas, editors of *Country Women Magazine*.

Yet, although I continued to write and publish poems about Women's Spirituality, I still faced immense barriers when it came to writing a novel based on women's spiritual experiences. It is a long, complicated story that involves the discrimination against and devaluation of women writers by editors, publishers, and critics, which was one of the hallmarks of the time. The short version is that, having been told that New York publishers, who essentially had a stranglehold on what did and did not get published, had decided novels about women's spirituality would not sell, I vowed to prove them wrong.

Sometime between 1974 and 1975, I began to search for a way to write a novel that would both portray God as a woman and bring this message to a larger audience. My first stroke of luck came in the form of Charlene Spretnak. Charlene, Susan Griffin, Valerie Miner, Sandy Bouchet and I had formed a writing group, meeting once a week to read our work to one another and offer feedback. To my surprise and delight, I found myself listening to Charlene read the early draft of *Lost Goddesses of Early Greece.*[5] As she recreated and restored the original Goddess-centered myths of the Hellenic world, I realized that I had found the first part of what I was looking for. Charlene convinced me there had been a time when God was female. So I decided to set my novel in pre-history.

Primed by Charlene's work and ready to take the next step, I came upon *When God Was A Woman,*[6] the second of the great books about Women's Spirituality to have had a profound influence on my writing. In this illuminating and ground-breaking study, Merlin Stone spoke eloquently about how the ancient Goddess-worshiping, matriarchal societies of the Mediterranean and Fertile Crescent were overwhelmed by patriarchal invaders bent on destroying all traces of Women's Spirituality. As a scholar, I knew that Stone's thesis was controversial, but as a novelist and writer of fiction, I had the luxury of not involving myself in academic arguments. The lost world of Women's Spirituality that Stone depicted spoke to my imagination. By the time I finished reading *When God Was A Woman,* I knew I had found my time (roughly 5,500 years ago), my place (Mesopotamia) and my plot (patriarchal nomads attack matriarchal Goddess-worshipping culture).

All I needed now was my Goddess, and I knew exactly where to find Her. Going to the library of my university, I checked out several books: *History Begins At Sumer* by Samuel Noah Kramer,[7] and three translations of the Sumerian legend of the Goddess Inanna's descent into the Underworld. For several years, I wrote and rewrote *The Last Warrior Queen,*[8] the first of my many novels about pre-historical Goddess-worshiping cultures and their struggle to survive patriarchal destruction. Modeled on a re-telling of the legend of the Goddess Inanna's descent into the Underworld—a technique I learned from novelist Mary Renault whom I greatly admired—*The Last Warrior Queen* was not only published by Putnam, it proved surprisingly popular.

Translated into a number of foreign languages, *The Last Warrior Queen* is still available thirty years later, living on both in hard copy and as an e-book. Just this week, I helped design a cover for a new edition of the e-book, which is going to be reissued and distributed by Vook.com, a New York-based company that publishes digital books that combine text and links to the internet and social media.

When it was originally published by Putnam in 1983, *The Last Warrior Queen* found an enthusiastic audience of readers, some of whom wrote me letters saying it had changed their lives and their concept of the Divine. At the time, I had created plot outlines for six more novels about ancient Goddess cultures, but publishers were not interested. "Women have peaked," they told me. "We do not want to publish any more novels about this Goddess stuff. Give us something else."

Unable to find publishers interested in publishing novels about Women's Spirituality, I pursued other interests, writing novels which, although not directly related to Women's Spirituality, featured stories about strong women taking control of their lives. Between 1983 and 1993, I had three novels published by major New York publishers: *A Grand Passion*[9] (Simon & Schuster, 1986), *The Kindness of Strangers*[10] (Simon & Schuster, 1988), and *Season of Shadows* (Bantam, 1992).[11] They were all serious creative works, and they all did well, particularly *A Grand Passion*, which made *The New York Times* Bestseller List and was translated into twelve foreign languages.

By late 1990, times had changed. Publishers had realized that women's fiction was not a transitory fad. I had just sent the manuscript of *Season of Shadows* off to my editor at Bantam when I received a phone call from the head of HarperSanFrancisco asking me if, as the author of *The Last Warrior Queen*, I would be interested in writing a novel based on a non-fiction book he was about to publish. The manuscript he sent to me turned out to be Professor Marija Gimbutas's *The Civilization of the Goddess*.[12] Eager to return to writing about ancient Goddess-worshiping cultures, I decided Professor Gimbutas's work was exactly what I had been looking for.

Before I outlined three novels based on her research, I visited her to ask if she had any objections to me turning her work into fiction. "On the contrary," she told me, "scholarly research is my field; fiction is yours. How can I help you do this?"

A remarkably warm, generous woman and brilliant scholar, Professor Gimbutas helped me in many ways as I wrote *The Year The Horses Came* and *The Horses at the Gate,* answering my questions and speculating with me on things for which there were no definitive answers. We were both always conscious that I was writing fiction, inventing rituals for which there was no firm scholarly proof, picking up the bones of those ancient cultures, clothing them in flesh, bringing them back to life, and making them dance. This is the way of novels: in fiction, as opposed to scholarly research, the writer is allowed to create, dream, and add imagined events to real ones.

When she received the final manuscripts for *The Year The Horses Came* and *The Horses at the Gate*, Professor Gimbutas was kind enough to tell me that the novels were beautiful, moving, accurate recreations of her research. Unfortunately, she did not live long enough to read *The Fires of Spring,* but it is my hope that she would have approved of it, too.

Without The Women's Spirituality Movement, I might not have written any of these novels. It has had a profound influence not only on my work but the work of countless other writers of my and subsequent generations. In this account of my own involvement with Women's Spirituality, I have left out a great deal: my seven collections of poetry, many of which invoke Goddesses; my scholarly articles; the graduate courses I have taught on topics like Women's Visionary Poetry, Women's Visionary Film, and Women's Visionary Fiction. I also instituted an interview series.[13]

Yet there is a pattern here, a circle of imagination and creation that has brought me from my mother's lap to a contemporary return to the themes I have been exploring in my novels for over thirty years. As I sit down at my computer tomorrow to write another chapter of *The Village of Bones: Sabalah's Tale*, my Muses will sit with me, old beloved companions now;

treasured and honored; living in my imagination although some of them no longer live in the physical world.

NOTES

1. Mary Mackey, *The Year The Horses Came. The Earthsong Trilogy* (San Francisco: HarperSanFrancisco, 1993).
2. Mary Mackey, *The Horses at the Gate. The Earthsong Trilogy* (San Francisco: HarperSanFrancisco, 1996).
3. Mary Mackey, *The Fires of Spring. The Earthsong Trilogy* (New York: Penguin, 1998).
4. Mary Mackey, *Immersion* (Berkeley: Shameless Hussy Press, 1972).
5. Charlene Spretnak, *Lost Goddesses of Early Greece.* (Berkeley: Moon Books, 1978).
6. Merlin Stone, *When God Was a Woman* (New York: Barnes and Noble, 1976).
7. Samuel Noah Kramer, *History Begins At Sumer* (New York: Doubleday, 1959).
8. Mary Mackey, *The Last Warrior Queen* (New York: Putnam, 1983).
9. Mary Mackey, *A Grand Passion* (New York: Simon & Schuster, 1986).
10. Mary Mackey, *The Kindness of Strangers* (New York: Simon & Schuster, 1988).
11. Mary Mackey, *Season of Shadows,* (New York: Bantam Books, 1991).
12. Marija Gimbutas, *The Civilization of the Goddess. The World of Old Europe,* ed. Joan Marler (San Francisco: HarperSanFrancisco, 1991).
13. http://marymackey.com/welcome-to-the-writers-journey-mary-mackey-on-writing-advice-and-the-writers-life/

CHAPTER 29

My Journey to the Goddess

Lydia Ruyle

Understanding my deep roots in women's spirituality took half my lifetime and led me on a sacred journey filled with lived experience, love of learning, and art. I was born to visionary parents who taught me by example the importance of acting on your visions. They believed in education, hard work, a strong family ethic, and a rich environment of experiences. Fortunately, they did not teach me religious dogma. When I was a child, I had a vivid imagination populated with fairies, and I was always busy with my hands. My mother majored in female action. She was a teacher, and she helped found the local Girl Scouts Council, the League of Women Voters, and a chapter of the American Association of University Women (AAUW). She even ran for the Colorado State Legislature during World War II and lost.

Women are born from a mother and over time most become mothers, the creation story in action. Women also give birth to ideas, causes, and institutions. The experience is both physically personal and universal. The process also has powerful psychic, spiritual dimensions (see figure 32).

Life is a continuous process of creation. As a woman lives her life, she gives birth to herself. She is a biological, experiential, intellectual, spiritual creatrix with the choices she makes consciously or unconsciously. She learns about others through relationships, which teach her about herself, other humans and glorious Mother Earth.

After graduating from the University of Colorado Boulder with a BA in Political Science and Economics in the 1950's, I married and birthed three children. The chaos of five children under four years of age, my three and two of my sister's, whom I babysat, drove me to art in the 1960's. I bought paint and canvas and worked on my kitchen counter above the reach of small hands. All five little ones survived and so did this fledgling artist. My choice to do art was a radical act.

My experiences as a woman did not fit with the stories I was told or had learned. It was my body that literally told me to search for spirit. I was initiated into the blood mysteries for five years in my twenties. I carried and birthed three children by cesarean and had two miscarriages. After the last birth, I had massive postpartum hemorrhaging, where I lost all my blood. Two courageous physicians stopped the flow. Floating weightless without feeling above my prone body, I had a near-death experience. I could hear the discussions of those around me. Someone put a wet rag in my mouth. The taste of water clicked me back into my body. I decided to stay and live. I needed my body in order to explore my soul.

When all three Ruyles were in school all day, I enrolled at the University of Northern Colorado and studied Visual Arts, graduating with a Masters of Art in 1972. At the same time, I was active in Democratic politics, state and local, and especially women's issues, also known as feminism. I helped start a pre-school still operating fifty years later. I founded the AAUW national art exhibition to raise money for women's scholarships, and I chaired three bond elections to build a community center for the city of Greeley. I was elected to the local school board twice. The

Governor of Colorado appointed me to the Colorado Council for the Arts and Humanities, and then to the Colorado Commission for Higher Education, which oversees twenty-seven institutions. In the 1970s, I was a woman of action, believing that I could make a difference in the cultural views of women.

I learned the voices, ideas and work of women were not valued; women were ignored.

Men and sometimes other women did not listen to my observations and experiences. I recognized that nothing in the socio-political realm would change until the spiritual story of women changed. The feminine divine called me to help change the paradigm. I set out to find the sacred images, traditions and stories that honored women and their work.

I love to make art, teach art, and study art. And that is what I do. When our children left the nest, I studied art history in Europe and Indonesia, learning and finding women's herstory. I worked with Judy Chicago on the Mother India quilt for the Birth Project in 1980. Women artists widened and validated my views of myself and art. Work with therapists helped me to understand my inner view. I did a series of self-portraits exploring my emotions, and another series on images and stories in Medieval Alchemy. Art helps us see. Learning from one's demons as well as her angels is a sure path. Finding the creative spirit within changes the paradigm without. Art became a spiritual path for me.

Although walking the path for decades, I first became aware of and involved in Women's Spirituality in the 1980s. Discovering Joseph Campbell, *The Power of Myth*,[1] Erich Neumann, *The Great Mother*,[2] Barbara Walker, *Women's Encyclopedia of Myths and Secrets*,[3] and Marija Gimbutas, *Language of the Goddess*,[4] opened an exciting world of images and ideas. They and many others gave me a language to find and tell "herstories" of the divine feminine with art.

For three decades, my art has focused on inherited images of women from the many cultures of the world; I call them Goddesses. I make icons, sacred images of women, to honor their power and archetypal energy. Why icons? Icons are soul images. All people and cultures create icons to honor the sacred dimension. Images revere, remember, revision us to wholeness, the sacred energy of divine mystery. That mystery is feminine for me. The Goddess symbolizes for me the highest possible development of each human being's potential on Mother Earth and in the cosmos.

In 1980, there were no women artists in the art history text books. I decided to find them and teach about them, which I did in my art history and art appreciation classes at the University of Northern Colorado. In 1989, this evolved into a course titled Women in Art, which, in the 1990's, became a course titled "Herstory of the Goddess." In 2010, The Lydia Ruyle Room for Women Artists was dedicated at the University of Northern Colorado (see figure 33).

Better Homes & Goddesses was born in 1987. The Goddess Has A Thousand Faces Mandala was my major contribution, and it is the opening page on my website today. Twelve images of Goddesses from western civilization surround a black and white etching of an egg titled, "Which Comes First?" In the eastern traditions, a *mandala* symbolizes the sacred dimension. It is about wholeness in the individual and the universe. I have used mandalas in my art since the 1960s and I am still creating them today.

In addition to teaching, I did exhibitions and led Goddess workshops in many venues for women, from young girls to wise crones, in schools, government offices, businesses, conferences, road trips, the College Art Association, and the National Association for Women in the Arts. Women continue to tell me today how much discovering the Goddess changed their lives (see figure 34).

My Goddess Icon Spirit Banners made their debut in 1995, at the Celsus Library in Ephesus, Turkey. Since then, the Goddess Banners, which began with eighteen and now number over 300, have traveled around the globe in over forty countries, at conferences, universities, sacred sites, museums, festivals, kindergartens, a golf course, a musical, a funeral, and a women's prison. They have hung at many sacred sites: Stonehenge,

Machu Picchu, Chartres, Kathmandu, Putuoshan, and Jeju Island. Today, the Banners average twenty exhibitions a year. Images of the Banners are in over thirty books and appear almost daily on digital media: the internet, YouTube, and Facebook. *Goddess Icons: Spirit Banners of the Divine Feminine*[5] was published in 2002; *Turkey Goddess Icon Spirit Banners of the Divine Feminine*[6] was published in Istanbul in 2005 (see figure 35).

In 1990, I showed up On The Trail of the Mother Goddess in Anatolia. I found when you show up, act, trust the process and let go of the outcome, magic happens! Anatolia is the ancient name for Turkey and means land of the Great Mothers. Bridging Asia and Europe, one can trace herstory for 14,000 years up to the present, from Neolithic Göbekli Tepe, Çatalhöyük, Hittites, Amazons, Lydians—the culture of my name—Persians, Greeks, Romans, Christians, Selcuks, Muslims, Turks. The Goddess has thousands of names and stories in Anatolia. We will celebrate the 25th Anniversary of the Goddess in Anatolia with a journey in 2015.

Reading about sacred females and seeing an image in a book are part of the process of discovery. Experiencing the image *in situ* with other humans is quite another. Making a pilgrimage to a sacred site is a long tradition. There are places in the world that have long been known for their power to energize, to heal, to transform humans, pilgrims, travellers, believers, skeptics. Sacred sites exist in nature and in human-made environments. I love being in the physical presence of art and images. The two-dimensional image—often black and white—becomes a three dimensional multi-sensory one of color, smell, sound, touch. When the image becomes fleshed out and embodied with my experience, it becomes part of me and I participate in the ancient tradition of honoring of the divine feminine.

Twenty-one years ago, I ventured into presenting Goddess Tours for women, focusing on the divine feminine at sacred sites. On the journeys, we sing, dance, play, and learn about the Goddess from very special wise women and each other. The journeys are soul journeys. They are about finding the divine feminine within and without in the culture of the particular pilgrimage.

With other women, I did fifteen journeys to Goddesses of England, Wales and Cornwall, Black Virgins of France, Goddesses of Germany, Turkey, the Southwestern US, Hawaii, and Mexico. Since 2000, I have been a resource for sacred travel to France, Hawaii, Italy, the Czech Republic, Mexico, and recently South Korea.

Sharing the divine feminine with my family and my lifetime partner, Bob, is part of my journey. His strong support of my work has been essential in teaching me about the masculine and the gift of relationship. As parents and grandparents, we continue to take all three of our children, their spouses and our six grandchildren, on sacred journeys, experiencing and teaching them herstory. Now they are teaching others about the Goddess.

Today, people are seeking a connection to the divine. Women and men are discovering herstory. There are dozens of women organizing journeys to sacred sites, teaching ritual and herstories of the divine feminine. Since the 1980s, hundreds of books have been published on women's spirituality. Conferences exploring women in mythology, religion, archaeology, and matriarchal studies are held throughout the world. Women are creating their own rituals, founding their own spiritual traditions, revisioning ancient pagan traditions celebrating Mother Earth and her seasons. The digital world is making it possible to teach, learn and participate in ritual with others around the globe. There are academic programs in women's spirituality and there are experiential venues and programs for women and men to be initiated and become priestesses and priests in women's spirituality. The myriad activities and actions are changing the paradigm.

What am I doing today? I am an elder approaching my ninth decade. I was called to find, create, teach, and exhibit Goddess Icons from the many cultures of the world, in order to make the images sacred. I will continue to search, create, travel, speak, support, and encourage women's empowerment and help change the paradigm for the next seven generations. Blessed Be!

NOTES

1. Joseph Campbell, *The Power of Myth* (New York: Anchor, 1991).
2. Erich Neumann, *The Great Mother: An Analysis of the Archetype.* Transl. Ralph Manheim. Bollingen Series XLVII (Princeton, New Jersey: Princeton University Press, 1955).
3. Barbara Walker, *Women's Encyclopedia of Myths and Secrets* (New York: HarperOne, 1983).
4. Marija Gimbutas, *The Language of the Goddess* (San Francisco: HarperSanFrancisco, 1989).
5. Lydia Ruyle, *Goddess Icons: Spirit Banners of the Divine Feminine* (Boulder, Colorado: Woven Word Press, 2002).
6. Lydia Ruyle, *Turkey Goddess Icon Spirit Banners of the Divine Feminine* (Istanbul: Yayımcı: Resit Ergener, 2005).

CHAPTER 30

KRISSY KEEFER, THE GENIUS BEHIND WALLFLOWER ORDER, DANCE BRIGADE, AND DANCE MISSION

Vicki Noble[1]

Krissy Keefer's brilliant life has always involved radical feminist dance and choreography, beginning with the activist Wallflower Order Dance Collective in late-1970's Eugene, Oregon, and when Wallflower Order imploded, like so many intense women-only political partnerships and collectives from the period, the group split up and Krissy, with co-founder Nina Fichter, moved to San Francisco and started Dance Brigade. For years they ran the popular annual holiday show, "The Revolutionary Nutcracker Sweetie," a feminist take on the Nutcracker Ballet in which a large cast (including numerous children, my son Aaron among them one year) revitalized the original story; the little Red book of Lenin was read by the Sugar Plum Fairy—originally Krissy and later, her daughter Fredrika, following in her footsteps.

Dance Brigade is a multi-racial feminist dance company expressing fierce wit and strong female movement, and fresh with creative originality. For two decades Krissy has run her own theater, first at Brady Street, and then Dance Mission Theater in San Francisco's Mission District. She runs a year-round schedule of dance classes and community performances, as well as evolving the award-winning Grrrl Brigade, a little sister program for girls and young women. Just as the powerful dancers of Dance Brigade, girls in Grrrl Brigade learn not only fierce feminist choreographies, but also leadership skills; they also do superb taiko drumming in their crowd-pleasing performances.

One of Krissy's gifts is narrative choreography; she usually weaves a text with a powerful, unapologetic political message as the structure for her dances. She says that Wallflower Order was the first dance company to use the word feminist to describe their approach to dance, including an explicit lesbian sensibility; they valorized strength, empowerment, and assertiveness as a contrast to the mainstream worship of a more demur beauty that depended on girls starving themselves in order to stay thin. Martial arts have always played an organic part in the training and performances of both Dance Brigade and Grrrl Brigade.

As Krissy became involved with Tibetan Buddhism in the 1990s, the dances became infused with lavish ritual and visualization expressing the sensibilities of yoginīs and Dākinīs from another time and place, in such works as "Cave Women," works that remained uncannily contemporary as well. Eventually she brought men into the pieces and, always doing her meticulous research, incorporated the aesthetics and teachings of

Buddhist and Indian Tantra into the work. Her "Great Liberation on Hearing" played in New York after a successful run in San Francisco.

In the early part of this millennium, as a response to 9/11 and the ongoing Gulf wars, she created and produced large, collaborative "Women Against The War" events, where the integration of all her interests and skills came together: political, aesthetic, and spiritual. For example, in between the musical and dance performances in one of the shows, Krissy let me bring in a large framed print of the Tibetan Black Dākinī and teach her "mantra of approach" to the audience as a magical formula for "subduing the demons" of war—quite an atypical possibility in a "concert" setting.

Building and sustaining community is Krissy Keefer's forte. The Dance Brigade has danced on the steps of government buildings and in parades down Market Street celebrating Gay Pride, and protesting war and rapacious capitalism. She even ran for public office a few years ago on the Green ticket, taking on Nancy Pelosi and winning 10% of her district. The community has painted a mural that features Krissy on the wall of the Horace Mann Middle School, a commemoration of the fondness the people of the city feel towards her. In the last decade, Dance Brigade has expanded to include a summer retreat center in the woods of northern California on the middle bank of the beautiful Eel River, where they hold sleep-over camps for the Grrrl Brigade, as well as other creative public events, such as "Cuba Camp" and "Summer Feast," an outdoor dance theater extravaganza that included dance, taiko drumming, stilt walking, political theater, and music on the land.

I used to think it was inevitable—only a matter of time—before Krissy Keefer won the coveted McArthur (genius) award, but now I understand that an "out-feminist" pretty much forfeits that privilege, like so many courageous whistle-blowers we see having to sacrifice so much, in order to get their radical and philanthropic messages out.

NOTES

1. During the period of our call for submissions, Krissy Keefer's professional activities kept her from writing her essay. As a board member of Krissy's non-profit organization, Dance Brigade, Vicki decided to write the piece for her.

PART V

PHILOSOPHER AND HUMANITARIAN

CHAPTER 31

PROMISES KEPT

Genevieve Vaughan

I was born in Texas in 1939. My family was Catholic but at 16, after much soul searching, I made the decision to become an atheist. However, I promised myself at the time that I would stop being an atheist if I ever found something that convinced me otherwise. I married an Italian and moved to Italy when I was 23. A couple of years after we were married my husband and I went on a vacation to Egypt. I had not become pregnant yet and I guess we hoped that the vacation might make a difference. We visited Luxor and Karnak and in one shadowy room at the bottom of a stairway, there was a lion headed Goddess, seated. The old tourist guide told us: This is the Goddess of fertility. Women come here; they make her a promise and they get pregnant. So I followed their lead. I wondered what the Goddess would like and I thought that since she was being ignored in this dark corner of the monumental complex, she might well like a temple of her own. So that is what I promised. I told her I would build her a temple. Then, in about a week's time my wish was granted. I became pregnant. It was 1965 and my oldest daughter is now 48 years old.

Back in those days there was no Goddess spirituality, especially in Italy, the land of the Vatican, and I did not know of any in the United States. I was convinced that I had to honor my promise but did not have the initiative and the independence of mind to build a temple at the time. It was the epoch of the Vietnam War and the student protests in Europe, which were more political and less counter-culture than those in the United States. My political consciousness was raised, and after my divorce in 1978, I became a feminist. In the country of the Vatican I began to believe that for social change to happen, there needed to be a women's religion, and I thought that perhaps we could invent one.

I came back to live in Texas in 1983, convinced that I should do whatever I could to create social change. I encountered the Goddess movement right away and realized that the women's "religion" had already been invented! I met women who chanted "Isis, Astarte, Diana" and who knew women like Starhawk, Margo Adler and Luisah Teish. There was a women's spirituality shop, Celebration, on the main street in front of the University of Texas, and one of the women who ran it was from my hometown. It was full of Goddess paraphernalia: crystals, tarot cards, books and statues. Someone read my cards, and I realized that if the tarot worked even a little, the exclusively realist mindset I had accepted until then must be false. I had the kind of positive culture shock I would have had travelling to the land of Oz. I read that one could become a witch by saying "I am a witch" three times, so I went into my back yard and did that—and it rained. Eventually, I joined a coven.

More years passed and I dedicated myself to social change, according to what I considered to be women's values. In Italy, I had developed a theory about the gift economy and communication as based in mothering and tried to put it into practice. I used the money I had inherited to start an all-women multicultural private operating foundation that ran a number of projects that I hoped would contribute to changing the values of the United States "from below." It was called the Foundation for a Compassionate Society. The purpose of its many projects was to change the values of the society from collective cruelty to collective compassion. I realized that Patriarchy and Capitalism together were causing the oppression of billions of people. In Europe, I had learned about classism, racism, and imperialism, and I realized how deeply we in the United States were oppressing other countries through our policies. I believed that women's caring values could change all this and I wanted to make the voices of women in the United States and other countries audible.

I had dreaded the date of 1984 because of George Orwell's novel,[1] and I had been glad to come back before then to try to do my part against a society ruled by Big Brother. I hoped that by speaking truth to power, the patriarchal surveillance society described by the novel could be avoided. I supported women's speaking tours and helped to start women's radio and television programs that gave a voice to women both in the Global South and in the United States. At the time, I met many indigenous women who were courageously speaking out, and I was able to hire some of them as well as women from other countries to work in the projects of the foundation. All the projects had women's leadership, although men came to many of the events. I opened a retreat center, Stonehaven Ranch, which was in operation from 1985 to 2005, a Grassroots Peace Building in downtown Austin, a women's radio program, FIRE, in Costa Rica, headed by Maria Suarez and Katarina Anfossi, and one in the United States which still exists, WINGS, started by Frieda Werden and Katherine Davenport. From the Peace Tent at the Nairobi conference in 1985 to the conferences on the gift economy in 2004 and on Matriarchal Studies in 2005, my co-workers and I brought women's thinking and women's values forward to the attention of the public. There were peace caravans, anti-nuclear gatherings, protests of all kinds that we organized or were part of. I will not explain them all here. They are described in some detail on my website.[2]

My hypothesis was and is that women have a different kind of economy from the mainstream capitalist Patriarchy. Since we may in our lives bear children, we are not encouraged to give up the nurturing economy and values that we learn as small children from our mothers or others who care for us. This is an economy of direct giving and receiving without exchange and its values stand in contrast to the values of the market that dominate our society, where every act requires an equal counter-act and there is no free lunch (In fact, women have always cooked lunch free for their families). Indigenous and matriarchal societies had and have gift economies of various kinds, and they respect the ways of the mothers and grandmothers. Many of those societies are highly functional and peaceful, whereas ours is dysfunctional and addicted to war.

So what does changing the economy have to do with spirituality? Creating social change is spiritual. I used to have the sense years ago that Mother Earth wept for all her children who were dying of starvation, war and injustice. Now she is crying out in pain directly for her own wounds as well as for us, who will not be able to live without her delicately calibrated gifts. Nevertheless, I believe that she is moving in mysterious ways, using all of our good initiatives for creative and life-enhancing ends, even if we do not see it immediately.

In the late 1980s, I started going to protests at the nuclear test site in the Nevada desert, and I thought that it would be a good place to build the temple I had promised to the Goddess I met in Egypt. After searching for some time, we found some land for sale in the desert on the highway that leads to the test site. I bought 25 acres in 1992, and I asked a group of young peace activists, called Chaos, to build the temple. I also asked sculptor Marsha Gomez to create a statue of the Goddess. I did not even know the Goddess's name, but I looked through a number of books and realized that she must be Sekhmet, as I remembered she had a lion's head. I was a little worried about scaring people with this ferocious Goddess, but I knew I had to be true to her. Some of the women who were working in the foundation at the time, especially Jody Dodd and Pamela Overeynder, organized the work. An architect from New Mexico, Molly Nieman, did the design, and builder Jole Reyes showed the young people how to lay the foundation in the shifting sand. They made the temple of straw bales and adobe. The roof is formed of copper hoops created by Richard Cotrell, and turrets were made of ceramic by Cynthia Dryflower. The first priestess was Cynthia Burkhardt, who lived on the land in a teepee while the temple was being built. In 1992, on the 500th anniversary of Columbus' invasion of the Americas, I gave the little piece of land back to the Western Shoshone, whose territory all that area used to be (including the nuclear test site). They allow us to have the temple there and we rent two buildings from them, one as the house of the priestess and the other as a guest house that visitors can use free of charge. Patricia Pearlman took over from Cynthia and was the priestess for 10 years. After Patricia stepped down, Anne Key was the priestess for 4 years and now Candace Ross has been there for 7 years. A growing community of devotees from Las Vegas and the surrounding area come to the rituals that honor the moon cycles and the Wheel of the Year. The temple is an outpost of peace in the middle of a war zone, in the sense that military bases have mushroomed in that area of Nevada; drones were developed and tested near there. Activists who protest pray at the temple and stay at the guest house. Passers-by travelling on Highway 95 sometimes find the temple by serendipity and stop to experience that place of peace and female energies (see figure 37).

I do not go to the temple very often. Since finally closing the Foundation, in 2005, I have spent a lot of time in Italy with my daughters. However, my daughter (the one Sekhmet blessed) and I just went there in the summer of 2014. We attended the ceremonies that were held for the installation of a new statue of Sekhmet. The original statue was stolen a few months before, and with the help of the community, we had a new statue made. The event was completely magical, with a beautiful all-women ritual one night and a potluck dinner for women and men the next night. The afternoon before the final dinner, it rained a little and a double rainbow appeared in the desert sky. Then the full moon rose.

Sunday morning, we did a special ritual to bring back the statue that had been stolen. Soon after, some young people who had taken it for a lark called Candace, admitting to her that they had destroyed it almost immediately out of fear. Fortunately, the mold of the original statue has now been found and we will make a new copy, which will be put inside one of the houses so that it will be safe.

I believe that practical action for peace is spiritual and that it is important to create long-term projects that can focus energies. However, at this time in my life I have realized that theory is as important as practice and creating theory is spiritual as well. Anyone whose brain and heart have not been injected with the patriarchal Capitalist immobilizing venom of denial surely mourns and opposes the destruction of Mother Earth happening all around us. However, I think that as a people, we have misdiagnosed the problem and I am still convinced that women's gift economy and its values are the keys to understanding and changing it. What is wrong, according to my theory, is not just Capitalism but the market itself—and yet our society keeps looking for solutions inside the market. Instead, the solutions must come from the so-called '"domestic sphere," which is outside the market, from Indigenous and matriarchal societies, and from Mother Nature herself. We have misunderstood what we humans are. We think we are greedy and warlike by nature, but actually we are a preeminently mothering species, whose processes of communication and community are all based on re-elaboration of the patterns of mother-child gifting interaction. Not everyone is a mother but everyone has to be mothered as an infant in order to survive: so everyone has that model (including men). We have been caught in a trap of a not-giving, accumulative economy where patriarchal domination prevails, but we are basically gift- giving and receiving beings. The problem is that the market economy is channeling the gifts of the many and the Earth to the few, creating scarcity where there should be abundance. Giving and receiving may even be the basic principle of the Universe, though perhaps not in such anthropomorphic terms. Our eyes receive the light of the sun, which has travelled far to nurture them, and they use it freely as a gift.

Our neurons send and receive impulses. Our hearts nurture our cells with blood, which circulates back to be oxygenated in our lungs. Breathing is receiving and giving air. Language too is based on gifting and it is now my challenge to try to prove that this is true, because I believe that if we recognize the patterns of gift giving in our most typical "mental" and interpersonal communicative activity, we will finally give them the importance they deserve. The economy, based on the market and money, programs us in the other direction, towards quantification, manipulation, and the exploitation and denial of gifts. Patriarchy has merged with the market to motivate economic competition for domination.

I have travelled on airplanes a lot. It always amazes me how few people look out the windows at the magnificent spectacle of the "big picture": the clouds, the water, the green and brown Earth, the tiny cities, the even tinier cars with invisible people in them. I remember once seeing a tiny spot of red in a car way below me and thinking that was probably the red sweater of a woman a lot like me whom I would never know. Yet I could imagine her thinking and perhaps hearing the airplane passing way overhead. These are something like the differences in dimensions between each of us and the planet. Still, we can locate ourselves in the context of the whole and think of what can be done in the different dimensions. It is important to keep promises and do long-term projects because they trace a deep alternative pattern. This negation of the mother and her economy is the cornerstone of patriarchal Capitalism. We need to be liberated from the market, not into it. The caption on the plaque on the Sekhmet statue is: A promise kept: May women be strong as a lion in giving birth to the future (see figure 38).

NOTES

1. George Orwell, *1984*. (New York: Signet, 1950).
2. http://www.gift-economy.com

Appendix

Figure 1. Snake Dancer.

Source. Photograph by Max Dashú.

Figure 2. Tchanumé at the Place of Initiation.

Source. Photograph by Max Dashú.

Figure 3. Calling at the Pictish Stone.

Source. Photograph by Max Dashú.

Figure 4. Transdancer.

Source. Photograph by Max Dashú.

Figure 5. *Dilukái,* originally from the Republic of Palau, Caroline Islands.

Source. Photograph by Starr Goode.
Note. A popular display figure placed over the entrances to ceremonial huts.

Figure 6. *The Crone,* mixed media, Fiona Marron.

Source. Photograph by Fiona Marron.
Note. A new vision of the medieval Sheela, a bone-white figure standing with the stillness of death; the ripeness of her vulva promises new creation.

Figure 7. Cavan Sheela na gig, Co. Cavan.

Source. Courtesy of Cavan County Museum. Photograph by Starr Goode.
Note. This dramatic Sheela once adorned a church. She has bony hag ribs and a
monstrous face, and the thick lips of her face echo her sexual labia.

Figure 8. Brooke Medicine Eagle Drumming for Ceremonial Dance.

Source. Photograph by Zane Williams.

Figure 9. Aboriginal Skills: Brooke Medicine Eagle Tanning Deer Hides into Soft Material.

Source. Photograph by Zane Williams.

Figure 10. Jane Hardwicke Collings, Going Within.

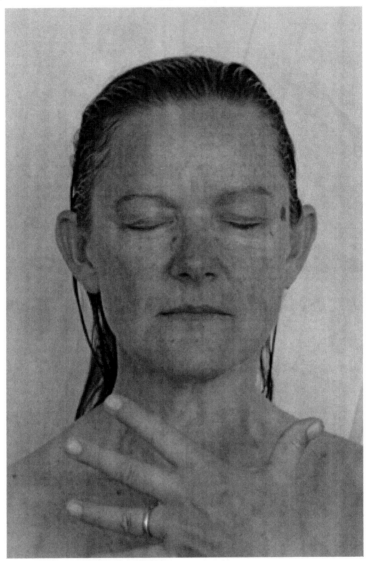

Source. Photograph by Paul Collings.

Figure 11. Jane Hardwicke Collings in a Thank-You Circle.

Source. Photograph by Kath Dumont.
Note. Red Tent gathering in Sidney, Australia.

Figure 12. Welcome to Womanhood Beltane Ceremony.

Source. Photograph by Kristan Lee Read.
Note. Jane Hardwicke Collings Drumming at a Welcome to Womanhood Beltane Ceremony.

Figure 13. PaGaian Cosmology altar/mandala: A "Womb of Gaia" map

Source. Photograph by Glenys Livingstone.
Note. An altar/mandala which represents Glenys Livingstone's PaGaian Cosmology.

Figure 14. MoonCourt - Goddess Ceremonial Space, Blue Mountains, Australia, 2008.

Source. Photograph by Glenys Livingstone.

Figure 15. PaGaian Cosmology - a gynocentric re-emergence.

Source. Front cover of Glenys Livingstone, *PaGaian Cosmology: Re-inventing Earth-based Goddess Religion* (Lincoln, Nebraska: iUniverse, 2005). Image designed by Julie Cunningham.

Figure 16. Cave: "Finally learning to merge with the Oneness."

Source. Photograph by Rob Hayden.
Note. Honaunau, Hawaii. Lava tube opening over the Ocean. 2004.

Figure 17. Hallie Austen Iglehart leading ritual at Glyptotek Museum, Copenhagen.

Source. Photograph by Romilly Grauer.
Note. The 1980 UN International Women's NGO Conference.

Figure 18. Horseshoe Cove beach clean-up, Sausalito, CA, September 2013.

Source. Photograph by Marcelina Martin.
Note. Three other All One Ocean volunteers and I went to the beach at Fort Baker
in Sausalito, just below the Golden Gate Bridge. In under an hour, we picked up 47
pounds of trash, including 40 plastic straws and three hypodermic needles. We were
shocked at the amount of debris, yet grateful that we could clean up this little area,
especially given the fact that it is home to families of harbor seals who feed there.
As I rested after the clean-up, I felt my body releasing the images of garbage, washed
away by the soul of the Ocean, thanking me and all of us.

Figure 19. Donna Henes as Spider Woman in her web.

Source. Photograph by Hans Deimel.

Figure 20. Arrival at the Isle of Avalon. Painting on the Glastonbury Goddess Hall.

Source. Painting by artist Jonathon Minshull. Photograph by Kathy Jones.

Figure 21. Septima. Ebony.

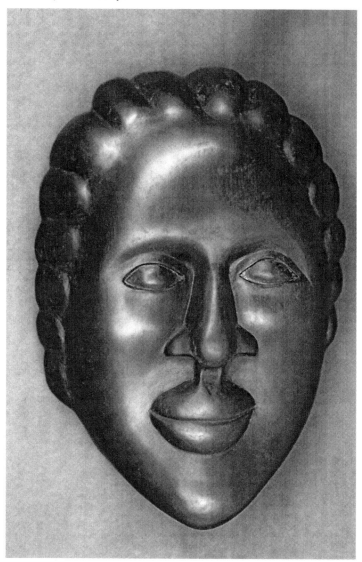

Source. Photograph by Karen Vogel.

Figure 22. Guardian of the Sacred. Black walnut.

Source. Photograph by Karen Vogel.

Figure 23. Temple of My Familiar. Kingwood.

Source. Photograph by Karen Vogel.

Figure 24. Puma and Coyote. Snakewood and pernumbuco.

Source. Photograph by Karen Vogel.

Figure 25. Forgiving Humans: Goddess of Forgiveness of our human follies. Douglas fir and woodburning.

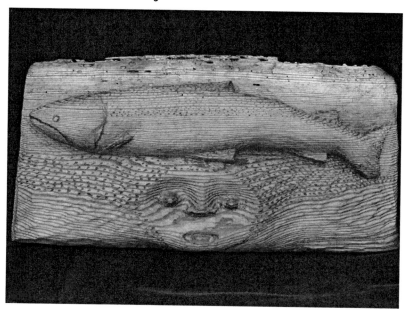

Source. Photograph by Karen Vogel.

Figure 26. Crucifixion Triptych I, 1977, 18.5 x 34 inches, black & white collage.

Source. Photograph by Cristina Biaggi.

Figure 27. Crucifixion Triptych II, 1983, 18.5 x 30 inches, black & white collage on wood.

Source. Photograph by Cristina Biaggi.

Figure 28. Crucifixion Triptych III, 1984, 30 x 29 inches, black & white collage on wood.

Source. Photograph by Cristina Biaggi.

Figure 29. Crucifixion Triptych IV, 1985, 17.5 x 19 inches, black & white collage on wood.

Source. Photograph by Cristina Biaggi.

Figure 30. Animal Crucifixion Triptych, 1986, large, 10 x 14 feet, small, 30 x 30 inches, color collage on canvas.

Source. Photograph by Cristina Biaggi.

Figure 31. Large Animal Crucifixion Triptych with Cristina Biaggi.

Source. Photograph by Patricia Walsh.

Figure 32. Mutti's Matrioshkas in memory of Lydia Alles Miller, 1908-1992.

Source: Photograph by Lydia Ruyle. Holiday greeting card by Lydia Ruyle, ©1992.
Note: Russian nesting dolls symbolize the continuing cycles of life through the mother-line. Ruyle has been creating family holiday greetings since 1950.

Figure 33. The Goddess Has A Thousand Faces Mandala.

Source: Photograph by Lydia Ruyle. Collagraph collage, by Lydia Ruyle, 54" x 54" ©1987.

Figure 34. Exhibition of Lydia Ruyle's Prayer Flags and Spirit Banners. Ephesus, Turkey.

Source: Photograph by Lydia Ruyle. ©1995 Lydia Ruyle photos. 1995.

Figure 35. Goddess Icons: Spirit Banners of the Divine Feminine book cover.

Source. *Goddess Icons: Spirit Banners of the Divine Feminine* book cover, by Lydia Ruyle. Boulder, Colorado. Woven Word Press. 2002.

Figure 36. Map of Life Self-Portrait. Watercolor monoprint on Fabriano paper.

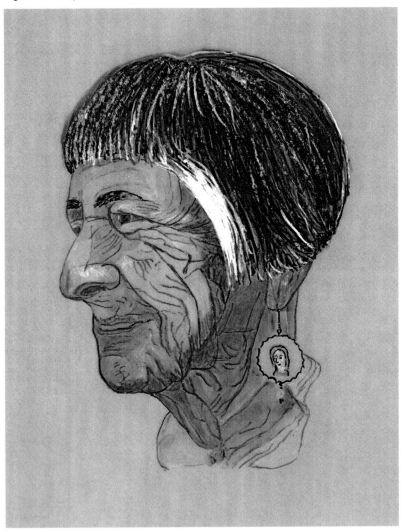

Source. Lydia Ruyle. 15" w. x 24" l. ©2011.

Figure 37. Sekhmet Temple, Cactus Springs, Nevada.

Source. Photograph by Candace Ross.

Figure 38. Sekhmet Statue and Genevieve Vaughan.

Source. Photograph by Amelia Rossi-Landi.

INDEX

About the Editors and Contributors

Miriam Robbins Dexter holds a Ph.D. in ancient Indo-European languages, archaeology, and comparative mythology, from UCLA. She has written scholarly journal and encyclopedia articles as well as books: *Whence the Goddesses: A Source Book* (1990) and *Sacred Display: Divine and Magical Female Figures of Eurasia* (2010) (Winner of the ASWM Sarasvati book award in 2012).

Vicki Noble is a feminist healer, teacher, artist, writer, and independent scholar; co-creator of *Motherpeace Tarot*; and author of eight books, including *Shakti Woman* (1991) and *The Double Goddess* (2003), both published in several languages. She travels and teaches internationally, is a grandmother and a professional astrologer, and lives in Santa Cruz, California.

Ruth Barrett is an ordained Dianic high priestess and elder, ritualist, educator, and author of *Women's Rites, Women's Mysteries: Intuitive Ritual Creation*. She is also an award-winning recording artist of original Goddess songs and contributor to the pioneering musical works in the Goddess Spirituality Movement. She is co-founder of Temple of Diana, Inc.

Cristina Biaggi, PhD, is foremost an artist and has exhibited throughout the US, Europe and Australia. She also has achieved significant recognition for her varied contributions to the field of Goddess-centered art and scholarship. Her art feeds her writings and her writing fuels her art.

Zsuzsanna (Z) Budapest is an author (*The Holy Book of Women's Mysteries, Grandmother Moon, Grandmother of Time, Goddess in the Bedroom*), priestess of feminist Witchcraft, public speaker and activist for peace and women. She travels to give speeches and workshops globally. Her goal is to bring back the Goddess culture, which supports and honors women. zbudapest@gmail.com.

Carol P. Christ, Ph.D. Yale, has taught at Claremont Graduate School, Columbia, Harvard, and California Institute of Integral Studies. She founded the Women's Caucus–Religious Studies. Her new book (with Judith Plaskow) is *Divinity in the World: Conversations in Embodied Theology.* She leads life-transforming Goddess Pilgrimages to Crete http://www.goddessariadne.org.

Jane Hardwicke Collings is a midwife, teacher, and writer. She gives workshops in Australia and internationally. She founded and runs The School of Shamanic Midwifery www.schoolofshamanicmidwifery.com. Her books include: *Ten Moons, the Inner Journey of Pregnancy, Thirteen Moons, How to chart your menstrual cycle, Spinning Wheels (a guide to the cycles), Becoming a Woman.* http://www.moonsong.com.au.

Max Dashu founded the Suppressed Histories Archives in 1970 to research global women's history, from ancient female icons to female leaders, shamans, and rebels. She is known for her expertise on goddesses, mother-right cultures, witches, and the witch hunts. Her dvds *Woman Shaman* and *Women's Power* are at http://www.suppressedhistories.net .

Riane Eisler is president of the Center for Partnership Studies, keynotes conferences worldwide, teaches university classes and webinars, and is editor in chief of the *Interdisciplinary Journal of Partnership Studies.* Her books have been translated into over 30 languages and include *The Chalice and the Blade* and *The Real Wealth of Nations.*

Elinor Gadon is a cultural historian, Indologist, art historian, and author notable for her examination of women in myth and culture in history. At the California Institute of Integral Studies in San Francisco, she developed and directed the program in Women's Spirituality. She is now a Resident Scholar at Brandeis University's Women's Studies Research Center Scholars Program.

Heide Goettner-Abendroth is a philosopher and researcher of matri-archal cultures and founder of modern Matriarchal Studies. She is Visiting Professor at the University of Montreal/Canada, and the University of Innsbruck/Austria, Director of "HAGIA. International Academy for Matriarchal Studies," and organizer of three world congresses on Matriarchal Studies and Politics. She was nominated for the Nobel Peace Prize in 2005.

Starr Goode, MA, is a writer and poet who teaches literature at Santa Monica College. Her book, *Sheela na gig: Dark Goddess of Europe, In Pursuit of an Image,* is forthcoming. Her previous work on the Sheelas has been published in *Irish Journal of Feminist Studies; ReVision: A Journal of Consciousness and Transformation;* the three volume encyclopedia, *Goddesses in World Culture;* and in *About Place Journal.*

Judy Grahn is author of thirteen books. *Blood, Bread, and Roses* can be read from a link on the www.metformia.com site. Most recent are *The Judy Grahn Reader* (Aunt Lute Press) and *A Simple Revolution* (Aunt Lute Press). Judy is currently a Professor-at-Large; she teaches writing and women's spirituality classes.

Donna Henes is the author of *The Queen of Myself, Stepping into Sovereignty in Midlife,* the groundbreaking book that addresses how women are reforming ideas about aging and power. She writes about an empowered midlife for the Huffington Post and Beliefnet and publishes a monthly e-zine, *The Queens Chronicles.* http://www.thequeenofmyself.com.

Hallie Austen Iglehart has taught throughout the United States and in Japan and Europe since 1974. She is the author of *Womanspirit* and *The Heart of the Goddess* (now online). Hallie is the founder of All One Ocean and a senior teacher of Wisdom Healing Zhineng Qigong. http://www.heartgoddess.net. and http://www.alloneocean.org.

Kathy Jones is a Priestess of Avalon, Priestess of the Goddess, Founder and Webster of Glastonbury Goddess Conference, Founder and Creative Director of the Glastonbury Goddess Temple. She is a ceremonialist, teacher, writer, wounded healer, initiator, Temple Melissa, sacred dramatist and priestess traveler, author of Goddess books, including *Priestess of Avalon, Priestess of the Goddess* and *In the Nature of Avalon.*

Mara Lynn Keller (PhD Philosophy, Yale University) is a Professor of Philosophy, Religion and Women's Spirituality at the California Institute of Integral Studies; former director of the Women's Spirituality graduate program (1998-2008); and a Rosen Method Bodywork teacher. Her articles can be found at http://www.ciis.edu/Academics/Graduate_Programs/Womens_Spirituality_/Womens_Spirituality_Faculty/Mara_Lynn_Keller.html

Glenys Livingstone, PhD, has been on a Goddess path since 1979. Her experience has included diverse spiritualities, a scientific perspective, inner and communal work, as well as academic scholarship. She lives in Australia where she was born in 1954. She facilitates seasonal rituals, teaches apprentices, teaches on-line, and writes. http://www.pagaian.org.

Vajra Ma guides women in directly accessing their female subtle body-knowing. She is author of *From a Hidden Stream: The Natural Spiritual Authority of Woman* and founder of the priestess lineage *Woman Mysteries of the Ancient Future Sisterhood®* and its womb-sourced, moving yoga, The Tantric Dance of Feminine Power® http://www.GreatGoddess.org.

Mary Mackey is author of 7 poetry collections including *Sugar Zone*; and 12 novels including *The Last Warrior Queen, The Year The Horses Came, The Horses At The Gate, The Fires of Spring,* and (forthcoming) *The Village of Bones: Sabalah's Tale* which recreate the Goddess-worshipping cultures of Old Europe and Mesopotamia. http://www.marymackey.com

Joan Marler is the editor of *The Civilization of the Goddess* (1991) by Marija Gimbutas, *From the Realm of the Ancestors* (1997), *The Danube Script* (2008), *Fifty Years of Tărtăria Excavations* (2014), and the online *Journal of Archaeomythology*. She is the Executive Director of the Institute of Archaeomythology.

Brooke Medicine Eagle is a legendary Earthkeeper, wisdom teacher, healer, visionary, singer/songwriter, catalyst for wholeness, and ceremonial leader. She is the author of the Native American literary classic, *Buffalo Woman Comes Singing*, and of *The Last Ghost Dance*. Her music recordings, teachings, writings, and wilderness spiritual retreats continue to touch the hearts and minds of people world-wide.   http://www.MedicineEagle.com.

Musawa is co-founder and priestess of *We'Moon: Gaia Rhythms for Womyn* (the datebook: www.wemoon.ws) and its sister organizations: We'Moon Land (a "mutual benefit" women's land community: www.wemoonland.org) and We'Mooniversity (a " public benefit" educational non-profit: www.wemooniversity.org). She hopes soon to complete *The Adventures of Mu* (a memoir), and a We'Moon Tarot deck.

Donna Read has been a filmmaker for almost fifty years, many of them at the National Film Board of Canada where she produced, directed, and edited dozens of films, including the acclaimed Women and Spirituality Trilogy. Read continues her work producing and directing independent videos and being a Great-Grandmother.

Lydia Ruyle, M.A. is an artist, author, scholar emerita of the Visual Arts faculty of the University of Northern Colorado in Greeley, Colorado. Her research into sacred images of women has taken her around the globe. Ruyle creates and exhibits her art throughout the U.S. and internationally. Her Goddess Icon Spirit Banners have flown in over forty countries.

Miranda Shaw holds a PhD from Harvard University and is the author of *Passionate Enlightenment: Women in Tantric Buddhism* and *Buddhist Goddesses of India*. Her research and writings focus on women's spirituality, embodied practices, and goddess traditions in India and the Himalayas. She is currently working on book manuscripts on Buddhist goddesses of Tibet and Nepal and Tantric Buddhist sacred dance.

Charlene Spretnak is author of *Lost Goddesses of Early Greece, Green Politics, The Spiritual Dimension of Green Politics, States of Grace, The Resurgence of the Real, Missing Mary, Relational Reality*, and *The Spiritual Dynamic in Modern Art*. In 2012 she received the Demeter Award as "one of the premier visionary feminist thinkers of our time" from the Association for the Study of Women and Mythology.

Starhawk is an activist and author of twelve books. Her novel, *The Fifth Sacred Thing*, is now in development for the screen. Starhawk directs and teaches Earth Activist Trainings, which combine a Permaculture design certificate course with focus on spiritual work, organizing, and activism. http://www.starhawk.org.

Luisah Teish is a writer, performer, and public speaker. She is the author of *Jambalaya: The Natural Woman's Book of Personal Charms* and *Practical Rituals.* Teish conducts workshops and delivers lectures and keynote speeches on many subjects, including "Goddesses, Queens, and Spirit Women of the African diaspora," Eco-Feminist Mythology, and Spiritual Life Guidance for Women.

Genevieve Vaughan created the international, multicultural all-women activist Foundation for a Compassionate Society (1987-2005), the Temple of Goddess Spirituality dedicated to Sekhmet in Cactus Springs, Nevada, (1992-present) and a network: International Feminists for a Gift Economy (2001- present). Her books and other material can be downloaded free from her website: http://www.gift-economy.com.

Karen Vogel is trained in anthropology, art, new construction and remodeling. In 1981, she co-created the *Motherpeace Tarot Deck* with Vicki Noble; there are over 300,000 copies of the deck in print. She currently tends the habitat garden at Ocean Song Farm and Wilderness Center. http://www.motherpeace.com.

Susun Weed is a green witch, a Peace Elder, a high priestess of the Goddess, and a joyous being. Her encyclopedic knowledge of herbs and health is available to you via online courses, correspondence courses, and apprenticeships.   http://www.susunweed.com, http://www.wisewomanmentor.com, and http://www.wisewomanbookshop.com.

Lightning Source UK Ltd.
Milton Keynes UK
UKOW04f2123141215

264733UK00001B/123/P